THE LAST UNDERCOVER

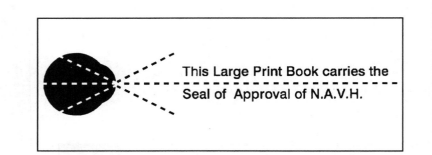

This Large Print Book carries the
Seal of Approval of N.A.V.H.

THE LAST UNDERCOVER

THE TRUE STORY OF AN FBI AGENT'S
DANGEROUS DANCE WITH EVIL

BOB HAMER

THORNDIKE PRESS
A part of Gale, Cengage Learning

Detroit • New York • San Francisco • New Haven, Conn • Waterville, Maine • London

GALE
CENGAGE Learning™

LIBRARY OF CONGRESS CATALOGING-IN-PUBLICATION DATA

Hamer, Bob.
    The last undercover : the true story of a FBI agent's
dangerous dance with evil / by Bob Hamer.
        p. cm. — (Thorndike Press large print crime scene)
    ISBN-13: 978-1-4104-1126-6 (hardcover : alk. paper)
    ISBN-10: 1-4104-1126-5 (hardcover : alk. paper)
    1. Undercover operations—United States—Case studies.
2. Hamer, Bob. 3. United States. Federal Bureau of
Investigation. 4. North American Man/Boy Love Association.
5. Large type books. I. Title.
HV8080.U5H36 2008b
364.15'36—dc22   2008036507

Published in 2008 by arrangement with Center Street, a division of
Hachette Book Group USA, Inc

Printed in the United States of America
1 2 3 4 5 6 7 12 11 10 09 08

CONTENTS

PREFACE

The simple words of A. W. Tozer in *The Divine Conquest* spoke volumes to my motivation in writing *The Last Undercover*. He wrote, "The only book that should ever be written is one that flows up from the heart, forced out by the inward pressure. . . . His book will be to him not only imperative, it will be inevitable."

After twenty-six years as an FBI agent, all of them as a street agent and many of those years spent in various undercover roles, I have experienced what most never will. I held a baby's arm . . . not a baby by the arm, just the arm, from the elbow to the fingers, an arm severed in a tragic accident. I saw a man's head detached from the torso, and attended autopsies. I comforted a woman with the brains of her boyfriend splattered on her blouse and confronted armed suspects. I've fired my weapon in the heat of a drug deal gone bad and have been threatened with death by disgruntled felons taken into custody. In my various undercover roles I have gone toe-to-toe with some of the most dangerous, notorious, and sometimes fascinating criminals in our society. Five years of working street gangs and more than twenty years working various organized crime groups exposed me to the best and worst of mankind.

Through all this, two things allowed me to withstand the day-to-day battles I fought. First was an unwavering belief that God, for whatever reason and however undeserved, had wrapped His protective arms around me. Second was a family who was there for me each and every evening when I returned home from work.

But with all the stories, all the incidents, all the assignments, only one flowed "up from the heart, forced out by inward pressure." That was my experience infiltrating NAMBLA. I needed to tell that story. I needed to share that experience to alert the world to an underground network of pedophiles targeting boys.

I first met my agent, Bucky Rosenbaum, at my brother Dan's Christmas party. Bucky had been on the staff at Saddleback Church in Orange County, California, and represented Rick Warren in the Purpose Driven

Life series. Bucky decided to launch his own literary agency and was looking for clients. He may now regret attending that party because I began to talk to him about my undercover experiences in NAMBLA and my desire to expose the organization. We agreed to meet later in the year once he got the agency off the ground and I began writing about the investigation. I wasn't interested in pounding my chest and bragging about my undercover exploits or in writing a tell-all exposé about the FBI. With missionary zeal I wanted to alert the world to the "boy lover" agenda. That was the book flowing up from within.

By the time we next met I had almost eighty-five thousand words on paper, detailing the three-year investigation. Bucky, too, captured my vision and agreed to help me find a publisher. We both thought the process would be easy. Child molestation was a topic that cut across the political aisle. *Law & Order: SVU* was a top-rated show on NBC and Chris Hansen's *Dateline NBC: To Catch a Predator* segments were drawing 10 million viewers with each episode. We assumed the publishers would be craving an exposé on such a hideous organization written from the perspective of an undercover FBI agent. Two dozen rejection letters later, we realized it was not going to be an easy sell. Many of the rejections were thoughtful, praising my writing and my willingness to target a notorious group of pedophiles. No one, however, wanted to take on the project. Several rejections even used "ick factor," which must be a literary term taught at our prestigious universities. But several publishers were helpful in encouraging me to expand the subject matter by including more undercover stories.

As I thought about what these publishers said, I knew that had I never had the undercover experience of twenty-plus administratively approved undercover operations, I would have never been successful in pulling off the NAMBLA assignment. Their suggestions to expand the manuscript made sense. Although I balked early in the process of including more stories, I knew that if I wanted to accomplish my mission of exposing the boy lover movement, I needed to add these other undercover investigations. I set about expanding the manuscript.

Bucky then called upon a friend in the publishing world, Gary Terashita at Center Street. The manuscript had been originally rejected by them but Gary agreed to give it another read. After a second look he caught our vision, bringing on board Thom Lemmons to help me work through the now 125,000 words and give shape to my story. A special thanks to Gary, Thom, and Harry Helm for believing in me and taking a chance with my message.

As I recounted my other undercover stories, I relied on memory and what few mementos I had from the investigations, mainly news accounts, court documents, and administrative write-ups either for awards or chastisements. For the NAMBLA account I relied not only on my memory but trial preparation materials, including reports, transcripts, and tape and video recordings.

As a condition of my employment with the FBI, it is necessary for me to obtain the Bureau's approval for any published material. This book has been vetted and approved under the provisions of the prepublication review policy. Upon the FBI's review of the manuscript there were only two requirements. First, I had to delete the names of any FBI agent mentioned in my original submission. Second, I had to clearly state that the views expressed in the book do not necessarily represent the views of the FBI. Although I hate not giving proper credit to those other special agents who worked with me throughout my career, I complied with the FBI's conditions. I hope those agents will forgive me since, for one of the few times in my career, I complied with an FBI mandate.

What follows is the true account of my career as an undercover special agent with the FBI culminating in my infiltration of NAMBLA. Thanks for joining me in the journey of *The Last Undercover.*

ACKNOWLEDGMENTS

Thanks to Harry Helm at Hachette Book Group USA and Rolf Zettersten, the senior vice president and publisher at Center Street, as well as Gary Terashita and Cara Highsmith, for their patience throughout the project. A special thanks to the rest of the Center Street team for making this a reality.

To Thom Lemmons, who helped me shape this into the book it is.

To Bucky Rosenbaum, my agent and friend. It was a longer journey than either of us expected.

To my friends Katie Finneran, Dawn De-Noon, Midge Raymond, Tracey Stern, Monika Baker, Paul Grellong, and Daniel Combs, who provided valuable feedback and encouragement on the original manuscript.

To Lawana Jones at the FBI Prepublication Unit for ushering the manuscript through the process . . . several times.

To Laura Eimiller with Public Affairs at the Los Angeles FBI, who offered support, encouragement, and great advice.

To Jennifer Corbett and Anne Perry, not only for leading the successful prosecution of the NAMBLA members but for providing me with court documents as I put this project together.

But mostly to a gracious God, who blessed me with a great family: parents who served as role models, a wife who stood by me for these past three-plus decades, and the two greatest children in the world. You are all my heroes.

1
A WALK TOWARD
THE BEAST

New York NAMBLA Conference

As my cab honked its way along the New York City streets, I stared out the window at the crowds on the sidewalks and tried to talk down the apprehension rising inside me. Don't get me wrong: I have known fear, and I have felt the temple-pounding rush of adrenaline pumping through my body. But this evening, a sense of anxiety enveloped me. The sensation was unlike anything I'd experienced in my more than two decades of undercover work for the FBI. This case was going to be the toughest I had ever tackled, for reasons I didn't fully understand . . . yet.

It was a clear Friday evening, Veterans Day weekend. I was in New York to infiltrate an organization known as NAMBLA: the North American Man/Boy Love Association, a society of men who professed sexual attraction to young boys. The plan looked

17

simple enough in the operations order but seemingly impossible to orchestrate; I would pose as an aging pedophile, work myself into a position of trust within the organization, and gain criminal admissions from its members — admissions that would lead to successful federal prosecutions.

But as the time neared for me to make my debut with NAMBLA, things were looking anything but simple. I was unable to view the group I'd be infiltrating with anything other than revulsion. How could I pretend to actually be one of them — without becoming physically ill or physically violent? I wasn't sure I knew the answer.

During my career with the FBI, I successfully targeted some of the most treacherous criminal groups in America: La Cosa Nostra; the Russian, Sicilian, and Mexican Mafias; Asian organized crime groups; black street gangs. In the early eighties I was the undercover agent in the Los Angeles Mafia family case that resulted in the imprisonment of L.A.'s top fifteen mobsters. I had worked street gangs. Picture a white man in South Central L.A. buying rock cocaine from convicted felons and known killers. While undercover, I shot two drug dealers who attempted to turn our $400,000 cocaine transaction into a "rip." As the undercover agent in more than twenty administratively approved operations, lasting anywhere from several days to more than three years, I have successfully posed as a drug dealer, contract killer, residential burglar, degenerate gambler, international weapons dealer, and white-collar criminal.

But tonight I was about to spend the weekend playing the role of a "boy lover," or "BL," as NAMBLA members refer to themselves. It was quite a journey that had brought me here, and tonight marked the next step in the FBI's efforts to target men who preyed on boys. NAMBLA was real — much more than an episodic joke on *South Park*. The group was celebrating its twenty-fifth anniversary and I was going to be present for that celebration. After all, I was a dues-paying member.

San Diego, 1980

My tour of humanity's dark side began in earnest back in 1980, just after I left the Marine Corps. I spent four years as a judge advocate, serving as prosecutor, defense counsel, and an appellate review attorney. Regardless of how glamorous they make the JAG corps look on TV, the military courtroom lacked the excitement I hoped it would bring. I worked on trials running the gamut from unauthorized absence to murder, but the cases were never "whodunnits." The decision always came down to whether the confession was admissible or the search was legal. For me, the excitement waned quickly. The 150 trials in which I participated did, however, prepare me for my work in the FBI. Better than most, I knew what was necessary to get a conviction. Often those requirements had nothing to do with Bureau-imposed administrative hurdles. Following bureaucratic regulations with no evidentiary value was never my strong suit and no administrator ever accused me of being procedurally pure.

After suffering through three years of law school and four years as an attorney in the Marine Corps, I knew the courtroom was not where I wanted to be. Neither did I aspire to spending the rest of my life tethered to a desk, drafting wills, divorce decrees, or other legal documents. The FBI, known for its recruitment of lawyers and accountants, proved to be a near-perfect fit. I would be getting paid to play cops and robbers, something I did for free as a kid. Never in my twenty-six-year career did I ever question my decision to join the Bureau. Sure, I had bad days, but knowing the next call might put me on the thrill ride of a lifetime made the momentary frustrations easier to handle . . . usually.

Hollywood envisions every FBI agent assuming an undercover identity and capturing crooks with some sophisticated ruse. In fact, very few FBI agents ever remove the suit coat and loosen the tie. Today, the FBI carefully screens every agent seeking to work in an undercover capacity. Few are selected, and fewer still successfully navigate the difficult path to undercover certification. From that small number, only a handful continue to accept undercover roles throughout their careers. For those who do, it can mean the most exhilarating challenge anybody could ever hope for.

But in 1980, receiving an undercover assignment was as easy as raising a hand. I was looking for excitement, variety, and, above all, a way to avoid being tied to a desk. Undercover work seemed the perfect means to all my ends. I wanted to enter the world of Serpico; I wanted the thrill of the chase and the satisfaction of the hard-earned collar at the end. I was fortunate enough to have a supervisor who encouraged me to pursue my dreams. And so it was, in 1980, after about six months in the Bureau, I found myself on my way to meet Dave, my first undercover target.

As the time for the meeting neared, my heart was pounding and my knees were shaking — less from fear than excitement. Still, I knew I needed to get my emotions under control; Dave was an accomplished criminal, and if he spotted the knees, my undercover career would be short-lived.

The San Diego office identified Dave as a subject through wiretap surveillance and an informant's tip. We were investigating an art theft ring and Dave was a major player with connections to the Bonanno crime family in Arizona. As is often the case in undercover work, Dave would end up taking us in directions we never anticipated.

My cover was pretty weak and not at all well thought out: I would be Bob Bourne. I kept my real first name, but took the last name of the character from Robert Ludlum's famous novels. My persona was that of a nouveau riche high roller. I would let Dave know I had made a bundle in real estate and was looking to invest in Western art, which we knew from surveillance to be his specialty. Dave would have bargains to offer simply because his inventory was hotter than the proverbial two-dollar pistol.

Dave was lean and athletic; he trained as a long-distance runner. His training served him well, since one of his favorite MOs involved escaping on foot from snatch-and-grab jewelry heists. He would research the shooting policies of local police departments to determine whether they were authorized to shoot a fleeing felon. After selecting his target area, he would fly into town, wearing a three-piece suit and carrying a ring with an empty setting. He would locate a jewelry store near the airport and wave the ring at the unsuspecting sales staff, asking to see stones that fit the setting. As soon as the clerk set a case of stones in front of him, Dave would grab the case and run, knowing police weren't likely to shoot. By the time a patrol unit arrived on the scene, he was back at the airport waiting for his return flight, now holding a pocketful of diamonds.

We set up an office front in San Diego's Sorrento Valley, a commercial/industrial area north of the city. It was the perfect ruse. The tech agents divided the oversized office into two separate units; a sliding bookshelf straight out of a Hollywood movie scene concealed the hidden room where my backup agents operated the audio and video recording equipment that monitored every meeting. Comfortable deep rich leather furniture, a fully stocked wet bar, and walls adorned with Western art prints provided a relaxed atmosphere in which to conduct business. Dave and his confederates never displayed much curiosity about what I did at the office, but several of my fellow tenants complained to the building manager that something suspicious was occurring on the second floor. I'm not sure if they were alarmed because I really sold myself as a criminal, or if I was just sloppy. In any event, I successfully lured Dave and his associates to the office, and as I waited for him to arrive for our first meeting — my first face-to-face experience undercover — I took deep breaths, said a couple of prayers, and tried to control the riptide of emotions surging through me.

As it turned out, the meeting was short and rather uneventful. Dave never noticed my knees and we actually hit it off. Our conversation was rather innocuous, but the important thing was Dave left believing I had money and was willing to buy at a five-finger discount. I came away with a stress headache and a lingering adrenaline jag. What a thrill to have successfully completed my first undercover meet! The target believed me — and I believed myself! I was a junky for the jazzed-up feeling, and I continued to chase that buzz throughout my career. I was invincible, or at least so I thought, and during that abbreviated meeting, I realized I had found my niche in the law enforcement world.

In reality, Dave and I had a lot in common: he neither drank nor smoked; he exercised regularly and was in great shape. I was an experienced runner having had competed in over a half-dozen marathons, completing several in less than three hours. Dave wasn't much of a talker, so running dominated much of the discussion during the several months I spent targeting him and his associates.

Starting out as a young agent was a blessing rather than a curse. I had yet to pick up the cop lingo. Cops said, "Have a good one." Bad guys said, "Later." I also didn't have the J. Edgar Hoover, everything-is-either-black-or-white mindset. As I learned throughout my career, the skills needed to successfully work undercover were self-taught, consisting mostly of common sense seasoned with lessons from the street. No school could adequately prepare you for the job — at least no school sponsored by the FBI. In fact, I tried to avoid such schools and seminars. Too often, I found that the rules promulgated by the various departments and agencies boxed you into a specific type of character that could easily be detected by the bad guys. My unorthodoxy proved valuable throughout my career as I negotiated with criminals from every culture and economic stratum. My best teachers were the informants I interacted with and the bad guys I arrested.

Shortly after meeting Dave, I saw the investigation hit pay dirt: he had a painting he had recently "acquired" and was looking to quietly dispose of it at a price well below its true market value. Just like something out of a TV crime drama, Dave showed up at the office with the painting, valued at more than fifty thousand dollars, and we negotiated a "fair" price, all on surveillance video. It was as simple as that. The Bureau put up the funds and with sufficient green, I became Dave's new best friend.

2
LIVING IN THE
SHADOW WORLD

Working undercover means more than donning a wig or growing a moustache. Despite what many FBI administrators think, it's not just a name change, a phony driver's license, and an untraceable credit card. The small cadre of successful undercover police officers and federal agents know it means being "one of them" without becoming one of them. It's one thing to immerse yourself in a character; it's another to be consumed by a criminal persona. Operating undercover means living with duality and praying you will recognize the ambiguous line between who you really are and the imposter you have become. It means adopting an alter ego antithetical to the real you and exploring the darkest side of humanity. It means being an actor in the ultimate reality show: one where there are no retakes — a drama where a botched line, a missed mark, or a dropped cue could mean instant death.

The FBI didn't instill a warrior ethos in its undercover agents. There was no secret handshake or written code of conduct. Heck, I'm still waiting for my secret decoder ring. We were part of a very loose brotherhood of single-minded individuals who seldom came together as a team. On only a few occasions did I work with another undercover agent posing as my confederate. More often than not I worked the high wire alone. Success depended upon individual ability, not the strength of teammates.

Much of my strength came from my family. I have been blessed with an understanding wife and two supportive children who have seen me through the difficult assignments. We often joke that I've been married to the same sweet, wonderful person for more than thirty years, yet she's tolerated life with a half-dozen personality changes and a variety of shady characters.

So who would choose such a life? It's not for everyone. The risks are enormous, physically and psychologically. The rewards are only personal, certainly not monetary; the pay's the same with or without a disguise. This life can mean wildly unpredictable working hours and bizarre assignments that interfere with any sense of normalcy. The skills are typically intuited rather than

28

acquired through training. You need to be autonomous and creative, yet remain a Bureau team player. Stress comes from all sides: from the FBI as well as the bad guys. Both sometimes make demands almost impossible to fulfill. For most of us who've lived in the shadow world, the primary motivation for working undercover is a sense of purpose — a strong, unyielding belief in right and wrong, a belief that the personal rewards and the sense of accomplishment far outweigh the risks. But regardless of the motive, there's a collateral benefit only an undercover agent can appreciate: when you have placed your life in harm's way and have successfully convinced the bad guys you *are* one of them, you experience a high few other experiences can top. I know of no comparable thrill.

After my first successful purchase, Dave became even more open about his activities. After all, he had just sold me a painting he stole from a Scottsdale, Arizona, art gallery and the police never pounced. What was not to like?

One afternoon, I met Dave for lunch at an ocean-side bistro. He brought along one of his associates, a penny stock manipulator from Salt Lake City. Although Dave and I had engaged in several criminal deals, Dave never asked me my last name and I never offered it. When his friend asked the question, I played the typical crook game and avoided an answer. Many times in my dealings with the bad guys, even in cases lasting months or more, we never exchanged last names. Criminals figure the less the other guy knows, the less chance he'll have of ratting you out if he gets snatched.

It was another area where I had to be careful. As an FBI agent I knew a great deal about my targets, but I had to compartmentalize what I knew as an agent and what I only "found out" while working undercover. To say something that came from an intelligence briefing and not from the lips of the bad guy could spell instant trouble, if not death.

However, Dave's buddy insisted on knowing my name. Finally I said, "Bourne — you know, like the book." Then I turned to Dave. "See, the book *The Bourne Identity* is really about me. I'm with the CIA."

Both of them let out a hearty laugh. Dave said, "Just as long as you're not with the FBI, what do we care?"

Although several agents in the San Diego office had undercover experience, most of it was the controversial targeting of radicals in the sixties and seventies. No one had worked the type of crime we were investigating so I didn't really seek the guidance of the older agents. Our efforts at targeting Dave were rather simplistic, almost naïve. I never had a good game plan and we seemed to be playing it by ear, allowing Dave to drive the investigation based upon whatever crimes he willingly discussed.

I did, however, get an enlightening look into the bureaucratic world of the FBI. At that time, all first-office agents not assigned to what the FBI called the "Dirty Dozen" — twelve large offices the Bureau had trouble filling with voluntary transfers — were subject to transfer after six months in their first office. San Diego was not on the Dirty Dozen list, and sure enough, orders came through for my transfer to Los Angeles, one of the offices on the list. Even though I was directly involved in an undercover assignment and had successfully targeted a proven, righteous thief, Washington was unwilling to allow me to stay in San Diego until the case played out. The Special Agent in Charge of the San Diego office worked out an arrangement with Los Angeles to keep me beyond the six months, but L.A. was unwilling to commit to an indefinite period of time. In fact, Los Angeles "needed" me as soon as possible for some undisclosed investigations being conducted by the "Hollywood" FBI. Despite efforts by San Diego, L.A. demanded that I report.

What made the transfer even more distressing was the fact my wife was seven months pregnant with our second child. Still, the Bureau was unrelenting. L.A. just had to have me and I had to report. We prepared for the move and I prepared Dave for my transfer.

I learned early in my undercover work to lie as little as possible. Cases are blown and agents get killed over the little lies, not the big ones. In my undercover role, I was married and my wife was pregnant. I stayed with those facts as part of my scenario.

One afternoon, while sitting in my undercover car equipped with recording devices, I explained to Dave the story I concocted. He knew my wife was pregnant. With tears welling up in my eyes, I explained that my wife had developed "inverted placenti." The medical condition caused previous miscarriages and the doctors ordered complete bed rest for the remainder of the pregnancy. In addition, I told him the most accomplished doctor familiar with this malady was in Indianapolis. It was going to be necessary to take her back to Indiana for hospitalization to save the baby. As a result, our near-daily meetings would have to be curtailed. Then I began to cry. Dave looked over at me, believing the tears, and patted me on the knee. With all sincerity, he asked me if I "believed in prayer." I was stunned by the question. At no time in our relationship did we ever discuss religion.

I said nothing, but Dave went on. "I've been studying this religion called Christian Science. You can call them up and they can pray for you over the phone and heal you."

I kept quiet, but turned my head away from Dave and bit my thumb, trying to keep from laughing.

"I'm seriously thinking of taking up the religion," Dave said, "once I give up stealing."

I bit harder, hoping my shoulders weren't shaking — or if they were, that Dave would think I was overcome with grief.

But as I later reflected on the conversation, I was touched. Dave was genuinely concerned with the health of my wife. Few agents ever expressed such feelings to me. When I later shared the story with an older agent, he went running to the supervisor, expressing concern that I was getting too close to my intended target and might cross the thin, blue line. The agent was wrong. I wasn't even close to switching sides, but it also taught me a valuable lesson about being cautious in sharing my true feelings with other agents. It was just the first instance of the double bind I would find myself in more than once during my career. A comment misinterpreted by an FBI supervisor could end your undercover career just as quickly — though, admittedly, not as violently — as a slipup in front of a bad guy. As a result, I often couldn't talk to anybody about what I was going through. Naturally, I couldn't tell the bad guys about the stress of pretending to be someone I wasn't; similarly, I couldn't give my supervisors — or even the FBI shrinks I had to see every six months for mandatory psych profiling — the whole story about what a particular case was doing to me emotionally. In other words, whether I was sitting in a room full of bad guys or sitting at a table with my Bureau managers, I was playing a role for somebody. Only with my family could I occasionally and selectively allow my true feelings to show.

As my wife and I prepared for the move, Dave dropped another bombshell. He had recently "acquired" fifty antique clocks worth more than $500,000, as well as gold, silverware, furs, and place settings valued at more than $300,000. The acquisition was the result of a successful Tucson burglary. I expressed an interest and we began negotiations. One afternoon he brought several clocks to the undercover office, allowing me to examine them so I could determine if I might know of an interested buyer. Again, the meeting was caught on tape as I examined antique clocks valued at more than my entire net worth.

Dave floated back and forth between California and Arizona. Following this most recent burglary he invited me to join him in Scottsdale to view the stolen silverware and place settings. I flew over on a Friday afternoon and that evening we met for dinner at an upscale Italian restaurant. Dave invited several of his mob friends to join us. It was a great meal with interesting conversation; each of the guys around the table tried to top the last with brags about criminal exploits. There was lots of laughing and good-natured ribbing, and as the dinner concluded I said I'd cover the tip. I threw a one-hundred-dollar bill on the table — which, by the way, earned me a butt chewing from a Bureau accountant when I got back to San Diego and vouchered my expenses.

One of the mobsters invited us to join him

at his office down the street, where we continued our conversation. Our host was already pretty drunk, but once we settled in his office he pulled out a silver tray and started cutting lines of cocaine. I remember thinking it was like a scene from a movie, only this was real. He grabbed a razor blade and began to chop at the coke, breaking it down into several fine, powdery lines, each a few inches in length. I was about to face my first true test as an undercover agent.

Drug use by undercover agents is only justified in a life-or-death situation and I had never been educated on how to handle this problem. Remember, I was the guy who just raised his hand for this assignment. I never attended the soon-to-be-required undercover certification school, and I certainly wasn't interested in putting any powder up my nose. My head was spinning as I tried to think of a response that wouldn't "blow" my cover.

As our host continued to make lines of coke, he presented me with another problem: he opened the top drawer of his desk and pulled a revolver from beneath several well-read porno magazines. As he laid the weapon on the desk next to the tray, my heart began to pound. I thought for sure those around the table could hear the deafening thumps now roaring in my ears. I did my best imitation of a nonchalant onlooker, but inside I knew I was walking through a minefield.

Of course, there was a method to our host's madness, even if he was three sheets to the wind. If everybody did a line of coke, he knew no cops were present. One by one the guests used a rolled-up hundred-dollar bill to snort the white powder. When it came my turn, I passed, trying to make my body language say it was no big deal.

But he didn't want to take no for an answer. He demanded I join him and his friends, suggesting only a cop would refuse. He then picked up the gun and pointed it toward my head.

With all the bravado I could muster, I looked him in the eye and with profanity-laced eloquence told him I was allergic to all "-caine" products. I couldn't even take novacaine at the dentist. "I'll do your lousy line if you want," I said, "but you might as well call an ambulance, because when that crap hits my system my heart's gonna freaking stop. Good luck explaining it to the medical examiner." Or words to that effect.

Dave, who was on my left and was next in line, came to my rescue. He wasn't about to put anything up his nose either. Our host relented and put the gun back in the drawer. I drew a slow, shaky breath, hoping everybody else was too drunk or coked up to care.

The rest of the evening was uneventful, and Dave and I negotiated a fair price for the stolen silverware, adding an additional count to the growing list of criminal charges.

Not long after the Scottsdale incident, my home phone rang, late one evening. It was Dave, calling collect from jail. He had been arrested for possession of a kilogram of cocaine and was being held in the Orange County Jail in Santa Ana, California. In light of his refusal to do a line in Scottsdale I was surprised by the possession arrest. Dave asked if I could help "raise bail." I promised to do all I could and immediately called my case agent. With a series of calls throughout the night, we were able to "raise the bail" to $1 million. I know that wasn't Dave's intent, but you have to admit, we did follow his spoken request to the letter.

The next day, as we continued to insure Dave would not be released, my wife became an important part of the investigation. Although the FBI was not new to undercover operations, we lacked some of the sophistication developed during the course of my career. For one thing, cell phones were nonexistent at this time. The number I provided the bad guys was merely a "cold" number at the FBI office subscribed to by my undercover company. I would have calls to that number forwarded to my home so there was no way anyone could identify where I lived, yet I would always be accessible. While I was in the FBI office, working with other agents on Dave's arrest, my wife received a call at home. I had forgotten to stop the call-forwarding feature on the office cold phone, and my wife, unsuspecting, answered the phone. The caller asked for me. She said I was "at the office." When the caller asked for that number, my wife had the sense to ask who was calling. The caller identified himself as a friend of Dave. Fortunately, she kept her cool and asked the caller for a number and told him I would call him later that evening. Had she not been so perceptive and instead given him the number of the FBI office, the case would have ended as soon as somebody at the Bureau answered the phone. My wife was developing the street smarts of an undercover agent. We also learned from that incident, and once we moved to L.A., we had two phones installed at the house. My children called them the good-guy phone and the bad-guy phone; I was the only person allowed to answer the bad-guy phone.

So there was Dave, my first undercover target, sitting in jail, no doubt trying to figure the circumstances by which his bail had gone up to a million dollars. As bad as his short-term prospects were, his long-term prospects were about to get even worse.

A subsequent search of Dave's storage facility resulted in the recovery of over $1 million in stolen property, including the antique clocks. Dave was sentenced to ten years in prison, after pleading guilty to charges of transporting stolen property across state lines. I never learned if he took up the Christian Science religion. And thanks to a very savvy case agent who negotiated the plea, Dave never learned I was an undercover agent. He and his associates thought I had slipped past the long arm of the law.

Operation Ruffcut, as we named the investigation, was only beginning and continued without me when I transferred to Los Angeles. Dave's arrest allowed me to bow out gracefully. We closed the Sorrento Valley undercover office and reopened one in another section of San Diego. Other undercover agents replaced me, targeting Dave's associates, and took the operation beyond anything we ever dreamed. Building upon my initial contributions and the continued outstanding work of the other undercover agents, the FBI broke a major interstate theft ring specializing in heavy equipment, art, gems, and weapons. In addition, the agents identified a cocaine trafficking ring operating out of Denver; over thirty individuals were indicted when everything was said and done. I was saddened by my inability to be a part of that portion of the investigation, but proud of my efforts at getting the investigation started and allowing it to proceed with such success. More importantly, I had become an undercover agent and was successful in my first foray into the criminal world.

New York NAMBLA Conference
As we weaved through molasses-slow New York traffic, the ever-constant blaring of horns and what I assumed to be curses in Arabic from my Middle Eastern cab driver interrupted my mental preparation for the NAMBLA encounter, but the moment of truth was quickly approaching. He pulled up in front of Grand Central Station, and it was time for me to meet my "fellow" pedophiles.

I hobbled from the cab using my crutch — my cover identity involved being a handicapped, "grandfatherly" type of independent financial means — and began the long walk around the train station. Even though the invitation said we would be meeting at 6:30 pm in the lower-level dining concourse, I wanted to be fashionably late. I continued walking around the upper level, with its fifty-plus retail specialty shops, and admiring the 125-foot vaulted ceiling, painted to resemble the evening sky. I ducked in and out of shops as commuters hustled home for the weekend. They were seeking refuge after a long week of labor; my job was just beginning.

I glanced at my watch; it was well past 6:30. It sounds like a tired, B-movie cliché, but I really did say to myself in a barely audible voice, "It's showtime!" More than twenty restaurants encircled the lower level, our prearranged meeting spot. I had no idea for whom to look or what to expect. Other than a few grainy photos of suspected or known members I found on the Internet, I wasn't even sure I would be able to identify the group.

NAMBLA wasn't the Mafia, so I wasn't looking for Al Pacino look-alikes congregating in a corner. Nor were they members of an outlaw motorcycle gang "flying colors," or an L.A.-based street gang like the Crips or Bloods, adorned in their respective blue or red. Instead, NAMBLA was an organization of men seeking to legitimize their sexual attraction to boys, and most members sought to hide their affiliation. What if I couldn't identify the group? What if they had already identified me as a special agent with the FBI and this was all part of an elaborate scheme to expose me as an undercover agent? Even if that were true, I didn't feel my life was in danger, not on this assignment. No, the risks of this investigation were far more subtle than dodging bullets.

3
CHINA WHITE

In the late eighties my partner and I were warned by an informant that a street gang had put out a contract on our lives. Word was disseminated throughout the hood that a financial reward awaited anyone who was willing to "blast on the two white dudes in the green Grand Prix." We fooled our adversaries by the less-than-sophisticated and clever ruse of switching cars. While I was undercover, members of the L.A. Mafia had on several occasions threatened to break my legs, run me over with a car, or bury me. Several men I arrested threatened to kill me once they completed their prison sentence — threats that never materialized but caused anxiety for my family when the men were released. The point is, I'd experienced enough real physical danger that I wasn't too worried about what a group of pedophiles might do. I was more afraid of being mugged in the subway than being attacked by NAMBLA members, and yet, apprehension gnawed ceaselessly at my stomach. The simple fact was, I didn't know if I was going to be able to play this part well enough to pull off the assignment. The prospect of acting and thinking enough like one of these child molesters to be taken for one of them was making my skin crawl.

The crowds seemed to grow larger as I limped toward the lower level. How would I recognize the targets? I couldn't exactly expect a big sign reading "NAMBLA MEETS HERE!" Although FBI agents from New York were covering me, I had little chance of communicating with them should I fail to spot the quarry.

Ten or fifteen steps down the ramp alleviated all my identification questions. My eyes were immediately drawn to several men congregating near a wooden bench. *Central casting, send me some perverts!* At first glance, they seemed so obvious — white men, poorly dressed, unshaven, overweight, some even wearing cheap, black, horn-rim glasses. But upon closer examination, not everyone fit my stereotypical image of a child molester. In fact, several of the men looked normal, not like creeps or monsters. They could have been your son's teacher, coach, or neighbor. But the group stood out like blue jeans at a formal dinner: clusters of men, chatting with each other — and not so subtly gawking at the occasional teen or preteen boy racing for a train. They reminded me of a bunch of fraternity guys at a wet T-shirt contest — except the objects of their hungry scrutiny were young men and boys, rather than gyrating, oversexed females. They were obviously out of place with the well-attired businessman or day laborer walking purposefully toward the subway. Their mere presence screamed "probable cause!" in my cop brain. I laughed inwardly at being so anxious about finding my new "soul mates."

Instead, I began to fear the group was so obvious the beat cops patrolling the area would hassle us on general principle and blow the entire operation before it ever got going. In fact, four uniformed police officers stood within twenty-five feet of where most of the NAMBLA members had gathered. The cops were probably talking about the Jets or the Giants, failing to even notice the boy lover assemblage congregating in their presence. At any moment, though, I expected the uniforms to swarm.

Rather than marching directly toward the men, I made my way to the restroom. As I stood at the urinal, a snatch of a Bible verse went through my head: the passage where Moses tells Joshua, as he leads his people toward the Promised Land, to not be afraid, since God would always be with them. I smiled and thought, "God, you and I are going to the NAMBLA convention."

As I walked out of the restroom, an FBI agent I recognized from the briefing sidled up to me. "They're in the middle of the concourse," he murmured, his lips barely moving. I gave an understanding nod but didn't need his help. They were pathetically obvious. I moved toward the belly of the beast.

By now about twenty men were gathered, all of them trusted NAMBLA members who had been with the organization at least three years and were specifically selected to attend this year's conference. I thrust out my hand and began greeting my new friends. Although I could tell I was viewed with suspicion, everyone returned the greeting. I did, however, keep an eye on the uniformed cops standing almost within earshot of our gathering. As an undercover agent, I was concerned they might disrupt the operation, but I also wanted to appear nervous about the law enforcement presence being so close. A member noticed my anxiety and tried to put me at ease. "Relax.

47

They're looking for muggers and terrorists."
Maybe I had passed the first test.

Most undercover operations are initiated
with an introduction by what law enforcement calls an informant, a source, a cooperating witness, or — a term I try to avoid —
a snitch. This person's motivation may be
revenge or money. More typically, though,
the individual is "working off a beef" and
has agreed to cooperate as part of a plea
agreement. Even though informants can
mean tremendous administrative and investigative headaches, they represent the life-
blood of many law enforcement operations.
An informant can provide much-needed
street "cred" and create the necessary
inroad into a criminal organization. Informants have covered my backside in many
undercover operations, vouching for my
authenticity and my reliability. A good
informant can be a valued partner, and I
often found myself siding with my source
over some bureaucratic bungler who had
little concept of what it means to work the
streets and risk your life. For the NAMBLA
operation, I had no informant to make the
introduction or accompany me to the conference. It was up to me to sell myself to
the targets; I could rely on no one if I made

an untimely slip.

Amid the buzz of Grand Central Station, I took a seat on a nearby wooden bench and conversed with several of the NAMBLA members. I was amazed at how open the men were, not in discussing criminal activity, but in talking about previous conferences, renewing old acquaintances, and making the occasional lewd reference to young boys who strode past.

I talked with Floyd, an older, white-haired man who walked with a distinct limp. He looked grandfatherly, and his tattered clothes belied his intellect. I listened intently to the conversations of Rowan, Ted, and Jim, all East Coast residents, longtime members . . . and retired schoolteachers. No one used last names in the informal introductions.

After listening to several long-winded reminiscences of previous conferences, I asked if Peter Herman was around. One of the men pointed to a short, thin, older man who looked almost professorial. I immediately recognized Peter from a Web site photo I saw in researching my role as a boy lover. "Peter Herman" was an alias for Peter Melzer. I knew quite a bit about him going into the conference, and here he was in the flesh — maybe not the Babe Ruth of BLs but certainly a member of the NAMBLA Hall of Fame. His appearance and stature hardly measured up to his notoriety.

Part of the thrill in assuming any undercover role is preparing to such an extent that I can pass myself off as knowledgeable in the chosen cover. I don't necessarily need to be an expert but I do need to "pass." By the time the subjects of our investigation have figured out I don't know what I'm talking about, I hope to have a nice, neat indictment to shove in their faces. I've had to learn about drugs, weapons, Western art, antique clocks, screenwriting, stunt work, real estate, import/exports, investments, horse racing, and, for this role, boy lovers. The Internet has been an invaluable tool in the last few years. In the early eighties I would spend hours at the library researching the various topics. Thanks to the Internet, most of that research can now be done in front of a computer screen.

As part of the preparation for the NAMBLA investigation, I read a sixty-three-page report titled "An Investigation into Misconduct Relating to Pedophilia by Peter Melzer, a Teacher at the Bronx High School of Science," dated September 1993. The report was thorough, well researched, and well written. Quite frankly, I didn't even care if it was true. I wasn't looking for evidence; I needed insight into the boy lover mindset. The investigation of Melzer and his role in NAMBLA provided a valuable peek into the world of the BL.

Melzer had been a teacher since 1963 and joined the faculty of the Bronx High School of Science in 1968, where he taught physics and science. His membership in NAMBLA came to public attention in March 1992. WNBC-TV aired a three-part story on NAMBLA showing him in a leadership role at meetings of the organization's New York chapter. When the news identified him as a teacher at the high school, the school board reacted quickly.

The written report also related the investigative work of Kevin Healy, a former NYPD detective who met Melzer in an undercover capacity. Melzer admitted to having sexual relations with "a young boy or boys in the Philippines." The report detailed articles in the NAMBLA *Bulletin,* their official magazine, when Melzer served as its editor. Articles published under his editorial leadership included one by an author who wrote,

My first suggestion [for initiating a sexual relationship with a boy] is to restrict your sexual involvement and overtures to boys who need you, boys who value you and your friendship. . . . Before risking any direct sexual overture, you can tell a lot about a boy with a few well-placed sexual jokes or comments. . . . Leave a pornographic magazine someplace where he's sure to find it. . . . Masturbation and pornography go hand in hand. An aroused and adventurous adolescent with a positive view of sexuality may try just about anything to get off. . . . The best way for you to pursue boys is to emigrate from the U.S. . . . to a country or culture where boy-love has greater acceptance. . . . Weigh the pros and cons of becoming involved yourself in sex tourism overseas. Seek and find love from American boys on a platonic, purely emotional level. For sexual satisfaction, travel once or twice yearly overseas. You might get arrested overseas . . . but the legal consequences . . . will be less severe.

The report also discussed a letter in the December 1992 *Bulletin* that provided advice on touching boys on various body parts, including the penis and the buttocks, and recommended taking warm showers together. Another letter in the *Bulletin*

52

began, "The penis of an adolescent boy offers the warmth and security of its size. . . . But we cannot place any less prestige in the young penis of the pre-adolescent."

All this information was running through my mind as I walked up to Peter Melzer, aka Peter Herman. I tried to block out the faces of my son and his Little League buddies on the team I'd coached years before, tried to empty my head of the nauseating suggestions Peter Melzer and his fellow NAMBLA members would have concocted about how to get such boys to acquiesce to their sexual advances. Instead, I pasted on a smile and stuck out my hand as I approached. "Hi, Peter. I'm Robert, from California."

Peter was cordial and welcomed me to my first conference. He acknowledged my participation in the holiday card and the pen-pal program for incarcerated NAMBLA members, and my apparent dedication to the organization commenting on two articles I submitted for publication in the *Bulletin.* We chatted briefly. His voice evidenced a slight Eastern European accent.

As many as twenty-five members had now gathered in the dining concourse. Peter organized us into informal groups based upon what each wanted to do for the evening. The majority chose a tour of Times Square Peter was conducting. Several groups, however, left to go to various residences. Most of those members were either from the New York area and had probably spent a lifetime in Times Square or were hesitant to spend too much time with first-time invitees. I chose the tour and it proved to be an eye-opening experience.

Los Angeles, 1983
Back in the mid-eighties, not long after the arrest of Dave, the marathon-running jewel thief, I was working in L.A. on a mob-run heroin trafficking ring. During the course of that investigation, we became aware of another trafficker, Darrel, a Canadian citizen living in Los Angeles. The Royal Canadian Mounted Police believed Darrel was responsible for much of the China White heroin trade in the greater Vancouver area. The RCMP was eager to cooperate with us in trying to nail Darrel and his associates.

The L.A. trafficking network utilized various individuals as "mules": couriers who delivered the heroin from the distributor to various dealers and other buyers. One of these mules was a strikingly beautiful woman we'll call Heather.

Heather not only worked as a mule for the traffickers but also practiced the world's oldest profession. Our evidence against her was insufficient to insure a conviction, but a profitable interrogation — especially if accompanied by a confession — could seal her legal fate. We had two alternatives: obtain a confession, and thus her conviction, or seek her cooperation. Heather's role was somewhat limited in the drug organization, and based upon her contacts in Los Angeles — and, as it later proved, in Canada — my FBI partner and I believed her cooperation would be of greater benefit to the government than another mere conviction stat. We were more interested in having her testify against her bosses and provide intelligence on other drug-trafficking organizations operating in Los Angeles than we were in seeing her incarcerated.

It was mid-December when we first met Heather. The fact she even agreed to meet with us boded well. Many subjects "lawyer up," preventing law enforcement officials from even making a pitch. She met us at an outdoor café on Ventura Boulevard in Studio City. Over coffee and Cokes, we explained in detail the accumulated evidence and told her that, just as an associate of hers had been arrested, she would be taken into custody unless she agreed to co-operate. Our strategy was nothing novel, nor was it something most people couldn't observe by watching crime dramas on TV. She seemed receptive and asked for a chance to think over our offer. Since we were unprepared to arrest her right then anyway, we gave her the opportunity to reflect. We agreed to meet a week later.

On December 23, my partner and I went to Heather's North Hollywood apartment. When we arrived, prepared to welcome our newest informant into a stable of very productive sources, we were shocked to see a packed bag sitting by the door. She arranged a babysitter for her eight-year-old son and was prepared to have us take her to jail. She decided she was unwilling to co-operate and was instead willing to face whatever consequences awaited her. The problem was, we had no authority to arrest her: the U.S. Attorney's office was unwilling to indict her based upon the evidence we had, and typically the FBI will not make an arrest without the prior authorization of the prosecutor. Heather didn't realize it, but she had our backs to the wall. With our stock of options dwindling fast, I asked if we could sit at her tiny dining room table and talk through her decision.

My partner and I started off slowly, using all our persuasive skills to convince her that jail was not an appropriate place for a mother, especially one who had an alternative avenue before her. Although we could see she was softening, she was unwilling to commit. Finally, in one last effort, I asked her to look me in the eye.

Heather was in her mid-thirties, a recovering heroin addict, a prostitute, a convicted felon, and a victim of parental and spousal abuse. Throughout her lifetime, she saw the damage drug abuse wreaked in peoples' lives; her own life was in shambles. With complete sincerity and — okay, I admit it — a bit of dramatic flair, I looked into her eyes and said, "Today, Heather, you can prevent another girl from going through the same hell you've seen. By agreeing to co-operate with us and targeting those people selling heroin to our children, you can help us save another Heather somewhere from the mess you've been through. Will you do it?"

She bowed her head, almost as if in prayer. When she looked up, tears were streaming down her cheeks. She choked as she spoke. "I'll help you."

My partner and I breathed a sigh of relief. Once Heather regained her composure, she asked us if we were Christians. I laughed when my partner said, "No, I'm Catholic," but I acknowledged that I was a Christian. She said she believed in God and believed He sent us. She said that while using heroin, she often prayed to God, seeking a vein in which to plunge the needle, and He always provided. I must admit, I was never convinced God was in the business of providing veins for junkies, but I was glad she saw us as God's messengers. I was pretty sure she'd fare better, over the long haul, with the choice she was making now, rather than the other less-favorable alternatives she'd already tried.

My partner and I wished her a Merry Christmas, told her we'd be in touch after the holidays, and began to think about how we could best utilize Heather's insider knowledge. Not long after the New Year, she would begin meeting — and exceeding — all our expectations.

4

THE WELCOMING COMMITTEE

After the first of the year, my partner and I received even more intel from the Mounties about Darrel, including details of his operation and several of his associates. Heather was unfamiliar with Darrel, as it turned out, but she did know several of the associates the Mounties identified. She was also familiar with a popular bar he used to frequent in Vancouver. We learned from Heather that one of Darrel's associates was a heroin dealer named John. His estranged wife, Kristi (not her real name), was living in L.A. and was a close friend of Heather. Both attended the same methadone maintenance treatment center, and like Heather, Kristi worked as a prostitute. Later in the year, Kristi and Heather moved in together, sharing the same North Hollywood apartment with their children. Eventually, my partner and I approached Kristi. She, too, agreed to cooperate. Neither woman knew the other was providing information to the FBI, but it was an excellent way of crosschecking the information each of them was giving us.

The information we were obtaining convinced us beyond any doubt that Darrel was a worthy target. Though a Canadian citizen, he'd been living in the U.S. since the 1960s. He was smart, evasive, and tough. Years earlier, we learned, he'd outmaneuvered a Drug Enforcement Agency team trying to nail him. In one situation, he'd agreed to a meeting with an undercover DEA agent only on the condition that they talk in the steam bath at a health club, where both men would be naked. Pretty hard to wear a wire into a situation like that. Eventually, Darrel wore out the DEA's patience and they moved on to other targets.

As I continued to talk with Heather about Darrel, she suggested that maybe she and Kristi could connect with him and pretend to know him from Vancouver. I realized we'd have to bring Kristi and Heather together in the operation, so I arranged a meeting in which the two women agreed to convince the other to work together as FBI informants.

In the summer of 1983, I received a call from my RCMP counterpart. He provided the flight itinerary for Darrel, who was returning from Canada later in the week. I hatched a plan to take both women to the Los Angeles International Airport, and, as Darrel got off the plane, we would orchestrate a "chance" encounter.

The scene that day, August 24, 1983, was like something you might view on the big screen. Both ladies showed up at LAX, dressed like they were working Hollywood Boulevard during convention season. One was in black and the other in red. As Kristi told me, "Black and red are the two sexiest colors." I don't know anybody — any man, at least — who would have disagreed. Actually, I was embarrassed just directing them to the gate. To say they turned heads is an understatement: chiropractors probably noticed a spike in business from men getting off planes that afternoon.

As part of their play, they pretended to be stranded and were engaged in a mock argument as Darrel exited the plane. They were so engrossed in their act they missed him as he walked past. He was well down the walkway when I approached them. "He's heading toward the baggage area," I whispered.

Heather and Kristi spun and started running — no small thing in spike heels — down the walkway, clomping like cloggers

61

in a speed competition. Had it not been so nerve-wracking and potentially dangerous, I would have laughed. Just as the two passed Darrel, they abruptly stopped and turned toward him. "You're Darrel from Vancouver, aren't you?" He bit and the game was on.

Over the next several months, Heather and Darrel occasionally dated. I continually warned Heather about getting sexually involved and she assured me he "wasn't sexual" — an interesting notion, given Heather's highly attractive qualities. My reason behind the admonition was twofold: morally, I had problems putting Heather in a compromising position; legally, I feared sex might torpedo the investigation, setting up an entrapment plea as an out for Darrel. However, as they continued to date, the fifty-eight-year-old heroin trafficker said all the right things, bragging of his overseas connections and eventually offering to sell Heather heroin for her out-of-town buyer. I intended to be that buyer.

For some reason, Heather decided to tell Darrel I was from Denver, even though that wasn't what we discussed and I'd never even been there. However, I figured I could do enough research to at least familiarize myself with the major landmarks. Later, at a critical point, my Denver "residency" would pose a temporary logistical problem, but for now, Darrel was going along with the story Heather was giving him: I was interested in purchasing large amounts of heroin.

As an initial transaction, we arranged a ten-ounce buy with Heather as my intermediary. The deal went smoothly, paving the way for my introduction. Once I was introduced, Heather's involvement was phased out. Darrel made few, if any, efforts to maintain contact with her, which pleased us all. For her part, Heather had no desire to maintain any relationship with him, and apparently Darrel's interest in her was also waning. Maybe she was right: maybe he wasn't "sexual."

At this time, the FBI was fairly new in the world of big-time drug traffickers, and Headquarters was dipping into the newly created Superfund for drug-buy money. The money in the fund was the result of the seizure and sale of forfeited items from various drug investigations throughout the country. It was an excellent idea: essentially, drug traffickers financed our narcotics investigations without the need of tapping into tax dollars.

As I began to have more face time with

Darrel, I came to realize his ego was almost boundless. I have a fairly robust self-esteem — some of my detractors might even suggest it borders on cockiness — but believe me, I paled in comparison to Darrel. I must have listened to a couple dozen sermons about his skill and acumen as a drug dealer. "I've been moving this stuff for twenty-three years and I've never been busted," he said. He based his operation in L.A. because the justice system in the U.S. was easier to beat, he told me. I just let him talk. I called him "Dr. D, the Doctor of Drugs," and he ate it up. Every time we met, the case against him got stronger.

One time, I decided to see how long he would talk without my saying anything. He started, and I just sat there, nodding my head at strategic moments, letting the tape roll. When it was transcribed, his soliloquy ran for over three pages, single-spaced. I don't think even Hamlet spoke that long in a single stretch.

Meanwhile, I was keeping up the Denver story line. The Bureau set up a cold phone in the Denver office and had the calls forwarded to my L.A. bad-guy phone. Darrel would call me from his Brentwood residence and I'd pick up the receiver in L.A., talking about the snow on the ground, or whatever the weather report from Denver said. To further the ruse, once I arranged to meet him at LAX long before 9/11 security rules went into effect. I waited for the plane from Denver to land and boarded through the rear doors, outside the terminal. I walked through the plane, grabbed a Denver paper from an empty seat, and walked out into the terminal, greeted by Darrel, who was standing at the gate. Subsequently, we had a very incriminating conversation at the airport.

Darrel talked of plans to travel to Australia and Thailand to solidify another heroin transaction. As I inquired about a future purchase, he said he still had thirty-two ounces available and once those ounces were sold he would travel. The FBI dipped into the Superfund a second time and we arranged the purchase.

Until this time, I had only discussed drug trafficking with him. Our previous buy was through Heather, working as my cutout. This was to be my first purchase. It was important that the transaction be recorded, but I was mindful of the DEA cohort who was forced to strip in order to discuss business. I decided to take the offensive with this purchase.

In November, prior to his December trip

to Australia and Thailand, I negotiated for the purchase of his remaining thirty-two ounces of China White. The day the deal was supposed to happen, Denver had a huge snow storm, closing Stapleton International Airport. Keeping with the ruse, I had to postpone the deal one day. When I called him that evening to delay the deal, he commented on how clear our phone connection was. He said it sounded as if I were across the street. Little did he know.

New York NAMBLA Conference

As I walked toward Times Square with Peter Herman and the rest of our tour group, I thought about all the things that could go wrong with the investigation, even if I were successful at obtaining ironclad evidence of criminal activity and executing a textbook arrest. Would some defense attorney successfully argue that I somehow intruded on a NAMBLA member's constitutional rights of free speech or freedom of assembly? How overt did a violation have to be to meet the standard of the courts? At the time, I had no idea I would be pursuing this investigation for two more years, nor how difficult it would prove to secure actionable grounds for arrest and indictment. But I was determined: these guys were sexual predators, and they had to be stopped, somehow.

Because this was my first in-person encounter with members of the organization, I chose not to wear a wire. I wasn't sure what was going to happen and wasn't completely confident they wouldn't make me strip or at least pat me down, looking for such devices. Several times during undercover assignments I have experienced the pat down or a subtle search or even a full-fledged frisk, but tonight there was a lapse in security — no pat down, no search, no apparent concern.

The members came in all shapes and sizes; their ages ranged from the mid-twenties to the late sixties. They had only two things in common: they were all boy lovers, and they were all white.

Peter showed concern at first; he looked at my arm crutch and questioned whether I would be able to make the lengthy walk to Times Square. I assured him I could. Floyd, who joined us on the walk, had a harder time getting around than I did; he actually had a medical problem that contributed to his hobbled gait. My "osteogenic osteomyelitis that resulted in spondylolisthesis" was more a condition of my imagination and a way to give fits to anyone who transcribed my recorded conversations. It worked, though; the condition's ominous sound never required further explanation. The $350 titanium crutch provided by one of my friends added authenticity to my claim of failing health.

As one member approached, my first impression was that he was a priest. I assumed there would be several at the conference, but I was wrong; there were none. Still, I wasn't too far off in my initial assessment: Jeff Devore was a chiropractor and an ordained minister from Orange County, California. As we began the walk, I struck up a conversation with Jeff. He was outgoing, easy to talk to, a fellow Californian, and it was his first conference as well. We had so much in common — except I carried a badge.

Prior to attending the conference, I spoke to a member who had previously attended the annual NAMBLA function. He told me that any criminal conversations would take place during the breaks and after the daylong meetings he described as "very boring." He told me I would be suspect at my first conference and should be careful. He cautioned me about asking too many questions and advised me to be more of an observer than a participant. He also said that if I attended a second conference I would be more accepted by the member-ship and would then have the credibility to ask more probing questions. With that caveat in mind, I did a lot of listening and very little probing. It was an easy plan. I really wasn't sure I could successfully convince "card-carrying" boy lovers that I was one of them, so the less I spoke, the less opportunity I had to reveal my true identity.

As we entered Times Square, elbowing our way through the thick Friday night crowds, I sensed a heightened anticipation on the part of my fellow travelers. Their interest and enthusiasm wasn't directed at the glittering, $37 million NASDAQ sign, the lights of Broadway, or Madame Tussaud's wax museum. No, the destina-tion on which they were fixed, homing in like starving men headed for a feast, was . . . Toys "R" Us.

Some of the men started to giggle as we neared the brightly lit store entrance. I couldn't figure out what was so exciting about a toy store until we entered and saw the sixty-foot-high indoor Ferris wheel — and all the children clustered around it. Several men rushed to the second-floor rail-ing and began an evening of gawking as young boys made their way onto the ride.

The Toys "R" Us visit truly opened my eyes to the BL mindset. Grown men, most in their forties and fifties, hung on the rail and described in rich, graphic, sexual detail what they would like to do to each boy. These men were predators, and they were prowling the streets. This assignment was dangerous, all right — but the danger wasn't to me. The danger was directed at innocent children, like the ones riding the Ferris wheel.

I'm often inwardly amused as I sit in a public place with a target and wonder if those around us have any idea that I'm negotiating a drug deal or a contract killing or an international weapons transaction. The passersby are oblivious to what is going on within a few feet of where they are shopping or enjoying a casual lunch. Now, though, I wondered what the parents watching their children enjoy the Ferris wheel would think if they knew they were unwittingly providing sexual predators with a public feast. The nervous dread I felt in my stomach earlier in the evening turned into waves of revulsion. What I was hearing from the men around me was so disgusting that had I overheard their conversations when I wasn't in an undercover role, I might have thrown them over the second-floor railing. I had to do this case right — whatever and however long it took.

5
GLOBE-HOPPING SMUGGLER

Los Angeles, 1983

Prior to making my way to Darrel's that day in November 1983, I carefully placed bundles of hundred-dollar bills around my waist inside my underwear and tucked in my shirttail. When I walked into Darrel's residence, we exchanged pleasantries for a few seconds, then I took off my shirt, dropped my pants to the floor, and watched the money cascade around me. Darrel stared at me in disbelief as I stood there in my underwear with my pants around my ankles.

"What are you doing?" he said.

I told him I wanted him to be comfortable dealing with me and to know I wasn't wired. Almost embarrassed, he ordered me to put my clothes back on and pick up the cash.

Darrel never saw the recording device I had strapped to my ankle. We completed the arrangements for the deal, and I got it all on tape.

Darrel's method of doing business was unlike any I had ever encountered. In fact, it's possible my unorthodoxy played into our eventual success.

Darrel saw the money, but the heroin wasn't there. Instead, it was in a hotel room in Canada, just outside Toronto in Scarborough, Ontario. I didn't balk at Darrel's plan, and my willingness to play by his rules enhanced my credibility. When the time came to make the pickup, an RCMP undercover officer, whom I had never met, posed as my Canadian associate and took the actual delivery of the drugs.

Once the deal was consummated, Darrel made final plans for his overseas trip. Surveillance confirmed he traveled with an associate to Sydney, Singapore, Rangoon, Bangkok, Hong Kong, Taipei, and Seoul. Overseas surveillance teams spotted the two of them meeting with known drug traffickers.

Darrel returned to the United States, prepared to deliver the two kilograms of China White I ordered at a cost of a $250,000 per kilo. As with most drug deals, the details had to remain fluid. Last-minute changes were standard, though my administrators seldom understood the need for any deviation from an approved operations order. This deal was no exception.

On February 7, 1984, Darrel promised to deliver the heroin to a hotel room at the Marriott Hotel near the Los Angeles International Airport. We set up surveillance equipment in the room and hoped to capture the transaction on videotape. When Darrel arrived at the hotel, though, he refused to meet in the room and insisted that all conversations take place in the lobby. I quickly strapped on a recording device and made my way to the lobby, carrying a briefcase containing $500,000.

Understandably, FBI administrators were apprehensive about letting me walk around the lobby of a hotel with that much money. I was specifically told the money was not to leave the lobby; agents, in and around the hotel, would be watching my every move.

When I arrived in the lobby, Darrel greeted me and began talking about his trip overseas and his future plans. He was growing more comfortable in our relationship and offered to put me in charge of his distribution network, provided I paid him a percentage of every completed transaction. He would introduce me to his Thai and Canadian connections and continue to educate me on the finer points of narcotics trafficking. It was a tremendous opportunity to fully identify his distribution network, but I knew there was no way I could allow the half-million dollars to walk out with him. I asked for more details and eventually agreed to his offer, but knew that once he delivered the heroin later that day, he and his associates would be arrested.

Again, however, the plan changed. Rather than flashing a half-million dollars in hundred-dollar bills in the lobby of the hotel, he wanted to walk with me into the restroom, where he could view the contents of my briefcase. The request made sense from a drug dealer's perspective. I knew I was in violation of my strict orders, but took the walk anyway. My cover team had no idea what I was doing but they had enough confidence in me and were sufficiently street savvy to remain flexible as the deal unfolded. In the restroom, Darrel viewed the money and we quickly returned to the lobby, much to the relief of FBI management.

Darrel continued to lecture me on the finer points of heroin distribution and periodically pointed out those in the lobby he suspected of being law enforcement. Ironically, agents were in the lobby, but he never picked out the right person. He continually pointed to people not affiliated with the FBI, many of whom were hotel workers. My cover was intact. He did, however, bring it all back to reality when he said that one of his partners was in the lobby with a gun and that if anything happened I would be the first one killed. He had previously played the tough-guy card with me, once saying that if anyone got in his way, he had no qualms about "blowing them away."

I was anxiously awaiting delivery of the heroin, which he promised would be within the hour. And then, while sitting in an overstuffed chair, listening to his bluster, I saw a situation arise from nowhere that could have caused Darrel's armed backup to start popping caps.

During the second semester of my first year of law school, I lived with a family in Cincinnati, Ohio. Pat and Don were a great couple from the church, and they gladly welcomed me into their home. I hadn't seen them in years, and as I sat in the lobby with Darrel, who should walk into the hotel but . . . Pat and Don! They had traveled over two thousand miles and just happened to stroll in, minutes from the takedown of a major international heroin trafficker and his associates, at least one of whom was armed.

My heart began to pound. I was wearing a body recorder with the microphone taped to my chest. When reviewing the tape after the arrest, I could actually hear my heart pounding.

Thankfully, I had stayed in touch with Pat and Don through the years, often by means of a Christmas newsletter in which I would detail some outlandish undercover assignment I had been on. Pat, a devout Christian, also told me later that I was on her mind as they flew into L.A. She knew my work and suspected I was probably doing something dangerous, so she had been praying for me earlier that day.

I leaned back in my seat, away from Darrel's view, caught Pat's attention and slowly shook my head. The look on my face must have communicated this wasn't the time for hugs and greetings. Thank God she understood and whisked her husband away in another direction.

Within minutes, Darrel said that the load car had arrived and I was to accompany him outside. I walked to the parking lot as his two partners, known to me because of our investigation, passed us. I said, "Now, those two look like cops." He laughed and told me they were his partners. He gave me the keys to the car. I walked over, opened the trunk, saw the two kilos, and gave the prearranged signal. In a perfectly executed arrest plan, FBI agents swooped in from every direction, arresting Darrel and his two partners.

I was pleased with our success and looked forward to the next investigation. The evidence was solid and the case seemed like a slam dunk. As we were fond of saying, Darrel and his cronies "were bought and paid for."

I only wish it had turned out that way.

New York NAMBLA Conference

It seemed as if we stayed forever at the railing in Toys "R" Us. Finally, Peter directed us toward a restaurant several blocks away. We continued the walk. Until this time, the location of the actual conference had not been disclosed. I was told earlier we would receive specific instructions later in the evening. NAMBLA feared that publishing the exact location of the meeting well in advance would allow law enforcement to set up appropriate surveillance and disrupt the yearly gathering. As we walked toward the restaurant, Peter stopped and pointed out New York Spaces, a building at 520 Eighth Avenue. "This is where we will be meeting tomorrow," he announced. "No one knows who we are. If asked, tell them we are with Wallace Hamilton Press, who is hosting the conference. This is a publishing seminar. Be very discreet."

We continued walking a short distance to a restaurant on Thirty-fourth Street where we broke up into smaller groups for dinner. After all I had already heard and observed, I didn't have much of an appetite.

I sat with Jeff Devore and Joe from Ann Arbor, Michigan. Joe was small and thin, with a "Mr. Clean," shaved-head, in his late forties or early fifties. Joe initially described himself as a composer. Later in the conversation, we learned he was actually a night lobby guard who had written two symphonies and an opera, none of which had ever been performed. Like many aspiring would-bes in Hollywood, Joe was a "slash" careerist: in his case, a composer/night watchman. He said he and his black lover were both BLs and, like Jeff and me, this was his first conference.

Joe's interests brought up another issue that troubled me as I played out my role. I have little interest in music, other than country and western. I see very few movies, unless they involve murder, mayhem, and mystery. And my tastes in literature run along the same lines, with an occasional biography to complement the fiction. Although boy lovers can cover the entire social and economic spectrum, many of those I interacted with were gay, and their interests were not my interests. I did not read the same books they read, nor did I see the same movies.

One night during dinner, when the question "Who's your favorite boy actor?" was asked, I had to fall back on an earlier answer — "Ricky Schroder, *Silver Spoons*" — even though I don't believe I ever saw an episode. I was often asked about specific movies with a boy lover theme and each time had to punt with some nebulous answer, usually responding with a question of my own. On other assignments, when interacting with gamblers, or with drug or weapons dealers, it was so easy to converse about *Monday Night Football* or the World Series, and if they didn't care it didn't matter. But the BL philosophy permeated the entire lifestyle. It was a part of them 24/7, but it wasn't a part of me. I was afraid that would show.

Remembering my earlier admonition from the disaffected NAMBLA member, I asked very few probing questions at dinner and was surprised when Jeff volunteered so much about his life. He was a fifty-two-year-old ordained minister from Orange County and taught at a chiropractic college in Whittier, California, one of the many smaller cities that make up the greater Los Angeles area. It was obvious he was relaxed among his like-minded, newly found friends, and he spoke openly of his quest to identify his sexual desires.

He admitted to being openly gay, spoke of his twenty-plus-year marriage that ended in divorce, and talked about his three grown children. He shocked me, however, when he admitted to having sex with a sixteen-year-old boy in San Diego's Balboa Park three years earlier. He described in graphic detail their meeting online, the arranged appointment, his drive from Orange County to San Diego, and the sex acts they performed once they met. Joe giggled with excitement as Jeff described the scene — I stopped eating. I regretted I wasn't wearing a wire and wondered if I would ever again have a chance to get such "smoking-gun" admissions on tape.

Across the narrow aisle at a larger table sat Peter and several longtime members of the organization. I glanced over at them occasionally, and we always seemed to be the object of their attention. My paranoia

81

kicked in, and I questioned whether my infiltration had been discovered. I also wondered whether they could hear Jeff describing his sexual adventures. Did they want to participate in the conversation, or silence him for being so open in a public place? I cautiously avoided any efforts to elicit admissions from Jeff or Joe, especially any questions Peter could overhear.

As dinner broke up, we went our separate ways. My disgust continued when I learned that many of the out-of-town attendees were staying at either the YMCA or the Youth Hostel, places that in my youth served as sanctuaries from evil, or at least so I thought. I was on the government dole and selected a very nice hotel with many of the New York amenities, located on East Thirty-first. I kept my location a secret from the other members by avoiding answering the question. I ambled back to the hotel — at a slightly faster pace once I knew no one from NAMBLA was watching — and prepared for the first session of the conference the next morning.

6
A NAMBLA
SAFETY LECTURE

Early Saturday morning, I entered the building at 520 Eighth Avenue and joined several other attendees I recognized from the night before. We waited in the lobby for only a few minutes before Peter Herman and Ted from New Jersey pulled up curbside and began unloading food for breakfast and lunch. Others helped carry the food as we boarded the elevator and made our way to the fifteenth floor. My "handicap" always prevented me from doing any heavy lifting, and I milked this aspect of my cover for all it was worth, whenever it suited me.

Apparently as part of the continued secrecy surrounding the entire organization, we took the elevator to the fifteenth floor, walked down a long hallway, and made our way up the stairwell to the sixteenth floor, where the meetings took place. This internationally recognized organization, celebrating its twenty-fifth anniversary, had to secretly access stairways to the conference venue.

The accommodations also failed to reflect the dignity the membership claimed society owed them. It was small and plain — a rehearsal room — with no wall decorations or amenities. Metal folding chairs circled the room. The floor had one restroom — a "one-holer" that was supposed to accommodate all the attendees — and the group of teenage boys rehearsing a play in a second room on the same floor. My fellow attendees were delighted when they learned they would be sharing bathroom facilities with teenagers. More eye candy for the predators.

Although it is unfair to say we were "locked" in the room for the day, Peter made it clear we would not be coming and going as we chose, which was the reason for breakfast and lunch being provided. His admonition was concise: "Nobody can leave the building." There was a fear someone might slip out and alert law enforcement of the locale of the meeting. Paranoia gripped this organization like no other group I ever infiltrated — just another reason I constantly had to be on my toes.

Approximately thirty men gathered that morning, more than had been at Grand

Central Station the night before. All were white and, with few exceptions, all looked as if the best accommodations they could afford would be the Y. Many appeared qualified for AARP cards; they were over the hill and, from what I could observe, they'd had a pretty hard climb.

Noticeably absent from the conference were boys. Although I never specifically asked in any communication I had with the NAMBLA leadership, I knew of no boys who were members. It seemed odd that this "First Amendment–protected" organization, so intent on "empowering" youth, would fail to have a single juvenile member. Why weren't boys lining up to join and seek their legal sexual emancipation? By contrast, the membership of Little League and Boy Scouts is dominated by boys. If NAMBLA was so intent on "the sexual liberation of boys" and, as the organization claimed, boys desired such liberation, it seemed that juveniles would be joining in droves, pressuring their parents and Congress for sexual freedom.

I was now wearing a wire, and as my recorder ran, Peter Herman called the meeting to order and welcomed us with a short talk. He then turned to Rock Thatcher, who was sitting near me, and asked him to give the "safety lecture." Rock was from Phoenix, in his late fifties, stocky, and articulate. At first I thought he was going to give an AIDS advisory. Wrong! Rock said,

> The most important, the most definite stand that we have ever taken is simply against any age of consent. We've debated, and we've never been able to draw a line and come up with a recommendation for a specific age of consent. So on principle, we say you can't draw a line and you have to take each case on its merits as to whether or not there was abuse, whether or not there was consent. That's our most basic position.

From all my reading, Rock's statement came as no surprise. NAMBLA's view was clear: The organization believed men and boys should be allowed to engage in mutual sexual relationships, regardless of the age of either participant, as long as both parties "consented." If the adult did not "abuse" the child or "force" himself upon the boy, that was understood as tantamount to "consent," and the organization saw nothing wrong with the actions of the adult. I wasn't quite sure why this was part of a "safety lecture." Rock went on.

We don't advocate that anybody break the law, even though we advocate changes in the law. We'd like to urge you not to break the law, and we'd like to urge you not to talk about breaking any laws while you're here on this occasion.

Rock was taking great pains to reinforce the position that NAMBLA was opposed to breaking the law. In other words, the organization believed sex with boys was morally okay but illegal by statute. I wasn't clear as to who was supposed to benefit from this admonition. His next statement provided the answer.

We have been infiltrated by the media. We've been infiltrated by law enforcement officials, and I have to say candidly, I don't know most of you well enough to say that you're not an infiltrator. There certainly have been times in the past when a similar warning has been given at our conferences . . . and the infiltrator sat right there [he gestured toward my seat!] and listened to it. One of them has even filed an affidavit against us in the lawsuit we are defending, so this is a concern. . . . Specifically this weekend we request that you not talk about anything that might even be considered illegal . . . even privately. If you don't know the person you're talking to, then you shouldn't be talking about anything that could possibly sound illegal.

Rock was playing to the infiltrator, and apparently I had chosen the "infiltrator chair." Skilled fiction writers disdain the use of coincidence to advance plot, but this was truly an instance of truth being stranger — or at least more ironic — than fiction. I have to admit, it was unnerving to see him pointing to my seat, but the membership didn't pounce, so the coincidence was apparently just that. It was obvious they anticipated some legal challenge to holding such a meeting and wanted to make the record clear that the organization did not "condone" criminal behavior. The point was made, but by all appearances it was a matter of form over substance. For most members, it was a "wink-wink, nudge-nudge" kind of thing, not a warning to be taken seriously.

Ted, the retired schoolteacher from New Jersey, apparently growing impatient with the standard caution, interrupted: "No confessions, no asking where to get child pornography in Manhattan, and no asking where you can travel someplace in the world — that's not why we're here. I think that's very clear."

Rock Thatcher continued. "We're here, basically, I would say, for two purposes: one is social, and the other is administrative. And there will obviously be a certain amount of sharing of information about items of interest that we all share, but they don't need to get into anything like discussing specific activities that could lead . . ."

Lead to what? I wondered.

Chris from Chicago interrupted. "Something we used to do at some of the old meetings was to make an announcement and ask anybody who's an agent or a case agent or a spy for the media, please stand up and remove yourself."

Chris, who I would later learn was a longtime member and on the steering committee, was serious in his request. Often while undercover, drug dealers would look me in the eye and ask point-blank if I was a cop. Jailhouse lawyers promulgated the rumor that a failure to answer that question honestly would result in convictions being overturned due to "entrapment." Once, after his arrest, a gang member, who asked that question while selling me drugs and heard my denial, laughed in my face and said the conviction would never stand. I responded, tongue-in-cheek, that the law required him to specifically ask if I "was affiliated with any federal law enforcement agency or working on behalf of any federal officer." Convinced by my meaningless officialese, he responded with an obscene invective critical of the jailhouse lawyer who advised him during his recent period of incarceration. Apparently, Chris was under the same misimpression. I didn't respond to his demand and remained seated.

Rock continued. "I personally used to advocate . . . that we invite the police regularly into our meetings so that they could see what we were doing. . . . We're not here to train people on how to seduce underage boys, and if you came for that, you might as well leave now."

Chris felt the need to chip in again. "We have a constitutional right to freedom of assembly and freedom of speech, and unless you're agreeing . . . to our principles, then you shouldn't be in the organization."

In one respect, Rock was going to get his wish. The "police" had been invited to this meeting — even though he didn't know it. The entire meeting would be recorded, and we would learn what did go on at these conferences.

I cannot imagine any other organization beginning its annual national conference with such a caveat: Don't break the law, but if you plan to talk about breaking the law, make sure you do it with someone you really know and trust; otherwise, he could be the press or, even worse, an undercover FBI agent who has infiltrated the ranks. And of course, we will be sharing, but when sharing information about "items of interest that we all share," don't get into discussing specific activities.

It sounded like double-talk, but, as Chris noted, it was constitutionally protected double-talk.

Within the first few minutes of the conference, NAMBLA had affirmed its purpose: to abolish age-of-consent laws. What would this "First Amendment–protected" organization do to further that aim, its primary purpose? In more than three years as a member of NAMBLA, I never once heard of any effort to campaign or lobby any political figure at any level of government to abolish or even modify the age-of-consent laws — not once. There was no talk of hiring a paid lobbyist in Washington; there was no organized letter-writing campaign; there was no endorsement of candidates. Even though most letters to the editor of the *Bulletin* were answered in some manner, the only letter I ever saw that asked which politicians should be supported in the upcoming election went unanswered. Odd, I thought, for an organization whose stated purpose concerned legalized change of accepted social mores. It wasn't the last inconsistency I would uncover during my membership in NAMBLA.

Los Angeles, 1984
One thing we knew we could count on with Darrel: he'd have plenty of highly paid legal talent to bring into the mix. In 1984, as we began preparing for the barrage of pretrial motions, Heather pulled me aside one afternoon.

Her former boyfriend, Robert, was a major player in the Mexican Mafia, also known as La Eme. Many in law enforcement believed that outside the penitentiary walls, Robert was the acting head of this prison-spawned organization known for murder, drug trafficking, and witness intimidation. One magazine article quoted a law enforcement official who described Robert as "a very intelligent, very crafty individual — almost bordering on genius."

Heather asked me if I wanted to "do"

Robert. He was truly a very worthy target, but I told her she'd already done enough and I didn't want to put her in that position. She got a tear in her eye and said I had been so nice to her and her son that, as a present, she would introduce me to the acting head of the Mexican Mafia. It was a gift I couldn't refuse.

I decided to pose as a movie stunt coordinator and lead Robert to believe I was distributing heroin to my Hollywood associates. On the morning of my first meeting with him, I called a friend who worked at Universal Studios. He told me they were shooting on location in Malibu. Any location shoot is a major production rivaling a military operation for logistics. Typically, there will be acres of trucks, cars, equipment, and people. I told Robert where "we" were shooting and asked him to join me just up the block. I would break away for a short time from filming to discuss "our business." The scene played well as he drove up and saw the massive trucks and lighting equipment so familiar to those around Los Angeles. He bought my act as a stunt coordinator and I promised him that one day I would invite him onto the set. He seemed pleased with his new Hollywood friend. Heather's introduction sealed my drug bona fides, but the extra little details of my story made me a valued customer.

On March 23, 1984, I purchased one ounce of heroin for eight thousand dollars. I paid him four thousand dollars and promised to make the second payment once I sold off some of the product. This arrangement allowed me more meetings with Robert and the chance to engage him in additional criminal conversations. At that time, street-level China White might only be two to three percent pure. The heroin Robert delivered graded out at nearly 100 percent, a powerful product by any trafficker's definition. On the street, it would have been pure poison, instant death for anyone who mainlined it. This also meant an actual drug dealer would be able to "step on" the heroin many times by "cutting" it with substances like sugar or quinine. He could then sell the diluted mixture at a very sizeable profit.

On March 28, 1984, I had a second meeting with Robert in which I paid him the additional four thousand dollars. Robert spoke broken English with a strong accent, and it was often difficult for me to understand him. I knew a jury might have just as much difficulty discerning his admissions. As we sat down that afternoon at an outdoor café,

I stood up and, feigning embarrassment, asked Robert to trade seats with me. I told him I "blew out an eardrum doing a fire gag" and was deaf in one ear. I re-seated us so he could speak directly into my "good ear." The ploy worked and allowed me to ask him to repeat his criminal admissions.

Robert was doing his best to improve his lot as well as that of the Mexican Mafia. He wanted to upgrade its image — less gang-banger more businessman. He envisioned La Eme to be the equivalent of the traditional Mafia, not the Crips or Bloods. His personal heroin trafficking clientele included doctors and lawyers. Unlike some criminals I targeted, I could take Robert out in public.

In a subsequent meeting at the Sheraton Grande, in downtown Los Angeles, Robert and I negotiated for a larger purchase. I asked a female agent to cover the meeting from inside the upscale hotel restaurant. My security inside the popular restaurant wasn't a real issue but additional eyes could corroborate that Robert and I did meet. I had my back to the main dining room. Robert sat against the wall and was able to see all the customers and their activities. The meeting progressed without a hitch. He made valuable admissions, including a discussion about the cost of a multiple-ounce purchase. As we lingered, Robert shocked me when he said to a patron, "Good-bye." I turned in time to see my female surveillance agent get up from the table and leave.

"What was that all about?" I asked him.

"I don't know, but that chica kept watching me the whole time she ate."

I quickly responded that I had recently worked with Erik Estrada, who played Ponch on the TV show *CHiPs,* and that Robert looked so much like him she probably thought he was Estrada. He bought the quick recovery, but afterward I reminded my colleague that subtlety was crucial while on surveillance.

Less than a week later, Robert called me, asking how many ounces of heroin I wanted to order. I ordered four and awaited delivery, which he informed me would take about a week. For the quality of heroin he was providing, a week's delay was not unusual.

On April 12, 1984, Robert and I agreed to meet at an upscale hotel near the University of Southern California campus. By this time, thanks to intelligence from a friend in the sheriff's department, we had identified the person we believed to be Robert's source for the heroin: Rick, a San Fernando

Valley bondsman who often posted bail for local mobsters, Hells Angels, and members of the Mexican Mafia. Because of his association with those in the criminal element, I had spoken to Rick several times in my capacity as an FBI agent. We knew each other on sight. In the grand scheme of things, Robert was the bigger target — much more important than his supplier. Since I knew Rick, I had no intention or desire to see him as Robert and I concluded our transaction. So, in keeping with typical drug dealer protocol, I told Robert, "I don't want to see any new faces," and if I did, I'd call off the deal. He said he understood.

Once Robert delivered the heroin, a team of FBI agents was prepared to take him into custody. His arrest would be a major blow to the Mexican Mafia and a tremendous victory for Los Angeles–area law enforcement.

I sat in the lobby of the hotel, dressed casually. I had a Pittsburgh Pirates cap in my back pocket. In the early eighties, the Pirates had one of the ugliest caps in baseball and, in a town of die-hard Dodger fans, the cap would make me easily identifiable should I get lost in a crowd. Once Robert delivered the drugs I was to don the cap, signaling the arrest team that I had possession of the narcotics.

I looked up from my lobby seat and my chest froze with apprehension when I saw Robert heading toward the hotel with Rick, the bail bondsman at his side. If they came in together and Rick saw me, I was a dead man and Robert would still be on the streets.

7

THE COURTROOM
CRAPSHOOT

I jumped from my seat and headed toward the rear entrance of the lobby. I grabbed the Pirates cap and stuck it on my head, hoping to break up my silhouette, should Robert or Rick see me. A transmitter was taped to my ankle, and as I ran out the back, hopping on one foot, I was shouting into my ankle, "The hat's not the signal. The hat's not the signal." If the moment could have been captured on camera it would probably have the makings of comedy — but at the time I was anything but amused.

As soon as I got to my undercover car, I alerted the arrest team that Robert had brought Rick with him and that Rick knew me to be an FBI agent. Within seconds the operation order changed. I sat in the car, trying to come up with an alternate plan. Soon I observed Robert — alone — in the parking lot, looking for me. I signaled to him and he came over to the vehicle.

He invited me inside to meet his friend. I repeated my earlier warning that if he brought in another person, I would back out. He tried to assure me that his supplier was honorable and that it would be good to meet him so I could do business directly with him in the future. I repeated my threats to withdraw from the transaction. He appreciated my caution but was also trying to placate Rick, who wanted to meet me.

Since I was insistent on not meeting Rick, however, Robert needed to return to Rick to discuss how the deal would happen. I showed Robert the money, assuring him I was capable of making the four-ounce purchase. He returned to the hotel lobby to tell Rick I had the money and to modify Rick's predetermined delivery plans.

Inside the hotel, the backup team observed Robert and Rick talking. When Robert left the lobby to return to my car, a third person entered the lobby and met with Rick.

Robert instructed me to follow him and said the deal would now happen in a restaurant next door to the hotel. I exited the undercover car and followed Robert. My Pirates cap was pulled down low and I feigned the same limp I had been using throughout our meetings. As Robert and I walked toward the restaurant, Rick and his associate followed a few feet behind. When I questioned Robert, he acknowledged that the two men shadowing us were his associates. And then, as I turned the corner heading into the restaurant, I heard the distinct and unwelcome sound of a shotgun racking.

I feared the worst, thinking this was a rip, until I heard a familiar voice holler, "Freeze, FBI!"

The on-site administrator had given the arrest order. My transmitter had been working only intermittently and the arrest team had no idea what was happening. All they knew was that I was walking with thirty-two thousand dollars to an unknown location out of their sight and outside the parameters of the operations order. Fearing a robbery or worse, the arrest order went out.

Hearing the rack of the shotgun and realizing the FBI had made an arrest, I quickly drew my revolver, hidden under my shirt. I had Robert prone on the ground, waiting for somebody from the arrest team to round the corner, since I had no handcuffs. One of my colleagues cuffed Robert, and a frisk revealed he was not holding the heroin. I returned to the other two who were in custody. Rick loudly maintained his innocence, incredulous that he had been arrested. The third person, who had been meeting with Rick in the lobby, was carrying a folded newspaper. Inside the newspaper was evidentiary gold — four ounces of uncut heroin.

Three people, including the acting head of the Mexican Mafia and a mob bondsman, were in custody. It was a huge victory for the good guys.

Meanwhile, though, what we had assumed would be a quick guilty plea from Darrel turned into a judicial nightmare. He and his boutique lawyers pulled out all the stops: lies, half-truths, and innuendo. I admit, as I view the situation in retrospect, that I made some errors in judgment. Even though my motives were pure, the appearance of impropriety felled our case.

Furthermore, as if the flurry of defense motions weren't enough, I learned through a reliable source close to Darrel that he had put out a $100,000 contract to have Heather killed.

Fortunately, we had the information early enough that we could whisk Heather and her son to safety, eventually placing them in the Witness Protection Program. Unlike what you usually see on TV, where the endangered person is ushered into the program immediately, the FBI paid for an out-of-town motel room for several weeks until all the necessary paperwork was completed. While awaiting the Marshals Service to approve her entrance into the program, we stored all of Heather's belongings in my garage — which led to an interesting situation.

Over the Fourth of July weekend, our church had a picnic. My wife went ahead, taking our two small children with her. I arrived a short time later escorting Heather — the drop-dead gorgeous prostitute — and her young son. I wasn't too sure how the folks from our church would react, but to their credit, they welcomed Heather and her son and treated her like an honored guest. It was quite a sight and, thankfully, my wife was still talking to me at the end of the day.

Darrel's motions hearing dragged on for weeks in the summer of 1984, with witnesses for both sides testifying at great lengths. As I had originally feared, sex became an issue; Darrel testified to falling in love and being intimate with Heather. He claimed he only sold drugs because of his love for her. He also said he learned everything he knew about heroin trafficking from library books.

Heather admitted to "sleeping" with him but denied ever having sex, claiming Darrel was impotent. At one point, during a break, Heather confided in me that she had been a prostitute for seventeen years and the first time she couldn't get a guy aroused, she had to testify to it in federal court. I had to smile — a welcome relief, actually, during a pretty somber summer. Still, the law was on our side and we were confident that despite the smoke and mirrors presented by the defense, we would prevail.

The judge waited several more weeks to issue his ruling. When he did, it was a bombshell.

As we walked into the courtroom, the prosecutor from the Organized Crime Strike Force, Blair Watson, turned to me and said he didn't have a good feeling about the forthcoming ruling. Blair had done a great job arguing our case, but his premonition turned out to be correct.

The judge said, "It would be easy for me to determine this, if I had some feeling that [Darrel] were not involved in drugs. I think the government has had every reason to look into his activities. I would think that they would be derelict if they did not. . . . [The defendant] is intricately involved in drug trafficking." But the judge was "troubled" and "offended" by our recruitment of Heather, whom the judge called a "tragic figure." He directed his comments to me on the sexual entrapment issues raised by the defense, characterizing my actions as a "deliberate closing of the eyes." The judge said he believed me when I said I instructed the informants not to engage in sex, but he didn't believe I meant it when I said it. Even though Heather and I testified that several times I warned her about engaging in sexual activities and she denied engaging in intercourse with the defendant, the judge broadened the definition of sex to include what a future president claimed under oath was not sex.

And so, the defense prevailed in its motion to dismiss the charges due to "gross governmental misconduct." In his written ruling, the judge based his decision on three aspects of our investigation: (1) the FBI's "manipulation" of Heather into becoming an informant; (2) the FBI's continued use of Heather after learning that she had become sexually involved; (3) the FBI's continued use of her after learning that she was still involved in unrelated criminal activity.

Ironically, in the same courthouse, the identical issues were raised in the Mexican

Mafia case. Since Heather was the former girlfriend of Robert, who had spent sixteen of his last twenty-two years in prison, and she introduced him to me, his defense thought they could also prevail with the same argument. I will never forget U.S. District Court Judge Laughlin Waters's words as he peered down from the bench at the defense counsel: "When the scene is set in hell, don't expect angels to be singing in the choir." Their defense motions were denied.

Once the initial shock of losing Darrel's case wore off, I was livid over the decision, as was the Strike Force. The government appealed the ruling. In the meantime, I was investigated by our Office of Professional Responsibility — the FBI's equivalent to a police department's Internal Affairs — because the judge had criticized my investigative techniques.

The local papers covered the story of Darrel's trial, especially the part about how the bad ol' FBI had exploited Heather and used sex to ensnare a wide-eyed, unsuspecting heroin distributor. The *Los Angeles Times* ran a front-page feature article in which they named me over twenty-five times, emphasizing my "outrageous" conduct and printing the story without benefit of even seeking comment from the FBI or the Strike Force. The *Orange County Register* misstated the facts and the evidence in their apparent haste to paint the worst possible picture of my actions. Not my best PR outing, for sure.

In 1987, three years after the dismissal, the Ninth Circuit Court of Appeals reversed the district court judge's ruling, stating that my conduct did not violate the due process clause of the Fifth Amendment. Even though Heather and I specifically denied that she engaged in sex with the defendant, the court still allowed that characterization of her relationship with Darrel. However, the court ruled that "the deceptive creation and/or exploitation of an intimate relationship does not exceed the boundary of permissible law enforcement tactics." Specifically, the court found nothing wrong in the recruitment of Heather as an informant. In words never reported in any newspaper that covered the story in 1984, the court said, "We hold that the FBI's conduct was not shocking to the universal sense of justice."

We still weren't out of the woods, though. When the case was remanded to the district court, the original judge dismissed the case a second time, using his "supervisory authority." The government again appealed and again the Ninth Circuit Court of Appeals reversed the district court judge. In language that strikes at the heart of the argument about an "activist judiciary," the Ninth Circuit ruling said,

Under the supervisory power, courts have substantial authority to oversee their own affairs to ensure that justice is done. They do not, however, have a license to intrude into the authority, powers, and functions of the coordinate branches. Judges are not legislators, free to make laws . . . nor are they executive officers, vested with discretion over law enforcement policy and decisions.

As expected, the defense appealed and sought redress at the Supreme Court. The Supreme Court refused to hear the issue. By the time the case returned to the district court, Darrel had died of cancer. Since the arrests took place prior to legislatively imposed mandatory minimum sentencing, the judge, in an obvious attempt to punish the government and send a message to the FBI, sentenced Darrel's two co-conspirators to ninety days in prison. The judge sent a message, all right — but what was it?

Think about it: The same undercover agent (me), working with the same informant (Heather), investigating the same federal violation, brought about six arrests and five convictions. (Darrel died before his two associates pleaded guilty.) All six defendants had their cases heard in the same federal courthouse, presented to two different judges by the same prosecutor. Three of those defendants, guilty of distributing four to five ounces of heroin, received sentences ranging from ten to fifteen years. Three other defendants, guilty of distributing approximately 115 ounces of heroin, received sentences of ninety days.

There must be a message in there somewhere.

8
MEET THE
PREDATORS

New York NAMBLA Conference
Peter Herman invited everyone in the circle to introduce himself and tell why he chose to attend. Prior to the actual introductions, he stated that no one need give his true name, and no one was forced to participate.

The men began, some using real names, some only first names, and some admitting to using aliases. Five or six of us were attending our first conference, but the others were veteran members.

Robin, an organist and youth minister from Georgia, began. He was tall and thin, with a thick Southern accent. A longtime member, he first learned about the organization from a *Reader's Digest* article. He spoke, as did others, about the need to recruit younger men with similar interests to join the ranks: "new blood with a new enthusiasm." He also talked about "young people who need our guidance. . . . When

110

you have a child who is not ready for a certain thing, you don't teach it to them. If you have a kid who is ready and is advanced, deal with him on a little higher level."

The group included Todd Calvin, a dentist who referred to himself as "Triple D . . . divorced dentist from Dallas"; numerous teachers; two ministers (Jeff Devore and Robin); and Bob, an attorney from Atlanta.

With a large girth and white beard, Bob could have easily passed for the real Santa Claus. A member for twenty years, he spoke with a closing-argument passion about what NAMBLA meant to him.

[The organization] fills me up. Helps me not feel bad about myself. Gives me confidence to understand this is what flavor was bestowed upon me. Coming to conferences like these and by knowing members, it has enabled me to see the way I am as a blessing, not a curse. . . . [Being here] is about filling my tank with self-worth.

Chris from Chicago described himself as a socialist seeking "to overthrow the capitalist system." His wild, unkempt hair and ragged clothes were reminiscent of a campus radical from the sixties.

One member complained that his father and brother were both BLs who were "doing" his friends but never came on to him. Joe P., a convicted sex offender and editor of the *Bulletin,* represented the Bay Area along with David M. and Floyd C., all three of whom were named in the Jeffrey Curley wrongful death civil lawsuit. But more about that later. In referring to NAMBLA, David made a remarkable but confusing comparison that would surely have made our forefathers proud: "Our ideas spring from the most basic ideas of the founding of the United States."

Mike came from Cleveland. Ian from Vermont sported a long ponytail and, despite the November cold, wore shorts the entire weekend. Tomas, who at twenty-five was the youngest, came from Denmark. Ray joined when he heard that "NAMBLA was a meeting about pedophiles." Joe, who was my dinner partner the night before and had been a member nineteen years, said, "I'm a boy lover. . . . It's a universal impulse. . . . The impulse to love the young is not immoral. It's an impulse to nurture, not something I'm ashamed of."

When it came time for me to speak, I had no idea what to say and was still apprehensive that anything I said might give away my true identity. I began by discussing my fear in joining the group the previous night at the dining concourse, and within a few sentences, as if on cue, began crying. It was perfect, an Academy Award–winning performance. Men on my right and left comforted me, and throughout the meeting, various members approached, telling of how scared they were at their first conference. They believed the tears and they believed me.

Tim B. arrived late. He wore a Green Party T-shirt and was a former NAMBLA membership chairman. Throughout the two days, he was one of the most vocal, bragging of his participation at the Stonewall riots of 1969 and challenging the membership to a more public stance. At one point in the meeting, Tim told me that in the nineties there were more than twelve hundred members, but many had dropped out since the filing of the Jeffrey Curley lawsuit.

I had little interest in the content of the meeting, either day. As I had been warned, it was boring, with no formal discussion that bordered on criminal admissions. The established agenda was only loosely followed, and Peter allowed the discussion to wander all over the map.

I heard lots of rehashing of old rallies,

some discussion about NAMBLA having been ostracized by the International Lesbian and Gay Association, and volleys back and forth about whether it was better to be "out" or "closeted." The vast majority feared that acknowledged membership in NAMBLA would have dire consequences.

The rhetoric flew thick and fast: "Ours is a liberation movement confronting the inequities of the system." Prison and state hospitals were referred to as "America's Gulag." Rock Thatcher stated that Atascadero [California] State Prison existed to "warehouse boy lovers." When Joe from Ann Arbor praised longtime active members who played such a pivotal role in the history of the organization and referred to them as "heroes," the room burst into applause. In yet another interesting historical interpretation, Joe compared the current day's boy lover activists to pre–Civil War abolitionists. He noted that every liberation movement went through three stages: ridicule, opposition, and acceptance. He was in the majority present who believed the boy lover movement was where the gay movement was in the early sixties: "It is only a matter of time before it is accepted by society." Tim hailed this period as a time when NAMBLA is on "the cusp of a new awakening."

Bob, the attorney, again made some interesting observations.

We're about consensual relationships. We're about people whose physical and sexual attraction take them in a certain direction. . . . Look, I've never been in the sack with anyone who didn't want to be in the sack with me. End of story. You know I'm not going after your son. . . . If he's not interested in being in a relationship with me, you've got nothing to worry about. If he is interested in me, then introduce us. . . . If your son wants a fifty-year-old, how are you going to stop him from finding another fifty-year-old on the Internet who may not be as decent as I am?

Bob's next comment was a bit less high-flown, but summoned a loud laugh:

The Internet is incredible. My big hobby now, I sit around in my boxer shorts . . . words come across the screen and the person typing says he's twelve; I get an erection.

Jeff Devore spoke up.

What can I do? I'm a gay minister, and I

have access to a pulpit, and so I can begin to or continue to . . . support the kind of values that we uphold without necessarily coming out and labeling it as, "Ooh, your son's looking really good today, Mrs. Smith, sitting back there in the pew."

Several members got my attention with no need for prompting. Jim and Rowan, both from New Jersey, were retired teachers, as was Ted, who taught for thirty-two years and was then sponsoring a school in the Philippines. Jim's hobby was photography, a subject that definitely needed exploration, I thought. Ted's school sponsorship was also troubling, since I knew that Peter Melzer, aka Peter Herman, admitted to an undercover police officer he molested a boy in the Philippines. I was also aware of the problems with child sex tourism in that country. I hoped to learn more about Ted's involvement as the investigation progressed. But I was fearful of probing too deeply — yet.

One asset to working an FBI-sanctioned undercover operation is the ability to be patient. Although progress must be shown during the course of the approved period of the operation, the need to "put powder on the table" or "bodies in cuffs" isn't as urgent as it might be with some departments or agencies. If we were to be successful in this operation, I needed to work without the pressure of developing a prosecutable case while at the conference. I had that leeway, and it proved invaluable as the investigation progressed.

Ted organized the conference and clearly had a leadership role at one time in NAMBLA. He was personable, charming, and radiated sincerity. He described himself as a "lover of boy lovers," and I believed him. He worked the room like a politician needing a few more votes. He was there in 1979 when the organization was founded and represented NAMBLA in the International Lesbian and Gay Association, where he wrote various position papers. Of all the members, he was one I would have wanted to invite to lunch. He was charismatic and lacked the paranoia I sensed in many of the members — but were these also the traits that allowed him to gain the necessary confidence of boys and their parents? In the black-is-white world of the pedophile, it was hard to know what to approve and what to distrust. The need to keep my own categories intact while maintaining my undercover persona was a major stress and challenge that only intensified as the investigation continued.

Although I had long ago learned as an undercover agent the absolute necessity of deferred gratification and emotional postponement, I realized to be successful in this assignment I was going to have to detach myself from my real feelings in a way I never had before. Posing as a drug dealer was child's play compared to the emotional and psychological roller coaster ride I was experiencing as I sat at the conference. I had to absorb all they were saying, yet at the same time, block it from my mind. To focus on the content of the conversation stirred in me emotions of rage, disgust, and hatred for the philosophy the members espoused. I could ill afford to allow those feelings to show. I had to smile, laugh, and offer positive reinforcement to ideas diametrically opposed to my personal belief system.

I began to play games to maintain my sanity. I knew I would have to view these men through the eyes of an unsuspecting boy or his parents. Like Ted, many of the members had positive qualities that made them interesting, endearing people. Although, those very qualities likely were what enabled them to gain access to their victims. Still, as long as I focused on the positive, I knew I could succeed.

Break time on Saturday was delightful for my fellow attendees. The "one-holer" provided them with a chance to stand in line with the boys who were also on break from rehearsing and waiting to use the restroom. Several of the men hovered around the boys, giggling and chatting. One member remarked to me, "Look at those chicken hawks swarming." I tried my best to watch the restroom to insure that no man went in with a boy. I saw no such incident and heard of no one bragging about a conquest.

The limited room in which I had to maneuver made it difficult to communicate with the Los Angeles case agent who accompanied me to New York and was the liaison with the New York surveillance agents. I used the brief time I had in the tiny bathroom with paper-thin walls to make hushed calls to her on the cell phone — multitasking as I spoke. The NAMBLA members were forced to eat lunch as a group in the meeting room — cold cuts and sandwiches. There was just no way to communicate safely with the outside.

The general tone of the meetings disgusted me. Although there was no direct criminal discussion, the BL philosophy permeating each speaker's presentation was more than I could take for an entire day. I was still nervous about being discovered and chose not to go out to dinner with my new friends that evening. To put it simply, I needed a break. My cover story was I was a financial advisor and was in New York to meet with a client, so I was "having dinner with her" that evening.

The Saturday session broke around five o'clock, and I welcomed the opportunity for fresh air — in fact, I had to exercise control to keep myself from bolting for the nearest door, using my arm crutch as a bludgeon along the way. I took a cab back to the hotel, where my case agent debriefed me. Even though I was recording the sessions, I wanted to give a detailed account of the activities that transpired that day. Recording equipment has been known to fail, and although I doubted I would soon forget my first day attending the NAMBLA conference, I wanted to get my observations on paper. After the debriefing, I went to dinner and used the time to decompress and prepare myself emotionally for the next day's fun and games.

9
WORKING THE HOOD

Los Angeles, 1988

One day in 1988, just after the noon hour, I got a call at my desk on the fifteenth floor of the Los Angeles Federal Building. Larry Lawlor, the Special Agent in Charge of the L.A. office, wanted to see me.

Visits to the SAC's office were nothing new for me. Trying hard to remember what rules I'd broken or which administrator's toes I'd stepped on most recently, I slowly climbed the two flights of stairs separating my floor from the seventeenth, where management was housed.

Larry Lawlor was one of the finest Bureau administrators under whom I served. He was a strong, articulate manager who wasn't afraid to admit to his mistakes or seek the advice of a street agent more familiar with the nuances of the investigation. His retirement party was one of the few I attended. He died of cancer not long after his retirement. The FBI lost a great leader when he retired, and the world lost a great human being when he died.

But I still couldn't figure out, as I climbed the stairs that day, if I was in for a commendation or a butt chewing. The Boss, as we called him, was equally skilled in both.

I walked into his office, he greeted me, and asked me to sit down. "I was having lunch with the chief of police today, Bob, and do you know what we talked about?"

I admitted I had no idea what he and Daryl Gates discussed over salad.

"He wants to attack the gang problem in South Central the same way we go after organized crime — like the LCN [La Cosa Nostra] case we just tied up."

Our office had recently successfully concluded an investigation of the L.A. Mafia crime family. I was the undercover agent, and fifteen members of the L.A. family were convicted under the Racketeer Influenced and Corrupt Organizations Act (RICO) and various other federal statutes. The investigation generated a great deal of positive publicity for the Los Angeles office and obviously caught the attention and accolades of HQ. Even the attorney general recognized our success in a press conference.

"Is that so?"

The Boss nodded. Always one to encourage cooperation among different branches of law enforcement, he told me he and Chief Gates discussed the possibility of a joint operation in South Central. "How do you feel about that, Bob?"

"Sounds like a good idea, I guess."

"Wonderful. Because I told Chief Gates I'd send him a couple of agents to help get things going, and I want you to lead the effort."

"No kidding?"

The Boss proceeded to tell me how much he needed someone with my qualities on this new joint operation: someone with innovative ideas, a self-starter, highly motivated —

"And dumb enough to think working gangs in South Central would be fun?"

"Something like that, yeah. And I'll let you choose your own partner."

"Sold," I said.

I make light of it now, but I was actually honored to be selected for the opportunity. I came away from the meeting very excited about the possibilities . . . but a little worried about how I was going to explain it to my wife. Sure enough, I spent most of that evening convincing her that a white man cruising around Watts consorting with black gangbangers wasn't all that much more at risk than an undercover agent in Hollywood or Beverly Hills hanging out with big-time drug dealers and known members of La Cosa Nostra. She didn't readily buy my argument, but eventually accepted my taking the assignment.

At the top of my list for partners was Tom, a new agent, only a few months out of the FBI Academy. He was a Naval Academy graduate, a former Navy officer, and an explosives expert. He had everything I was looking for in a partner: he was enthusiastic, willing, and just goofy enough to buy the same sales pitch the SAC laid on me the day before.

Within a few weeks, Tom and I reported to the LAPD South Bureau's CRASH (Community Resources Against Street Hoodlums) unit. Although the program would later come under political fire, the South Bureau was manned by some of the finest police officers with whom I ever worked. My partner and I joined a team of plainclothes detectives whose offices were above a supermarket in South Central Los Angeles. We answered to a sergeant and his lieutenant and for the next several months played real-life cops and robbers.

For both Tom and me, it was a side of police work we had never seen. No longer federal agents wearing suits and ties, knocking on doors, and interviewing witnesses, we got down and dirty. We kicked in doors and braced gang members on the street. We rode side by side with the detectives; we joined them in foot pursuits and a few high-speed chases. At least two or three times a week, we assisted with search warrants issued for gang members' residences and hangouts. It was not unusual to round up several dozen gang members in a single evening.

Tom and I worked alongside our LAPD team members but spent each evening on the commute home figuring out ways to make a federal impact.

The general public perceives Los Angeles–based black street gangs as being two distinct organizations, the Crips and the Bloods. In fact, those two terms represent over a hundred separate entities. Within the broad umbrella of the Crips or the Bloods are individual gangs or, as they are known on the street, sets. Often the gangs are designated by a geographical or territorial marker. The Five-Deuce Hoover Crips are in the general neighborhood of Fifty-second Street and Hoover Avenue. The Seven-Four

Hoovers are located near Seventy-forth Street and Hoover. The Compton Pirus and the West Side Pirus, Blood sets, hail from Piru Street in Compton.

Although I heard from a number of OGs (Original Gangsters or senior members of the gangs) a variety of stories as to the origin of the Crips, most credit Raymond Washington with founding the gang in 1969. They were initially called the Baby Avenues, but when a Los Angeles paper reported that crime victims described their attackers as youths with canes, the term "crips" — short for "cripples" — was adopted. The gang grew, and other neighborhood gangs began to adopt "Crip" as part of their identity. The loose confederation of Crips soon became the most powerful street gang in South Central.

Other gangs, known as the Pirus, from the city of Compton, refused to align themselves with the Crips and responded by uniting under the general heading of Bloods. The two gangs were fierce rivals. The knives and chains of a *West Side Story*–style street battle gave way to guns. Killing became a way of life and gang-related murders dominated the homicide landscape. The Crips far outnumbered the Bloods, but for a reason no one could ever adequately ex-

126

plain, the Crips often fought among themselves, even killing each other; the Bloods usually managed to maintain a united front.

In the 1980s, with the rising popularity of crack, or rock cocaine, a simpler alternative to freebasing, the gangs moved into drug trafficking, marketing the cheap high in the lower-income neighborhoods. Rocks could go for as little as two or three dollars and the gangs profited from their semisophisticated distribution networks.

Compared to La Cosa Nostra, the street gangs of South Central had a somewhat looser organizational structure. No single person ran a set. There was no formal hierarchy within each gang, nor was there any sort of interset commission of representatives from the various sets. The leaders in each set were known as "shot callers." More often than not, the shot callers were those with the money, the drugs, and the women. The ranking was fluid: today's "pu-butt," or novice member, might be tomorrow's shot caller, if he developed a lucrative source for cocaine or performed a necessary criminal deed that advanced the gang's stature.

When Congress became convinced of the highly addictive nature of rock cocaine, they responded with what many defense counsels believed to be draconian criminal provisions. Distribution of five grams of rock was equal in punishment to the sale of five hundred grams of powder cocaine: a minimum mandatory five years in prison. Fifty grams of rock, an amount which could easily fit in the palm of your hand, was equivalent to five kilograms of powder, roughly the size of five large Tom Clancy hardback novels. Conviction carried a minimum mandatory ten-year sentence. If the distributor had a previous felony drug conviction, it was a "double-up," the punishment was doubled. Although I have heard sociologists attribute declining crime rates to such liberalized practices as legalized abortion, I am more inclined to believe that the federal sentencing statutes played a major role. The thirty-three gang members I eventually convicted under federal drug statutes, most of whom were responsible for at least a felony a day, were unable to commit their criminal deeds on the street while tucked away in federal prison for many, many years. And I was just one agent. Multiply my successes by the many other federal agents working gangs and you begin to understand the basis for my belief.

Tom and I began working closely with two of the best detectives I ever met — Rick and Mike. Rick was a stocky, street-smart white cop and Mike was a rail-thin African American with the fortitude of a Samurai warrior. On many a slow night, Tom, Rick, and I would station ourselves at the far end of a gang-infested housing complex. Mike would begin running through the complex, scattering drug-dealing gang members, who often ran into our waiting arms at the opposite end of the complex.

Rather than take a shotgun approach to the South Central Los Angeles gang problem, we initially narrowed our investigation to two Crip sets, the Seven-Four Hoovers and the Backstreet. We began to develop as much intelligence as possible on the most notorious members of these two gangs and identified the shot callers within each set. We also discovered who had prior felony drug convictions and who was currently believed to be distributing.

Concentrating on the drug distribution made sense. The sentencing statutes proved a tremendous incentive for cooperation with anyone we caught dealing. A strong network of informants working off beefs from a federal drug arrest would allow us to solve many crimes and possibly gain freedom for a neighborhood presently in the stranglehold of street gangs.

We created our target list and sought

funds from the FBI to make a series of drug buys. Once we had our money in place, we were ready to begin. Our only problem was finding an entry into the gangs. Tom and I were white and Rick and Mike were well known as CRASH detectives.

Rick and Mike introduced us to an informant who was willing to make buys from those members we targeted. The informant, however, had a criminal record and his credibility could be attacked if called upon to testify. If we hoped to be successful and convict those members we targeted, we were going to need an undercover agent.

Although the FBI had talented black agents, many were lawyers and accountants who came from middle-class backgrounds. They were no more anxious to work undercover in South Central than anybody else. Our first attempts at using FBI agents proved disastrous: the first two agents we attempted to introduce lacked the experience to successfully pull off the assignment. In our third attempt, the informant could not get along with the agent. Finally, one Friday evening, the black informant looked at me in desperation and said — and I quote — "Leave the niggers at home. I'd rather take you in." When I asked if he could sell it, he offered a huge smile. Thus began my undercover experiences in South Central.

The cover I developed was simple. I knew that most of the gang members we targeted stayed within the boundaries of their own gang territory and few, if any, would ever travel to "Boystown," in West Hollywood. My story was that I worked in a tire store on Santa Monica Boulevard and sold rock to the gays. "They eat that stuff up" was my standard line. Actually, to sell my act in the tough streets of South Central L.A., I used slightly stronger language, but you get the idea. We had an old pickup truck as our undercover vehicle. My daily attire was already pretty grubby and I rubbed grease on my hands and clothes, making sure my fingernails were filthy. I looked like I'd been changing tires all day.

The informant made the initial introduction and after that the sales came rather easily. Typically, once I entered a neighborhood, I turned away youngsters who ran up to my car, hoping to sell me rock. I'd ask for the person we had identified as being a viable target and within a few minutes he would appear. After consummating a sale, I'd leave the area. Within a half hour or so, police units would arrive in the neighborhood, not an infrequent occurrence, and conduct an FI (field identification) of the

131

gang members congregating on the street. Our target was often milling about with the others. Rick and Mike would take photos of the gang members and maybe even pat them down, discovering the marked bills used to purchase the rock. No arrests were made, but the evidence began to mount.

10
PATIENCE IS A VIRTUE

Some nights in South Central proved more nerve-wracking than others. Late one evening while making a purchase, a drive-by shooting occurred up the block from where I was parked. The recorder I was wearing picked up the distinct *pop, pop, pop* of the firearms.

A community source identified Eligh as a prominent shot caller. He had an extensive criminal record with multiple narcotics convictions and was a major street-level distributor. He became a prime target.

Accompanying the informant late one Friday evening, we drove through the hood seeking Eligh. We came upon him and the informant introduced me. We made a quick buy and the stage was set for further business. Several nights later I returned alone and made a quick purchase. When I returned to the office to review the evidence, I realized the sale took place so quickly and with such ease there was almost no audio of any evidentiary value. The sole evidence was my testimony; the U.S. Attorney's office would require more if we were hoping for a federal prosecution.

I decided the next purchase would have to involve more conversation. The problem was, Eligh wasn't much of a talker. He wanted buyers and wasn't looking to make a white man his best friend. Although the purchase prices were minimal, often just a few hundred dollars, I decided that rather than pay him in hundreds, fifties, and twenties, I'd use small bills. I planned to purchase an ounce and a half of rock, at a total cost of nine hundred dollars. I would make the payment in tens and fives, figuring I could capture Eligh counting the money on tape.

Late that evening I drove down into the heart of South Central, only a few blocks from the famous Watts Towers. I always made my purchases while remaining in the truck and had no plans of ever leaving the sanctum of the well-worn vehicle. I also kept my .38 on the front seat between my legs, available for quick access should it be necessary. As I slowly rounded the corner and made my way down the street, a young boy who had not yet reached puberty rushed the vehicle and offered to sell me drugs. I told him to get me Eligh and then get his tail home. Or maybe I didn't say "tail." South Central, remember?

Within moments Eligh and an associate approached the truck. I told Eligh I wanted an ounce and half and he instructed me to wait in the truck, an order I had no problem following. When he returned he demanded to see the money. I handed him seven hundred dollars in fives and tens. He handed me two clear plastic sandwich bags, each containing chunks of rock cocaine, each rock the approximate size of a baby's tooth.

I patiently waited as Eligh and his associate attempted to count the money. It was dark and not only did they have trouble discerning the fives from the tens, they had trouble counting. My recorder picked up the two counting the money, then becoming confused, dropping a few f-bombs, and beginning the counting process anew. Finally they announced I was a hundred dollars short. Knowing I was actually two hundred short, I handed over another hundred dollars. After counting that, Eligh announced I was still a hundred dollars short. When I protested, he ordered me out of the truck. That was all the incentive I needed to pony up the remaining hundred.

I had achieved my goal. I had purchased an ounce and a half of rock for nine hundred dollars and recorded the lengthy counting process on tape.

Weeks later we did a sweep, arresting all the thirteen gang members who sold us rock cocaine. Eligh was one of the thirteen, having sold me drugs on five separate occasions.

We brought each of the thirteen back to the CRASH off-site building for interviewing and processing prior to taking them to the federal lockup. When I confronted Eligh, I looked him in the eye and asked, "Eligh, you had to suspect a white guy coming down here and buying rock, didn't you?"

His answer was priceless. "I talks it over with my homeboys and we figure the police would be too stupid to send in a white guy."

Eligh was the only one of the thirty-three gang members I arrested and subsequently convicted who went to trial. Everyone else pleaded guilty. Eligh was convicted in a jury trial and sentenced to thirty-one years.

Los Angeles, 1989
Going into the NAMBLA operation, I had to constantly remind myself and my case agent that sometimes, to make the collar

happen to maximum advantage, you've got to wait for matters to unfold in the right way. Had I rushed into the New York conference wearing a wire and pushing members to make criminal admissions, it's likely the case would have ended right there. Despite my almost continual disgust with what I was hearing and with the social agenda NAMBLA espoused, I had to remain patient and in character as I slowly but surely built the government's case.

Similarly, the advantages of patience made themselves known in my 1989 investigation of a drug operation centering on an upscale restaurant in the heart of Beverly Hills. In fact, patience and my unwillingness to renege on a commitment to my son — coupled with a brazen bluff and dumb luck — actually served to enhance my credibility with a fairly sophisticated drug distributor.

Peter was Sicilian and opened a posh Beverly Hills eatery, his second. His first establishment was in New York, and intelligence reports we received from there stated the New York restaurant was used as a way station for mob fugitives waiting to escape the country. Peter was a worthy target and my supervisor was hoping we could ensnare him in an FBI-orchestrated sting.

A confidential informant reported that Peter, who had a prior felony narcotics conviction, was involved in drug trafficking. With that piece of information, I began frequenting the restaurant. Peter was outgoing and appreciated my regularity; sometimes I ate there for lunch and dinner on the same day. The food was overpriced and not really that good, but I continued to praise the chef, who just happened to be Peter's mother.

Often Peter would join me at the table, especially when business was slow. He eventually inquired about my business. The vague description I gave of my source of income intrigued him and fueled further questioning. Because this was 1989, any high roller in Beverly Hills with a vague economic history was presumed to be involved in the drug trade. After several of these beat-around-the-bush conversations, I finally confirmed my interest in purchasing high-grade cocaine. Peter took the bait and negotiations commenced.

Due to limited drug budgets, many law enforcement agencies at the time were unable to do "buy-walks": transactions where the officer purchases a quantity of drugs, then walks away to return another day for a larger purchase. In fact, most deals were "buy-busts": the supplier shows up with the negotiated drug and is arrested on the spot. Such a less-expensive tactic obviously removes one drug dealer from the streets, but unless he cooperates, the full scope of the distribution network is never determined.

Thanks to the Superfund and the priority narcotics and organized crime took in the FBI investigative agenda, we often did buy-walks. This was especially true when the federal forfeiture statutes came into play. Under the statutes, any piece of real or personal property used to facilitate a drug transaction or any property purchased with drug funds could be forfeited to the federal government. Often this property was sold at public auction, the money going into the Superfund or to the U.S. Treasury. However, at times, the actual property was used in undercover scenarios. Even my wife admitted I was better looking with a forfeited fifteen-thousand-dollar Rolex watch on my wrist and driving a Porsche or BMW, compliments of an unlucky narcotics dealer. Such props certainly made me more attractive to hustlers like Peter.

He agreed to sell me a kilogram sample of cocaine in anticipation of a larger purchase. We established the ground rules for the purchase and Peter readily agreed to consummate the deal in the safety and security of the upstairs office above his restaurant. Once the deal was complete, we had a solid count on Peter. To further sweeten the deal, his restaurant had been used to facilitate the transaction and was now subject to forfeiture. Peter's product tested positive as high-grade cocaine and the wheels were set in motion for a larger purchase.

I continued to meet with Peter and spoke of my desire to make the larger purchase. Although I pride myself on being cognizant of my surroundings, one evening I proved just how focused I was during my undercover role. The human ear can discern a particular noise or voice, shutting out the surrounding sounds. Often by concentrating on someone speaking to us, we can become oblivious to other ordinary noises. Recording devices usually lack that very human capability. I always scoff at the movie scene in which the cop and the bad guy are talking in a crowded restaurant and the tech team easily and clearly monitors every word from the van across the street. Even quiet restaurants are often anything but quiet to the sensitive technical equipment that picks up the sound of every dropped dish, every clang of silverware, and every slammed door. Often in those days we had to send out the tapes to be "enhanced," the technical term for separating the tracks and isolating the conversation.

One evening, Peter and I sat at one of his tables for nearly a half hour, discussing in hushed tones our next transaction. We laid out the details and the incriminating conversation proved a valuable piece of evidence. The equipment, of course, picked up every word and noise in the restaurant. When I returned to the office and began reviewing the recorded conversation, I realized the device I was wearing also picked up the conversation occurring at the table behind me. The two diners were discussing a money-laundering scheme. I was so focused on Peter I had no idea what was being discussed right behind me — a lost opportunity.

I sometimes feared I looked and acted like a fed. I would often modify my appearance in some manner — longer hair, unshaven, temporary tattoos, and even the crutch I adopted later in my career. Similarly, in an effort to throw Peter off any "cop" scent I might inadvertently be leaving, I ordered up seventeen kilos of cocaine for the larger purchase. I figured most cops ordered in ones, fives, tens, or a hundred. Seventeen seemed like an odd number for a purchase, and sure enough it threw Peter when I placed the order, as I counted out who was to get what and added up the figures to seventeen. He bought the act and placed the order.

Back at the office, we started the cumbersome paperwork to have Headquarters send us the "show" money for a seventeen-kilo buy-bust. Unlike on television, the money wasn't waiting in a neat bundle in a safe. In fact, it was always nerve-wracking to hold off my targets until "my money guy arrived," or I "liquidated my stock position and the clearing house sent a cashier's check to my out-of-state bank," or because "my banker in Grand Cayman is out of the office until next Tuesday." Greed usually trumped fear, and the bad guys almost always bought the delay.

Another major problem with any buy-bust involving a large amount of cash is the fact that a team of FBI agents must cover — *swarm* might be a better word — the buy and effect the subsequent arrest. As a result of our negotiations, I now had in excess of a quarter of a million dollars in a briefcase that I would be flashing at Peter sometime prior to the delivery of the cocaine. As with the previous transaction, Peter was most comfortable consummating the deal at the restaurant. I was only too happy to oblige, making an even stronger case for forfeiture of the property.

Many FBI agents shied away from drug investigations because of the long and uncertain hours. I made it a point to set up almost every transaction during the day, however, arguing with my dealers that the police were easier to observe in the daylight hours.

We had initially arranged for the deal to go down at Peter's restaurant at noon on Monday. As I learned early in my career, drug dealer time is not the same time most of us observe; Peter and his associates were no exception. FBI agents were staked out throughout Beverly Hills on Monday, awaiting the "load car" transporting the cocaine, but noon came and went with no load car. After waiting several more hours, Peter received a call. The load car had broken down somewhere on the freeway and we would be unable to consummate the deal that day. Los Angeles is the second largest city in the United States and its 915-mile freeway system made it pointless to try to locate a broken-down load car. I agreed to postpone the deal until Tuesday.

But now a personal problem arose. I have a son who loves baseball as much as I do. I had two tickets to see the Angels play Tuesday evening; the seats were located right behind the Angels dugout. Our home was almost one hundred miles from Anaheim. In order to make the game, I would have to drive almost fifty miles to my house, pick up my son, and then drive the hundred miles to Anaheim Stadium. So, to make sure I'd have enough time to make the opening pitch, I told Peter, "I don't like playing games. I'll be at the restaurant at noon tomorrow, but if the supplier can't produce by 1:30, I'm gone."

All of the agents regrouped at the FBI office, we returned the money to the safe, and prepared for tomorrow's buy. No one else knew I had box-seat tickets to the Angels.

On Tuesday, I was back at the restaurant with agents milling around Beverly Hills. Once again, noon came and went. Finally, at 1:20 pm, Peter emerged from his office. His face beamed. "I just got off the phone. My man will be here in a half hour," he said.

"That's fine," I said. "But I won't be here. I told you if he can't deliver by one thirty, I'm gone. Unlike you and your supplier, I'm a man of my word." With that, I threw down a tip on the table. I told Peter, "You've inconvenienced me enough today. Lunch is on you." And I walked out.

I know Peter and his supplier were shocked, but my credibility soared. After all, no cop would walk away from a multi-kilo dope deal because the supplier was going to be twenty minutes late. I knew Peter would call back; he was hungry for a sale . . . at least, that's what I told myself.

My son and I made the game, enjoyed baseball up close, and had a great time. Not long after, true to my hunch (and to my relief), Peter called, profusely apologizing for any misunderstanding. He arranged for his supplier to meet me directly on Wednesday at the supplier's house. How fortuitous! The fact that I placed my son and baseball ahead of the FBI meant we would be able to not only identify the supplier but, if he used his house to "facilitate" the transaction, acquire some more real estate under the forfeiture statutes.

I have to admit, my refusal to cancel my baseball outing with my son had as much to do with my unwillingness to allow my work to intrude on my family as it did with maintaining an image for my targets. And even with my determination to keep my family as a priority, those dearest to me sometimes suffered because of my job.

My daughter provides an example both amusing and, in a way, heartbreaking. When she was five, she knew I went to work every day with the bad guys and pretended to be someone else. But she also feared they might kidnap me and send someone home in my place. Of course, at the time, I didn't know this was what she was thinking; I only knew that when I came home in the evenings, she was a bit standoffish for a while. My son would rush to greet me, but my daughter would take her time. I attributed it to the difference between boys and girls, but that wasn't her reason.

In her childish imagination, she believed the impostor would wear a plastic mask — a Halloween mask held on by an elastic band — that looked like her dad.

"So, he would come home every night and he would sit in this one blue chair we had," she explained, years later. "And I would walk around behind him before I would give him a hug, just to make sure he didn't have the string across the back of his head. That's how I knew that it was really him."

I, of course, didn't get the full story until she graduated from college. The point is, my family made sacrifices I never even knew about. But I knew my son loved baseball, and this was one time my job wasn't going to interfere.

My squad mates and supervisor, however,

weren't exactly pleased that I'd missed the Tuesday buy. Wednesday meant another day on surveillance, covering me for yet another deal that might or might not happen. In addition, the dealer lived near Ontario, California — almost sixty miles east of the FBI offices. Still, because Peter was considered a big target and his supplier even bigger, everyone supported me one more time.

So, the stage was set. The deal would surely go down this time . . . wouldn't it?

11
Improvise
to Survive

On Wednesday, I met with Onofrio, Peter's supplier, in a shopping center near his home. I had the funds to close the deal secreted in the trunk of my undercover car. When I met Onofrio for the first time, we spoke briefly and he agreed to take me to his house to show me the cocaine. I was amazed at his boldness and his stupidity. Peter vouched for me and Onofrio was aware that the one-kilo sample purchase went down without a problem, but using his home as the base of his operation seemed naïve at best.

Because the money was in my car, I thought quickly and decided to have Onofrio drive me to his house, leaving the car in the shopping center parking lot where I assumed agents could keep it under tight security. It also provided me another opportunity to have Onofrio or one of his associates drive me back to my car to get the money, allowing me to engage others in conspiratorial conversations. It also provided a chance for a surveillance team to follow me more than once, just in case they lost us going to the residence.

We arrived at Onofrio's home, a large house in an upscale residential neighborhood that didn't allow on-street parking. It was neat and well decorated, unlike the homes of the South Central gang members I'd been chasing recently. Onofrio had obviously been successful and now owned some valuable California real estate.

Onofrio and I were alone, as far as I could tell, which surprised me. He had me sit in his living room while he attended to business in the back of the house. He had yet to ask to see any money, so I assumed I was safe from being ripped, but still his actions differed from drug dealers I previously encountered.

Within a few minutes he returned from the back of the house and escorted me to the master bedroom. His house was much larger than mine. We walked down a long hallway. As we turned into his bedroom, I saw a cardboard box on the bed. In it were seven kilograms of cocaine wrapped in red cellophane. Peter told me earlier we could do seven, and then after that deal Onofrio would deliver the remaining ten I ordered. I pulled a switchblade knife from my back pocket, activated the spring-loaded blade, and slit open a corner of one of the kilos. I tested the product, using a standard field test kit I told Onofrio I purchased at a head shop in the Valley. Onofrio didn't question the small hard plastic pouch, no bigger than a cigarette lighter, that contained three clear plastic vials. With the knife tip I took a small sample, placed it into the plastic container, and systematically broke the three vials, watching the substance change color with each broken vial. The small container lit up like a Christmas tree, indicating high-quality cocaine.

I announced my pleasure with his product and told him we needed to return to my car at the shopping center to retrieve the cash. He gave me an ear-to-ear smile and we both returned to his car. As he was backing out of the driveway and began to proceed toward the shopping center, we both spotted a lone male sitting in a four-door car that screamed "government vehicle." It was the only car on the street in a neighborhood that prohibited on-street parking. The reason it looked like a government car was simple: it was.

Onofrio noticed the car immediately and

commented on the driver, strongly suggesting he was a cop. Trying to defuse the situation, I said he was probably a real estate agent, and then, practically yelling into the transmitter I was wearing, I said, "The cops couldn't be that stupid. No cop would sit in front of your house if he was watching you." I was livid, and to make it worse, my efforts proved futile. Onofrio got on his cell phone and called someone in the house we just left — a person I had never seen or heard — and ordered him to take the drugs out the back. Onofrio called off the deal and drove me back to the shopping center, dropping me off near a phone booth.

By this time, the surveillance team lost me, and my transmitter was out of communication range. From the phone booth I called dispatch and told them where I was and what happened. I also called Peter, complaining that his supplier called off the deal because of a real estate agent. As hard as I tried and as hard as Peter tried, we were unable to complete the transaction that day. Three days, three attempts — all failures.

I returned to the "barn" and debriefed. I placed the show money in the safe and assumed that at some point we would indict Peter, but that Onofrio would walk. No-dope conspiracies weren't real popular in federal court, and without the drugs Onofrio showed me, there was little chance the U.S. Attorney's office would indict him. I began to worry that maybe my cavalier attitude about taking my son to a baseball game cost us a defendant and the seizure of seven kilos of cocaine. I had to prepare for court the next day. I was testifying in a trial stemming from a previous investigation we'd concluded. The courtroom and testimony meant a suit and tie, none of which were on my all-time-favorites list.

The next day, during my testimony, my pager vibrated; Peter was calling. During a court recess, I went to a pay phone down the hall from the courtroom.

The excitement in Peter's voice came through the telephone. Onofrio had just delivered the seven kilos of cocaine to the restaurant, he told me, and he wanted me to come over right away and complete the deal. I knew there was no way I could walk off the witness stand in the middle of a trial. Peter thought I was a freelance screenwriter who supplemented his income with drug trafficking, a cover accounting for my unpredictable schedule. I told Peter he "jacked me around for three days," his supplier saw cops masquerading as real estate agents, and I wasn't about to walk out of a rewrite conference in Culver City for another no-show drug deal with him and his buddies. I would be at the restaurant sometime after seven, I told him. He bought my tirade and agreed to meet me in his office.

Following my testimony, I rushed back to the FBI offices, attempting for a fourth time in four days to secure the drugs and build a solid case against Peter and his supplier. My supervisor, however, was unmoved by my pleas to retrieve the cash from the safe. He was right when he said I had tied up the squad all week and he had little faith in Peter's assurances that he would produce this time. I understood the supervisor's reluctance but still I stormed out of his office, as I was prone to do, vowing to handle the situation "my way."

Fortunately, two young agents were still in the squad bay, completing mounds of Bureau paperwork. Everyone else had left for the evening. Knowing that both these men, who eventually rose in the ranks and became two of the finest agents in the FBI, carried the same fire in the belly I did, I asked if they wanted to go make an arrest. They eagerly agreed and we left — without notifying the supervisor.

Once we got to Beverly Hills, I explained the situation. We briefed in the alley behind the restaurant. I changed into casual clothes as I explained the plan. Both knew this was somewhere far outside the volumes of regulations pounded into young agents at the Academy, but even before I assured them I would take full responsibility for any mishaps, they agreed to help. I really liked these guys.

I went into the restaurant using the alley entrance. My cover team remained in the alley several hundred feet from the door. Peter met me downstairs and we spoke briefly before he escorted me through a locked metal door and up the stairs to a locked storageroom. Once up there, he walked to a large floor safe and removed the same cardboard box I saw the day before in Onofrio's bedroom. After opening the box, he allowed me to examine the contents. It was the same seven kilos of cocaine; the knife slits I made on one of the packages were clearly visible.

I told Peter I was satisfied and asked him to accompany me to my car where he could count the money and we could complete the transaction. He balked at that request, saying, "This is Onofrio's stuff; God help me if anything happens." He told me to bring the money to his office. His request made perfect sense from a drug dealer's standpoint — except I had no money. But I headed for my car, anyway.

I had just left seven kilos of high-grade cocaine on the table in the upstairs storeroom and had no money to complete the buy-bust. I needed to find an acceptable means of payment — or to convince Peter I found one.

I returned to the car and my two young cover agents. As I began unpacking my gym bag I explained the plan. They thought I was kidding. I wasn't.

For years, I had enjoyed boxing and worked out at a gym where many professional fighters trained for upcoming bouts. I regularly had my head beaten in by guys with world-class skills and some might say it knocked loose a few too many brain cells. However, I had a plan. I placed a pair of ten-ounce boxing gloves in a small gym bag, which would be my proxy for the cash I didn't have for this evening's transaction. I looked at my watch and told my confederates to come up to the storageroom in exactly five minutes.

I began walking down the alley, hoping I could pull this off. As I got to the back door, I noticed one of the cooks standing by the door, holding a meat cleaver — not a particularly auspicious symbol. I entered through the caged door and began to ascend the stairs. The door slammed behind me. Once I entered the storage area, I observed Peter sitting next to the cardboard box still on the table.

I walked toward the floor safe. I knew time was running out and I also knew the door to the storage area locked when it slammed shut. I looked at Peter and using my Marine Corps command voice told him, "I don't like having the money and the dope together in one place. I just counted the cash; it's all here. If I'm short, I'll make it up next time." I walked to the safe, shoved my gym bag inside, closed the doors, spun the tumbler, and did an about-face. I walked over to the table, picked up the cardboard box, and marched down the stairs before he could say a word.

My brazen attitude caught him so off guard he allowed me to walk away with the drugs. As I descended the stairs, my cover team awaited. I opened the door and walked out into the alley as they rushed up the steps and placed Peter under arrest.

The deal was completed. I had swapped a pair of ten-ounce boxing gloves for seven kilos of high-grade cocaine. Final tally: two arrests and two indictments; for the taxpayers, the seizure and forfeiture of the restaurant, Onofrio's house, and the car he used to pick me up at the shopping center. Seeing a baseball game with my son from seats behind the dugout: priceless!

12
A NAMBLA
History Lesson

New York NAMBLA Conference
Sunday marked a new day. I successfully sold my undercover persona during the first day of meetings and doubted I raised any suspicions. The Sunday session provided a chance to spend more time with the members in a somewhat smaller setting.

We broke into committees to help draft various pamphlets NAMBLA wanted to publish. We were encouraged to participate on one or more committees. I volunteered to be on the "Privacy" pamphlet committee with Joe P. from California and Rowan and Jim from New Jersey. Other committees included such topics as "Coming Out," "Responding to the Media," "How to Handle Arrests and Police Inquiries," "Age-of-Consent Position," "SVP (Sexual Violent Predator) Reporting," "Treating Kids as Adults in the Court System," "Power Differences," "Families and Friends," "Famous

Boy Lover Figures," "Legal Counseling," "Religious Aspect of Boy Love," "AIDS Advice," "Are You a BL?," and "Do You Love a BL?"

As I found out during my multiyear membership, the organization was poor on follow-through. To my knowledge, no pamphlet discussed at the conference was ever published. In my experience, the conferences had little to do with any organized political agenda. Instead, they were basically conclaves for boy lovers to gather, encourage each other in their "lifestyle," and share criminal fantasies.

It was during our breakout session that Jim and I spoke at length. Jim, a former teacher from Bergen County, New Jersey, admitted to being arrested in 1982, but the charges were dismissed after three hung juries. The boy he was charged with seducing eventually testified that his psychiatrist coerced the admissions. Jim, however, never denied the seduction. He also discussed his hobby: photography. The conversation was enlightening — and infuriating — as he spoke of photographing students at an all-boys' school, his hands gesturing to emphasize his points.

There's a Catholic high school in the

area of my neighborhood. . . . So I'm watching the soccer games . . . I mean, they're out on the field . . . scratching, pushing their [genitals] down like they have [an erection], right on the field. One day this one kid, the most beautiful legs you'd ever want to see . . . he's sitting there on the bench . . . like this [Jim gestures as if playing with himself], right out in the open.

When Paul interrupted our conversation I was somewhat irritated, but Paul elicited answers to questions I dared not ask. Paul introduced himself as being from Sussex County, New Jersey, and a friend of Tim B., the former membership chairman and Green Party member. He was clean-cut and looked to be in his early to mid-thirties. With his buttoned-down appearance, I would have suspected him of being an undercover FBI agent. His dialogue with Jim was enlightening.

Jim: We used to have chapter meetings in New York. . . . But it was so easy to infiltrate then. People show up you don't know.

Paul: I think Peter tries to screen who comes here, hopefully.

Jim: Yeah, obviously the only reason I

came here is because I knew how tight Peter was screening everyone.

Paul: He told me there were some people he decided not to invite. . . .

Jim: This is part of the problem with trying to spread the work out. . . . Someone seems to be all gung ho . . . then turns out to be a very skilled undercover operator.

Paul: Yeah . . . So we can all look at each other like that [with mistrust].

Jim: You know we do. . . . My only credential is I've survived twenty-three years in the organization.

Paul: Some people . . . have gotten out of it altogether. Won't even show up to something like this.

Jim: Well, actually, I did quit; I guess it was back in eighty-three or something. I didn't like the way they were going.

Paul: Politics?

Jim: Yeah . . . I was doing the publications, which got me well known to the FBI, I discovered later.

Paul: Yeah, well, it's good maybe that you didn't keep your name on the list there because you might be part of the lawsuit that's going on now, the Massachusetts thing [the Jeffrey Curley wrongful death civil lawsuit].

161

Jim: I don't know who's on there, but I suspect it's the executive . . .

Paul: Although I doubt if it will go anywhere.

Jim: Yeah, but it can be very expensive even if it does not go anywhere. That was my trouble.

Paul: The two guys [convicted of killing Jeffrey Curley] who had the NAMBLA *Bulletin* around and murdered the kid.

Jim: That's the other thing. . . . Some of your members could be undercover guys. Some of the members are not the kind of members you really want.

Paul: Right, they could be other things.

Jim: There's boy lovers and there's predators.

Paul: Right . . . I wonder what the percentage is?

Jim: I have my own feelings.

Paul: What are they?

Jim: Seventy-thirty.

Paul: More are predators?

Jim: Yeah . . . There are people who are only interested in sex and go after it in whatever way.

I could not have been more interested in the exchange I'd just heard. My ego was fed by their belief that only a "skilled undercover operator" could fool Peter. But most important, a longtime member had just opined that sexual predators comprised 70 percent of the membership. The need for the "safety lecture" may have been valid. Rock wasn't playing to an "infiltrator"; as it turned out, he was genuinely concerned about those in attendance doing something criminal while at the conference.

My cover was confirmed intact a bit later, when Peter Herman pulled me aside and asked if I wanted to be on the steering committee. I thought briefly about the invitation, smiling inwardly at my success, but respectfully declined. I knew FBI Headquarters would erupt in an administrative furor had I been elected, especially given all the discussion clarifying my investigative role prior to my attending the conference. It was made very clear that we were seeking to identify the criminal activities of individual members, not become a part of the organization's inner sanctum. To that end, and to avoid even the appearance of attempting to interfere with the men's legitimate First Amendment rights of assembly, I declined Peter's invitation, then left the conference on Sunday before voting on any propositions or the selection of the steering committee members. My purpose in attending the conference was not to direct or influence or sabotage the organization, as such; my mission was to determine if members were engaging in criminal conduct. Staying focused was the only way to be successful.

As a part of my preparation for infiltrating NAMBLA, I delved into the beginnings of the organization, which lay in the late sixties, a time when the traditional values and institutions of this nation were publicly questioned and scrutinized. Sex became political and sexual liberation was at the forefront of the counterculture movement.

On June 28, 1969, around 1:20 am, in New York City's Greenwich Village, officers from the New York Police Department's First Precinct conducted an all-too-typical raid on the Stonewall Inn, a West Village converted garage serving as a gay disco. It was an easy target for law enforcement, because the establishment operated without a valid liquor license.

Just a week prior, Judy Garland, deeply loved by many in the gay community, died. As many as twelve thousand men attended her June 27 funeral on the Upper East Side. A wake at Stonewall followed, and emotions were still running high as the police entered, armed with a search warrant.

Although accounts vary as to what actually precipitated the violent disturbance, by the end of the evening an estimated two thousand rioters fought with four hundred police officers. For three consecutive nights the disturbance continued — and a movement was born.

Within a month, the Gay Liberation Front was founded. The sexual revolution was at its height. This revolutionary movement spawned the opportunity for a more open discussion on all aspects of sex, including sex with minors. Among the early participants in this new movement were the founders of NAMBLA.

Almost seven years later, a December 1977 raid on a home in Revere, Massachusetts, a quiet Boston suburb, generated extensive media coverage of the twenty-four men arrested. Described as an interstate sex ring, the men were charged with child pornography and having sex with boys. Allegedly, the men lured boys to the house to participate in sexual activity that was subsequently photographed and then distributed. The allegations made headlines; news outlets published names, addresses, occupations, and photos of those arrested.

Members of the gay community saw this law enforcement effort as a witch hunt and rallied to support those arrested. One activist, Tom Reeves, organized a meeting at the Community Church of Boston on December 2, 1978. As the evening progressed, about thirty men mobilized and formed NAMBLA, the North American Man/Boy Love Association. NAMBLA was born for the express purpose of abolishing age-of-consent laws, legalizing consensual sex between men and boys.

Initially, NAMBLA was welcomed into the radical gay community and was an active member of the International Lesbian and Gay Association. The ILGA was founded in 1978 and currently consists of over four hundred member organizations seeking equality throughout the world for lesbians, gays, bisexuals, and transgendered individuals.

NAMBLA delegates participated in the drafting of ILGA's early positions on the sexual rights of youth. The ILGA adopted resolutions calling on member organizations to implore their respective governments to abolish age-of-consent laws, to support the right of young people to sexual and social self-determination, and to support the right of every individual, regardless of age, to explore and develop his or her sexuality.

NAMBLA delegates participated for a

decade in the association and considered themselves bona fide participants in the radical gay movement, even though many gay rights supporters distanced themselves from NAMBLA and its professed goals. But support by the ILGA waned when, in 1993, the ILGA learned the United States government was seeking its removal from the United Nations' Economic and Social Counsel as a "consultative body" unless NAMBLA, the Dutch Vereniging Martijn, and Project Truth were expelled from the ILGA. The United States took the position that these three organizations promoted and supported pedophilia; a bill passed unanimously in Congress that threatened to cut off United Nations funding unless NAMBLA was expelled. Even though the ILGA subsequently voted to oust NAMBLA along with the other two organizations, ILGA's consultative status was revoked, never to be reinstated. However, this action by the ILGA spelled the end of NAMBLA's acceptance within the gay community.

Through the years, several significant efforts against NAMBLA have taken their toll on the organization's credibility and viability. NAMBLA did manage to survive the efforts of Mike Echols, a child advocate, who infiltrated the organization and in 1985 published a membership list. His strategy — exposure — had some effect, and would soon be utilized by others.

In January 1992, KRON-TV in San Francisco aired hidden-camera video of NAMBLA meetings being held in San Francisco's Potrero Hill Public Library. An outraged public balked at a group of admitted pedophiles using tax-supported buildings for their scheduled gatherings. CNN and Geraldo Rivera ran with the story. Two months later, John Miller of WNBC in New York aired the New York chapter meetings. This public exposure caused NAMBLA to end its public chapter meetings in several cities — events alluded to in the conversations I heard at the New York conference. Membership began to decline. Public exposure and the threat of public exposure were powerful disincentives to remaining with the organization.

In 1994, Adi Sideman's controversial documentary *Chicken Hawk* debuted. The film exposed the organization through one-on-one, intimate interviews with members. Later, the 1995 NAMBLA national conference, held in Seattle, elected undercover detective Tom Polhemus to the steering committee. The 1996 conference was held in the offices of Denny Mintun in Hayward,

California. Mintun later announced via the Internet that he was a government source who had provided information about the membership to law enforcement and Mike Echols' child advocacy organization.

The event that would prove most damaging to NAMBLA was, however, the murder of ten-year-old Jeffrey Curley on October 1, 1997.

Los Angeles, 1990

January can be beautiful in Los Angeles, especially when the Santa Ana winds blow in from the desert. The smog is cleared from the sky, resulting in a scenic view of the often snow-covered San Gabriel Mountains. In 1990, I was enjoying just such a view from the fifteenth floor of the Federal Building when an agent from another squad approached. He needed assistance with a narcotics investigation.

An informant identified Michael, the manager of a local strip club, as desiring to move ten kilos of cocaine. My FBI colleague needed an undercover agent to meet Michael and negotiate the transaction. It seemed like a quick hit and I readily agreed. At the time I was working another investigation with John, an informant who identified numerous L.A.-based gang members dealing street-level quantities of rock cocaine. John had a linebacker build and arms tattooed with obvious indicia of his gang affiliation. Although he had an extensive prison record, he was likable and I enjoyed our time together. He was educating me as much as I hoped I was positively influencing him. We had been successful in our investigative endeavors, and I wanted to reward him whenever possible with a payday. I decided to bring him along with me to meet Michael. If I was able to put some powder on the table, I could compensate John for his assistance, making him even more grateful to me and the largesse of the federal government. I was hopeful such generosity would advance future investigations where his skills would be needed.

John and I worked out a backstory that seemed plausible. I posed as a tough Hollywood producer who was distributing drugs throughout the industry. Our story would be that we met while doing an after-school special on gangs and soon discovered we both were involved in the drug trade. No one who looked at John would ever question his gang affiliation. The black-and-white team of John and me seemed strange — a gangbanging linebacker and a tough-talking cross-country runner — but once again, the unconventional played well and our "odd couple" act befuddled our target.

Our initial meeting with Michael was at a Denny's restaurant on Sunset Boulevard, just off the Hollywood freeway. We were within walking distance of several studios and just across the street from the Fox Television Center, home to *Mama's Family* and *Married . . . with Children.* While sitting next to me in the vinyl-covered booth with John facing us, Michael laid out his plans to become a big-time Los Angeles cocaine trafficker. His wannabe act was weak; I'm not sure he had what it took to make it to the show. Throughout his spiel, I kept eating the french fries on his plate without asking his permission. I could tell he wanted to protest, but my boldness caught him off guard. At one point I even slapped his hand as he reached for one of his own fries.

After Michael left the table, convinced we were interested in purchasing whatever quantity of drugs he could produce, John looked at me and shook his head. "You are one cold mother. You're gonna put the boy in jail and you sit there eatin' his fries!"

Michael bought our act and never questioned our bona fides. His attempts, however, weren't nearly as productive. Like many I met in L.A., Michael "knew of someone who knew someone" who wanted to move the ten kilos of coke; he wasn't sitting on his personal stash. I played it tough with Michael, but I also played it fair. If Michael couldn't produce the product, I wasn't interested in making him a drug dealer. After several more unproductive meetings, I moved on with other investigations, believing Michael would become a distant memory who was more suited to being picked up by the local police on a possession charge than being the target of a federal inquiry.

Apparently, though, my tough demeanor made a lasting impression on Michael. The next spring, more than a year later, I was enjoying an annual tradition celebrated by many members of the L.A. FBI family: a large group of us was attending opening day at Dodger Stadium. Just a few minutes before the opening pitch, my pager went off. I looked down and saw an unfamiliar number. I reluctantly decided to find a pay phone and answer the page. To my surprise, it was Michael. Without fanfare or pleasantries he came to the point: he wanted me to kill two people.

Not having a recorder to document the call, I gave him a terse response, suitable for my bad-boy image: "It's opening day.

Nothing interferes with baseball. I'll call you tonight after the game."

Despite giving Michael the impression I was blowing him off, I was so caught up in the excitement of the potential of a new case — a contract killing, at that! — I had trouble concentrating on the game.

By the way, the Padres beat the Dodgers, 4-2.

13
The Murder of Jeffrey Curley

He could have ridden across your screen in a McDonald's commercial or been cast in a local youth production as Huckleberry Finn. By every account the blue-eyed, freckle-faced ten-year-old Jeffrey Curley was "all boy." He lived in East Cambridge, Massachusetts, and his trouble began when he lost his bike. Losing a bike is not an uncommon experience for many youngsters. Barbara Curley wanted to teach her son responsibility and told him he would have to wait until Christmas to have it replaced.

Salvatore Sicari, twenty-two, a house painter, who lived a block away from the Curley home, and Charles Jaynes, twenty-three, an auto detailer, befriended the youngster — though "targeted" might be a better word. Jaynes and Sicari intended to recruit Jeffrey for sex. Jaynes had recently joined NAMBLA. Sicari and Jaynes learned of the lost bike and devised a scheme to lure Jeffrey into Jaynes's 1983 gray Cadillac with the promise of a new bike.

On the afternoon of October 1, 1997, Jeffrey left his grandmother's home after telling her, "I have to go do something. I'll be back in a little while." He never returned.

Ten-year-old Jeffrey Curley met with Jaynes, accepting the bait used to lure him for sexual seduction. After a short drive, the 250-plus-pound Jaynes tried to sexually assault Jeffrey, who resisted. "Don't fight it, kid, don't fight it," said Jaynes, according to Sicari. But Jeffrey kept fighting, and when he refused to submit, Jaynes suffocated the ten-year-old with a gasoline-soaked rag.

Sicari and Jaynes then drove the body to Jaynes' Manchester, New Hampshire, apartment. According to Sicari, it was there that Jaynes sodomized Jeffrey's dead body. Sicari then helped Jaynes prepare the body for disposal, placing it in a cement-filled Rubbermaid container and using lime to speed decomposition. They drove Jeffrey's body to South Berwick, Maine, and disposed of him in the Great Works River.

When Jaynes was arrested, police found receipts for items purchased on the day of Jeffrey's disappearance: a Rubbermaid container, cement, lime, and a bicycle. They also found eight copies of the NAMBLA

Bulletin.

Following the three-week trial of Sicari, a Middlesex Superior Court found him guilty of first-degree murder and kidnapping and sentenced him to life in prison. A month later, Jaynes was convicted of second-degree murder and kidnapping. He was also sentenced to life in prison. (It may seem as if Jaynes got off easier, but because Massachusetts has no death penalty they faced the same punishment. The Curley case brought the death penalty issue to a head. A measure to reinstate capital punishment failed by one vote in the State House of Representatives.)

The case, however, didn't end with the criminal verdict. The Curley family filed a $200 million wrongful death action against NAMBLA and its individual members. They charged, in the twenty-one-count lawsuit, that NAMBLA incited Jaynes to commit the crime. The suit alleges that NAMBLA "encourages its members to rape male children . . . and serves as a conduit for an underground network of pedophiles in the United States." The suit also claims that "as a direct and proximate result of the urging, advocacy, conspiring, and promoting of pedophile activity by . . . NAMBLA . . . Charles Jaynes became obsessed with having sex with and raping young male children." After a lengthy legal process, the civil lawsuit was dismissed in April 2008.

Jaynes joined NAMBLA in the fall of 1996 and allegedly viewed the Web site shortly before murdering Jeffrey Curley. The family claims the NAMBLA Web site provided psychological comfort for what Jaynes was planning. These claims are bolstered by Jaynes's diary, in which a handwritten entry reads, "This was a turning point in discovery of myself. . . . NAMBLA's *Bulletin* helped me to become aware of my own sexuality and acceptance of it." The lawsuit cites a statement from the *Bulletin* that says, "Call it love, call it lust, call it whatever you want. We desire sex with boys, and boys, whether society is willing to admit it, desire sex with us."

Affidavits filed in support of the lawsuit include one by Mike Echols, whose Web site I accessed in researching my role as a boy lover. He described NAMBLA as a "quasi school for training its members on how to profile children," how to gain the confidence of children, and how to have sex with children without being detected by parents or police.

Fairfax County, Virginia, police detective Thomas Polhemus filed a separate affidavit in which he described his membership on the NAMBLA steering committee.

The ACLU agreed to defend NAMBLA, citing First Amendment free-speech and freedom-of-association issues. According to ACLU attorney Harvey Silvergate, "There is room in this country for people who believe man/boy love is okay. There is room for people who believe it, who say it, but not who do it."

The lawsuit named individual members, many of whom I encountered at the conferences.

Despite all the public relations embarrassments and legal battles of the past several years, few arrests resulted. As I sat among the members of NAMBLA and listened to their sickening conversation and self-justification, I had to wonder, would my results be any different?

Los Angeles, 1991

Michael's surprise phone call in 1991 wasn't my first experience at assuming the identity of a contract killer; several years earlier, I was hired by an attorney to kill his father and a business associate. I always derived a special satisfaction from nailing any attorney who stepped outside the law, and I enjoyed that brief undercover stint. I offered the attorney several ways of satisfying the contract: an ice pick through the eardrum to the brain ("not easily detected," I told him) or a gunshot (always sure to send a clear message). He chose the clear message and, upon my insistence, even furnished an automatic weapon to do the dirty deed. Following several meetings, he told an associate I had "killer eyes." I'm sure that was what drew my wife to me as well. The attorney was convicted by a federal jury who quickly rejected his claim that he had a brain dysfunction stemming from hyperactivity.

All these memories cascaded through my mind as I thought about Michael's call. It was going to be fun to play a killer again.

Later that evening, with my recorder running, I placed a call to Michael. He didn't disappoint me. In unambiguous terms he laid out his desires. A former girlfriend had sicced some gang members on him to collect money for a debt he presumably owed her. The collection efforts went beyond a mere "please and thank you" and Michael wanted payback as soon as possible. He was also the object of a local police search of his apartment for narcotics. He suspected one of his small-time drug clients of ratting him out and providing probable cause for the warrant. He wanted both of them killed and thought that either I could do it or could at least arrange for it to be done through my street gang affiliations.

When we met the next day, Michael's face was bruised from the recent collection efforts. He reiterated that he wanted the female killed but modified his position on the informant: he just wanted him "hospitalized." When the issue of money arose, I was incredulous when he asked that I kill on his behalf for free. He explained that if I did so, I could count on his lifetime loyalty.

Apparently, my new "client" had watched the *The Godfather* one too many times. As I pointed out to Michael in no uncertain terms, my generosity did not extend to contract killings. I had no problem with his request but I expected to be compensated for my efforts. Besides, I knew the case would be much stronger if money actually exchanged hands or a quid pro quo was negotiated. Michael's cash reserves were minimal. No surprise there; if he'd had money he would have paid off the collectors before they inflicted the beating. I wasn't sympathetic to his plight and was preparing to leave when he arrived at a possible solution.

He knew two guys who were attempting

to move twenty kilos of cocaine. He would introduce me and we could split the profits. He would then use his profits to pay me for my "work." I had trouble concealing a wicked smile and he noted the upturned curve of my lips. "You like that idea, don't you?" said Michael.

He was right, I did. What started as a failed cocaine transaction over a year ago morphed into a contract killing that led us back around to cocaine and possibly would ensnare more perpetrators.

Michael seemed content to hold off on the killings pending the completion of the drug deal, so my FBI associates and I believed we were justified in foregoing any warnings to his intended targets. It isn't always wise to believe convicted felons or soon-to-be-convicted felons, but I was confident Michael was too weak to pull the trigger himself nor would he seek to employ someone else to do his bidding. This was especially true because he had no funds to pay another hit man.

We decided to move quickly with the drug deal for two reasons: the most pressing was to preclude the opportunity for Michael to find someone else to kill his intended victims; second, we wanted to begin negotiations with the drug traffickers before they found a more suitable customer. Michael agreed to introduce me as soon as the others agreed.

Within a day Michael arranged for the meeting with his two associates, Noel and Steele. Michael admitted doing drug deals with Steele in the past and assured me both of his associates were righteous cocaine traffickers with international connections. Michael and I agreed to rendezvous before the face-to-face with his associates. He surprised me when he brought a shotgun. Since Michael was vouching for his associates, I wondered why he thought he needed to bring that much firepower. Something wasn't right, and my already high caution level ratcheted up a notch.

Although I had no money, we were to begin negotiations for the deal that day. Still, this first meeting was more than merely a meet-and-greet. All parties expected to get to the nuts and bolts of the transaction.

Michael and I returned to the Denny's restaurant across from Fox Television Center. I had previously transacted an undercover deal on the lot. Since I was posing as a TV producer I thought meeting across the street from "my office" would provide that extra touch of authenticity that might sell the case. This was before 9/11 and studio security was more relaxed. Just to make sure, prior to the meeting I attempted to enter the lot by merely waving to the gate guard and driving through the employee entrance. It worked twice, so I thought I might take a chance with my newest targets.

In my two separate meetings that day with Noel, he played the tough guy role even better than I. He threatened me and said if I turned out to be a cop, he'd be my "worst nightmare." He seemed tense, and I thought it best to put him at ease. I suggested we drive onto the lot and I'd show him around the sound stages, where we could continue our negotiations without the constant distractions of the Denny's employees and customers. We climbed into my car and made our way to Fox. I waved to the gate guard and drove through the employee entrance. I drove around the lot, pointing out Vicki Lawrence's parking spot before I parked. We quickly hopped out of the car, and I showed him the *Mama's Family* soundstage. He didn't seem too impressed, so we returned to the car.

I was driving a seized BMW I was only using for this investigation. Unfortunately, I really hadn't thoroughly checked out the vehicle, other than searching it to make sure it was clean of any government-issued paraphernalia and to familiarize myself with most of the bells and whistles. I did not, however, notice a microphone just above the driver's-side visor. To this day, I'm not sure what it was for. While sitting in the car, Noel noticed the device above my head. His face reddened as he pointed to the microphone.

"What's that?"

I looked up and thought quickly. "It's a speaker for my car phone, what do you think it is?"

"Where's the phone?"

Cell phones were just coming into vogue and I didn't have one for this case, but I still had to make my bluff stick.

"The stupid thing never has worked right. I sent it back to the dealer."

Inwardly, I was kicking myself for not being more careful. Noel had caught me; I had no idea what the device was, and until he pointed it out, didn't even realize it was in the car.

He said again, "If you turn out to be a cop, even if I get ten years, my people will get you."

Although menacing, his bravado was hardly anything new. I had been threatened by the Mafia on more than one occasion.

You never get used to it, but having survived in the past made it easier to handle Noel's bullying.

As is often the case in a drug deal, the negotiations broke down when I refused to show him the cash and he refused to show me the cocaine. Neither of us was experiencing that warm fuzzy feeling.

Subsequently I continued to talk with Michael and Steele, leaving Noel out of the loop. The first transaction is always the toughest, as each party waltzes around the details and attempts to force the other to show his cards first. I have found this minuet to be typical regardless of the quantity of the purchase. I couldn't really expect the three to deliver twenty kilos merely on the word of an untested buyer. The most we could hope for would be that I could convince them to have the entire amount readily available for delivery once I purchased a smaller sample I found to be of sufficient quality. Once again, I had to play the sophisticated buyer who would be unwilling to show the entire pay out before seeing the negotiated quantity.

I agreed to initially purchase two kilos of cocaine. Upon delivery of the two, they would produce the remaining eighteen, once I showed them all the money. The only problem was, once again, I had no money. Contrary to what is seen every evening on prime-time television, getting buy money or even show funds for a buy-bust can be an administrative nightmare, and even those officials willing to accommodate the street agent realize the paperwork can be daunting. I didn't think my boxing-glove ploy would work this time, so I kept to the usual stall tactics: "My offshore banker is on vacation"; "My money guy is out of town until Saturday"; "I've got to sell off some stock to raise the cash."

After completing our negotiations dance, we settled on May 6 as the date to finalize the twenty-kilo purchase of the cocaine Michael, Steele, and Noel claimed to possess. The cost was $400,000.

We geared up for the May 6 buy-bust. That morning I briefed the arrest team, consisting of FBI agents and officers from our Beverly Hills Police Department task force. A surveillance team tailed Noel and Steele. The plan was simple: We were to meet at the Denny's restaurant at 10:00 am. I would demand the sellers show me the two-kilo sample before I showed any cash. Once I saw the sample, I would give the arrest signal, indicating I had seen the cocaine, and the arrest team would pounce. We planned on picking up Michael later, since for some unexplained reason he didn't want to be present for the transaction.

Everyone was in place and we waited. Patience is not one of my virtues but most drug deals are waiting games; that morning we waited. At 10:00 the surveillance team had Noel and Steele under their watchful eye as the two were meeting with a third party, a Colombian. Our deal was definitely not happening at ten. I eventually left Denny's and waited on a side street. Finally at 11:30 am, Steele contacted me and said they would be ready at noon. I returned to Denny's. At 12:45, they still had not arrived. I called Steele and said I was calling it off if they couldn't put it together. Steele said they were loading the car then, and would be there shortly. I knew from the surveillance agents they were not loading a car but had, in fact, met with the Colombian, who was now in the area.

Shortly after one, Steele and Noel arrived at Denny's. The mood was tense. Both Noel and I were trying to "out-bad" the other. He demanded to see the money and I demanded to see the powder. Since I didn't have $400,000, I had every incentive to be demanding. Noel relented and the three of us left the restaurant for his car. Steele went directly to his pickup, which seemed odd.

Noel and I sat in the front seat of his car. I was wearing a transmitter and a recorder; only later did I learn the transmitter wasn't working. Noel portrayed himself as a major player in the L.A. coke trade, but his car certainly didn't reflect that: it was a Volkswagen Jetta. His sample also didn't reflect the big time. The cocaine was wrapped in duct tape and plastic, not the fiberglass packaging often seen with coke directly shipped from South America. His package looked more like something that could have been stepped on. Continuing to play up my macho image, I complained about the packaging. Noel didn't back down; he told me it came "packaged all different ways." I wanted him to continue his taunts and his brags, telling me how much he knew about drugs and how naïve I was. His expertise would play well with a jury.

"This is the *reina!*" he insisted. *Reina* is Spanish for "queen," a street term indicative of the highest-quality goods.

Finally, I acquiesced and told him I'd accept the sample. We agreed to go to my office to complete the deal. I exited the Jetta and headed toward my car where they thought I had the $400,000. And then, things began to go quite awry.

Noel jumped out of his car and screamed toward Steele. Steele gunned his engine and came barreling toward me in his pickup truck as I crossed the parking lot.

14
SEXUAL ADDICTION

As Steele's pickup bore down on me in the parking lot, my training took over. I pulled my five-shot .38 revolver from beneath my shirt and fired once, striking Steele in the neck. His vehicle veered to the right. Almost simultaneously I heard the screeching of tires and turned to see Noel's car racing toward me. I fired two more shots, and then jumped out of the way. Noel sped off, leaving the parking lot and his wounded companion, now lying on the pavement. I rushed over to Steele, blood pouring from his neck.

Mike, an FBI agent and a member of the arrest team, ran over to Steele and with no regard for his personal safety — especially in light of the AIDS epidemic plaguing L.A. — cradled Steele and applied pressure to the neck wound; Mike wasn't wearing gloves. Sirens wailed in the background as LAPD units and paramedics responded.

Mike's quick action saved Steele's life.

Within minutes an LAPD unit reported they found Noel, who wrecked his car several blocks from the scene. One of my rounds penetrated his chest, bounced around inside, and punctured both lungs. Both he and Steele were rushed to the hospital.

Controlled chaos prevailed at the shooting scene as FBI agents, police officers from Beverly Hills, and LAPD officers conducted their respective shooting inquiries. As policy dictates, they took my gun from me but left my recorder. So, as I sat in a surveillance van, waiting for various investigators to interview me, I called Michael.

"Everything went great," I told him. "I got the entire load. I know I can move it quickly; come on over and I'll give you your cut now. Oh, by the way, just to avoid any problems, meet me a few blocks west of the restaurant. That way, if any heat is hanging around, they won't put us together."

Once again, greed prevailed over fear and Michael hustled to our prearranged location. News copters and police units surrounded the parking lot of Denny's; every passing motorist and pedestrian strained to view the commotion — every driver, that is, but one. Michael drove past the scene in his distinctive black Firebird, oblivious to the law-enforcement presence, as I watched from the surveillance van. Greed and stupidity proved his downfall. When he arrived at our meeting spot, he was quickly taken into custody. The Colombian, who had been under surveillance by FBI agents since meeting with Noel and Steele earlier in the morning, was also arrested a few blocks from Denny's.

As we tried to unfold the story, it appears the suppliers believed I was easy pickings. The plan was to steal the $400,000 and kill me in the process, if necessary. Steele admitted as much.

Steele and Noel pleaded guilty. Michael and the Colombian went to trial and I spent several days on the stand. The first day was especially nerve-wracking as three of the Columbian's relatives sat in the back of the courtroom. His cousin glared at me throughout my testimony. At various times when I looked to the back row, the cousin would discreetly put his finger to his head as if simulating a weapon and pull the trigger. The meaning was clear.

During a recess, I approached the defense attorney and asked if I could speak to his client. It was an unusual request; at first he balked, then I told him he could be present.

I approached his client in a calm manner and resorted to some language I learned in the Marine Corps. My message was equally clear: I wasn't intimidated, and if his friends didn't knock it off, I'd have people in prison make his stay most unpleasant.

The attorney thanked me for not making it an issue with the judge, and the Colombian's friends never returned.

The trial took an interesting turn when at one point the prosecutor, Chris Johnson, who while a Navy judge advocate actually participated in the trial upon which the film *A Few Good Men* was based, attempted to introduce yet another tape-recorded conversation between me and Michael. The judge balked at the request, loudly proclaiming he was sick and tired of the profanity on the tapes. "Everyone is swearing and I'm sick of it. The defendant is cussing and so is the undercover agent." With that remark one the jurors blurted out, "No, Your Honor, the agent hasn't sworn yet." I was glad the juror was paying such close attention and thankful I hadn't been caught on tape swearing — this time.

Both Michael and the Colombian were convicted, and all four spent substantial time in federal prison for their part in the drug conspiracy.

I never really got to play contract killer, but the four arrests sort of took away the sting.

Los Angeles, after the New York Conference
Following the New York NAMBLA conference, I wanted to maintain my credibility with the organization. I decided the best way to do this would be to quickly follow up with the "Privacy" pamphlet project; I naïvely thought the membership actually expected some sort of finished product. Using cut-and-paste skills and the Internet, in less than a day I prepared a multipage document discussing privacy issues. I e-mailed a copy of my work to each of the members on the committee, including Peter Herman. I heard nothing from anyone but Peter, who suggested my article was too detailed and requested I condense it to a one-page format. I had little interest in editing the pamphlet. I decided if I were ever questioned, I could lay blame on the rest of the committee for not responding to my initial work product.

One matter that did require further inquiry was Jeff Devore, someone in whom we had an investigative interest. He was a NAMBLA member, a resident of Orange County — within the Los Angeles office's jurisdiction — a youth minister, a medical professional, and an admitted traveler who used the Internet to meet and set up a sexual encounter with a sixteen-year-old boy. The predication was perfect and we opened a case.

Once I returned from the conference, Jeff and I traded e-mails and agreed to meet for dinner.

I was deeply involved in another undercover operation at the same time, targeting Chinese, Russian, and Iraqi organized crime figures. For that assignment, my chosen cover was that of someone who lived off an inherited family trust and managed several private financial accounts. It was an almost perfect cover because there was no way for any subject to verify my employment or challenge my story. I could also be somewhat nebulous about my daily activities, and I had sufficient "wealth" to live comfortably, but not extravagantly. My business card reflected a Beverly Hills address, a private post office box. I maintained the same cover for the NAMBLA investigation, even keeping the same name and phone number. The only difference was that as a "straight" organized crime associate, I was "Bob." To my NAMBLA friends, I was "Robert." Moving from one persona to the other could give a guy whiplash, if he wasn't careful.

I scheduled dinner for Jeff and myself at a Beverly Hills restaurant, one I frequented in an undercover capacity while working organized crime cases a decade earlier. The outdoor tables and paparazzi provided a perfect atmosphere. The ownership had not changed nor had the menu. They had no idea I was an agent, and as I had in the past, I ordered something not on the menu. The waiter always accommodated my unique request, and it appeared as though I was a regular with special connections. It all played into my role and provided that little something extra that added to my credibility.

Hollywood types frequented the restaurant. On one occasion, as Jeff and I were eating, Jon Voight walked in and sat one table away. I think Jeff was impressed. I know I was.

Jeff seemed to have a gentle spirit but was sad and troubled, something I hadn't seen in our limited contact at the conference. His mental anguish became clear at our first dinner.

I did little talking that first evening and dug into my capellini puttanesca. Jeff expressed a real struggle with his sexuality. He

196

admitted to being gay but wasn't sure he was really a boy lover. He spoke of trying to find himself and had hoped his four-year participation as a member of NAMBLA would answer a lot of questions, or "fill in missing pieces of the puzzle," as he put it. In fact, it created more uncertainties for him. He grimaced as he talked about trying to identify his real sexual desires.

Unlike some boy lovers I met or read about, Jeff characterized his desires as a "sexual addiction" rather than age-specific targeting. He openly talked of upping his age of preference into the legal range. Even his pornography collection ranged from preteen to adult. Many boy lovers were quite specific in their preferences: pedophiles desired prepubescent boys; pederasts were attracted to boys who had entered puberty. Once a boy exceeded a specific age he was no longer desirable and would be cast aside for a younger target. Jeff was confused as to where he drew the line and occasionally expressed an interest in drawing that line beyond the long arm of the criminal law.

As part of his quest for answers, he joined a 12-step sexual addiction program. I certainly wasn't expecting this when we opened the investigation. Despite his participation in this program, he admitted to being in regular Internet contact with a fourteen-year-old in Canada with whom he engaged in online sex. He claimed they never physically met but Jeff was contemplating a trip.

Jeff also talked of an online relationship with an eighteen-year-old in Missouri. Jeff was planning a trip after Christmas to visit relatives and was debating whether he would try to set up a meeting with the boy. Sex with the teenager was part of the plan, if they met.

An ordained minister in the United Church of Christ, he was still active in his church, yet maintained a full-time job as a chiropractor, taught at a chiropractic school, and worked with chiropractic interns at a West Hollywood AIDS clinic. He denied ever seducing or molesting anyone at the church. He claimed the senior pastor was aware of his boy-lover desires and approved of Jeff's conduct as long as the acts were consensual. It was an area I wanted to explore with the senior pastor but knew we were treading on thin legal ice since we had no evidence the senior pastor committed a crime.

Divorced with three children, Jeff was quite candid when he talked about having homoerotic fantasies during intercourse with his ex-wife. "When making love to my wife, I wished a man was doing to me what I was doing to her." If the investigation ended with Jeff's conviction, I thought, he just might get his wish — but not in the way he imagined.

Jeff was a tragic figure. He summed it up best in an e-mail to me.

I've been running from my own BL tendencies. I've wanted to leave it behind, yet I stay in almost daily e-mail contact with the young man in Canada. I'm not sure if I'm running toward sanity or away from a wonderful opportunity. I don't expect you to sort this out for me, but it's good to reach out to a fellow traveler.

In January, we met again. Jeff maintained his participation in the 12-step program. In furtherance of that participation, he said he "destroyed 98 percent" of the pornography on his zip drives, a portion of which was child pornography. Once again, he surprised me — his actions weren't typical. Most individuals who collect child pornography rarely dispose of it; the material becomes a cherished possession, often hidden in a secure place, but kept for years. Although the Internet has made the task somewhat easier, collections are still difficult to obtain. Efforts to accumulate the illegal images may take years and usually aren't destroyed with a single act. But maybe Jeff was different.

Jeff repeated the story he told me at dinner at the NAMBLA conference, about his sexual encounter with a sixteen-year-old in San Diego. Jeff said the two met again on the boy's seventeenth birthday and had recently met with a third person from Nebraska, involving a three-way tryst in front of a fireplace. His detailed account was more than I really wanted to hear.

Interacting with Jeff was somewhat easy. He enjoyed sharing his experiences and didn't really delve too deeply into my history, desires, or orientation. Usually I could counter any personal questions with a disjointed answer followed by a question, throwing the conversation back to him. Since most of us really prefer to talk about ourselves anyway, it wasn't too hard to keep Jeff's discussions turned most advantageously for me.

Jeff again spoke of the Canadian youth with whom he was having online sex. He also mentioned another sixteen-year-old with whom he had renewed an online relationship. The previous night, Jeff and the boy had a sexually explicit chat. According to Jeff, the boy "got off" but Jeff did not masturbate, believing that abstinence was in keeping with his 12-step "sobriety" promise.

I had mixed feelings about the first two encounters. Although Jeff admitted to having downloaded child pornography on his computer, a federal violation, he also said he deleted it. Seldom, however, does "delete" really mean delete; our computer experts could probably still recover the deleted images and we would have a prosecutable case. But Jeff said he was seeking help for his sexual addiction. Did we want to interfere with any recovery that might be possible for him by maintaining contact or by arresting him? A more pragmatic problem was the fact that, should we arrest him, my identity would be compromised and any attempt to target other members of NAMBLA would be futile. Based on his statements, if he could be believed — and I did believe him — he was not involved with any of the youth at his church, so that was not an immediate issue. Besides, he said the senior pastor knew of his orientation and took no action.

The decision was made somewhat easier because the U.S. Attorney's office was not prepared to charge Devore or issue a search warrant for his computer. We didn't have enough. Arrest warrants on TV crime dramas are issued on the basis of partial fingerprints or the word of a highly suspect witness. No such luck with any U.S. Attorney's office in the Ninth Circuit Court of Appeals, not-so-affectionately called the Ninth Circus because of its highly controversial decisions and record of reversals by the Supreme Court. If we wanted a warrant, "proof beyond a reasonable doubt" was usually the standard, rather than the "probable cause" requirement of almost every other jurisdiction.

In late January, Jeff sent me an e-mail and attached a couple of stories. Although the stories were not pornographic in the federal criminal sense, they were sexually explicit and disgusting. One was entitled, "No More Bananas," the story of a man's sexual encounter with a twelve-year-old. It featured the tag line, "Better than seducing a boy is allowing him to seduce you." Each time we thought of backing off, Jeff provided this sort of extra incentive to continue. The stories demonstrated to me that his rehabilitative efforts were failing.

15
THE FIX IS IN

Los Angeles, 1995

I have often told agents new to undercover work that a successful undercover assignment is one from which you return alive. Obviously, that is melodramatic, but success truly is a relative term. Not every operation results in front-page news or mass arrests. Instead, successful undercover operations go where the evidence leads, where the targets direct. This can be troublesome in the FBI, where a detailed and approved operational plan must be followed and permission obtained to deviate from the investigation of crimes listed in the initial paperwork.

I had no idea where the NAMBLA investigation was going to lead. I knew that to date we were unsuccessful at identifying significant prosecutable criminal activity, but I believed that if I continued in my undercover capacity we would be successful. In the mid-nineties I worked a case that was not as expansive as we initially thought, but it did take us in directions we did not anticipate.

In the summer of 1995, I had just returned to an organized-crime squad after my second round of working gangs. A thirty-day "temporary" assignment following the 1992 Los Angeles riots that lasted more than three years. I welcomed the opportunity to return to investigating mobsters and was hoping to find an undercover assignment with a wallop. Instead, I found one with a gallop.

Less than a week after my return to the OC squad, a colleague approached. She was investigating fixed races at Los Angeles–area horse racing venues and thought an undercover operation might be the best way to prove the violation. I had only been to the track on one previous occasion and I didn't know a quinella from a gelding, but by the time the investigation ended I had become a successful handicapper and actually won a lot more money than I wagered. Initially, I wasn't even sure I wanted the assignment and questioned why we were getting involved in the investigation: There was no apparent organized crime angle and the California Horse Racing Board (CHRB) had primary jurisdiction over horse racing matters. Our squad did, however, handle sports bribery investigations — thus the reason for FBI involvement. Finally, I figured working the paddocks had to be better than being saddled to a desk.

The FBI learned that several gamblers who frequented the tracks were bribing jockeys to alter the outcome of races. Contrary to what many people believe, a fixed race doesn't usually mean the gambler knows which horse is going to win, but rather he can eliminate the probable winner by paying the jockey riding the favorite to hold his mount back. In a typical race, certain horses have little or no chance of winning. The favorites, however, can often be narrowed to two or three horses. Of course, the thrill of placing a winning bet on a long shot makes for an exciting day at the track, but the odds overwhelmingly prefer a given race's two or three favorites. When one or more of these horses are eliminated from consideration, picking the winner is much easier.

The Pick Six is a bet in which the gambler wagers on the winner of six selected consecutive races. For as little as two dollars per bet, a gambler tries to select the winner in each of the six designated races. The payoff on a winning Pick Six ticket is often in the thousands of dollars, if not hundreds of thousands. But tickets could end up costing a lot more than two dollars: by selecting multiple horses in each race as possible winners, the cost of the wager is multiplied exponentially. It was not unusual for our targets to place bets costing several thousand dollars, thus increasing the odds of successfully winning the Pick Six. If no one places a winning bet for the Pick Six on a given day, all of the money in the wagering pool is carried over until the next day of racing. It was on these carryover days our crew began working in earnest.

As soon as a carryover was announced, they began their homework, attempting to identify the probable winners for the next day's racing. More importantly, these gamblers also identified which jockeys were riding the favorites. By paying those jockeys not to win, the crew increased their odds of winning, while at the same time decreasing the cost of the ticket — they knew which horses *not* to bet on. While the gambling public busily wagered on the favorites, wasting their betting dollars and beefing up the wagering pool, our crew eliminated those horses from their tickets.

An informant identified the targets but

refused to testify against them or introduce an undercover agent. It was going to be up to me to infiltrate the betting ring and sell myself as a gambler. Convincing professional gamblers I was one of them was going to take a great deal of preparation. I began studying gambling and horse racing, poring through books, newspapers, and magazines.

Mike Kilpack of the CHRB provided me with considerable intelligence on the suspects. I also spoke with an older man with strong mob ties whom I convicted in the early eighties and had since become an informant for the FBI. He was a sports gambler, and once he learned the FBI was paying his admission to the park and would provide him with betting money in exchange for educating me, he was on board.

My mentor had a reputation for being a sophisticated gambler with connections all over the country. In his younger years, he was close to the Kennedys, Jimmy Hoffa, and well-known organized crime figures. I always enjoyed his company and loved listening to his stories, but I soon learned that even sophisticated sports gamblers had a tough time picking the ponies. We went to the track several times and never came home winners. In fact, I'm not sure he ever won a race. Each afternoon with him was an enjoyable experience, but I realized just how hard this assignment was going to be.

My two female case agents went with me to the track several times as we familiarized ourselves with the various venues and identified the key players. I watched and I listened. The track had a vocabulary all its own and I needed to learn it quickly. Soon I not only knew what a gelding was, but I knew the difference between an exacta, a quinella, a trifecta, and a supertrifecta. I realized a "nickel" was five hundred dollars and a "dime" bet meant you had wagered a thousand dollars. I learned to read the tote board and the *Daily Racing Form.* I learned how to "wheel" a bet and even wager beyond the "chalk." I was becoming fluent in track talk.

I also tried to pick up the habits of various gamblers — how they held their programs, how they marked their selections, which periodicals they purchased, how they dressed, when they arrived, when they left. To be successful, I needed to present the authentic appearance of a degenerate gambler who lived for the track and the next big score. I had about a month to accomplish what most of these men learned to do over a lifetime.

Before the actual undercover operation began, we received information that on September 28, 1995, several races were being fixed at the Los Alamitos racetrack in Orange County, California. Arabian horses and quarter horses, rather than Thoroughbreds, were running that night. The Pick Six carryover that evening was eighty-one thousand dollars, a large amount for a smaller track.

According to sources, Fingers, someone identified as a major race fixer, paid off two jockeys to fix three races. Fingers was banned from every track in California, but he could bet the race in Mexico, where the wager would not appear in the pari-mutuel pool.

Fingers was truly a character. A golf hustler and a professional gambler, he prided himself on being an excellent handicapper. A favorite trick of his was to tout different horses in the same race to several different gamblers, then collect his percentage of the winnings from the person who placed the winning wager.

In 1991, he was with an associate who was fatally shot outside a hotel following a successful night of gambling at Hollywood Park. Fingers was initially a suspect, but was eventually cleared, although rumors abounded at the track. Many still believed Fingers was involved in the murder.

At the Los Alamitos track that evening in one of the suspected races, the even-money favorite came in fourth. The horse jumped at the starting gate and at one point was ten lengths behind the lead. In a second race, a horse that went off as the favorite at 7-5 odds, ridden by the same jockey, finished third and was disqualified to fourth because of interference. Even to my untrained eye, the race looked funny. The jockey we suspected was starting from the number one post, next to the inside rail. Before the race ended, his horse had run across the track to the outside of the pack, blocking several of the other favorites from advancing. It seemed pretty clear to me. But afterward, in discussions with the steward, a state employee paid to officiate the races, he claimed that particular horse had a history of "lugging out" — running to the outside — so the steward could not say with certainty the race was fixed or the horse's conduct was unusual. Would the steward's opinion sink the investigation before it began? Just how difficult was it going to be to prove race fixing?

Once the administrative approvals were in place, I began a six-month undercover assignment, never returning to the office. My only contact with the FBI would be weekly meetings with my case agents at some discreet park or restaurant. I spent every race day at Santa Anita or Hollywood Park, two of the most famous racetracks in America. It was like living inside a Damon Runyon story.

Los Angeles, after the New York Conference
In February, I met again with Jeff, this time at a casual Beverly Hills restaurant he recommended. My case agent and I had decided to make one more attempt to obtain sufficient facts for the probable cause we needed to get a search warrant for his computer. We reasoned that the wording in a search warrant affidavit could be written to conceal the fact I was an undercover agent. Should we find prosecutable images, Jeff might even confess and agree to plead guilty without any need for disclosing my identity.

At dinner, he told me he was no longer attending the 12-step sexual addiction program. The program defined "appropriate" sexual intercourse as the act between a married man and his wife. Jeff was gay, he said, and couldn't or wouldn't accept that premise, so he dropped out of the program and refused to seek help elsewhere.

Two probationary agents were providing backup during the meeting, and I suggested they cover us from inside the restaurant. Let the Bureau buy a meal; the pay's not that great and I figured they deserved the perk. I didn't have to work too hard to persuade the agents; they sat several tables away in the very crowded restaurant.

Shortly after we arrived, while we were waiting for our dinner, Jeff excused himself to go to the restroom. When he came back, he had a big smile on his face.

"Do you see those two guys sitting over there?" He nodded in the direction of my surveillance team.

"You mean those two?" I said referring to the agents.

"Yeah. When I went to the bathroom, the cute one couldn't take his eyes off of me."

I laughed and said they were both a little old for me, but maybe I could fix him up for the evening. Once again, my surveillance agents lost points for lack of subtlety. The agent's interest played well with Jeff, though; he never suspected.

I told Jeff my computer crashed and I lost my entire collection of child pornography. He said he would like to help, but once he began the 12-step program, he deleted the pornography on his five-year-old computer. I probed, trying to determine exactly how he deleted the images. He said he merely pushed the delete button, and they were gone. I knew then the images could probably be recovered if the FBI decided to pursue the matter with a search warrant. He did volunteer that the images would be "of interest to law enforcement," a comment that clearly signaled child pornography.

Jeff returned to the theme of our previous meetings: he seemed confused, was questioning his boy-lover orientation, and suggested he didn't even think he was a BL. As much as I hated everything NAMBLA stood for and as vehemently as I disagreed with their efforts to justify "Greek love," I was beginning to feel sorry for Jeff. Maybe the FBI should back away, I thought, and give this guy a chance to sort himself out.

Before I could go much further along that line of thought, he dropped a bombshell: "But, if you said you had a fourteen-year-old boy in your apartment and I could have sex with him without getting into trouble, I would do it for the experience — but I don't feel like I have to."

What kind of statement was that supposed to be? Suddenly he sounded like the predators Jim from New Jersey feared were part of the membership. Apparently, Jeff was no closer to rehabilitation than before he entered the 12-step program.

Jeff and I ended the evening with a promise to meet again, but it would be almost ten months before we had our next face-to-face encounter. Though Jeff certainly wasn't making a concerted effort to leave his problematic behavior behind, the evidence for prosecution just wasn't there.

We did exchange a few more e-mails. In a February 23 communication, he complained that the Canadian fourteen-year-old "verbally assaulted" him. A discouraged and ambivalent Jeff wrote, "Sometimes I think this BL is a crock of shit, and other times I realize it's such a part of me."

In a second e-mail following the dinner, Jeff said he had another friend he met online who was a BL and lived in Long Beach. He suggested the three of us get together. I was ready, hoping to rekindle the investigation. I tried to pursue the invitation but Jeff was never able to arrange for the three of us to meet. Once again, my case agent and I realized we lacked the evidence to go forward, so we put the matter of Jeff Devore on hold.

16
KEEPING
MY SHIRT ON

Los Angeles, 1995

My favorite track was Santa Anita, situated on 320 acres at the foot of the San Gabriel Mountains in Arcadia, California. There I could easily envision the excitement during the days when racing was truly the "sport of kings." Even though the grandstand could accommodate twenty-six thousand patrons, the days of capacity crowds had long passed. I frequented the clubhouse level, where all of our targets congregated.

Racetracks abound with unique characters. From the wealthiest in society to the unemployed, thousands spend afternoons at the track. Grown men who have not won a race in years still brag of the time they hit a "big one," even if it was decades earlier.

The crowds increased on the days following the issuance of welfare checks; young children were dragged to the track by parents hoping to extend their state-issued monthly stipend into a windfall. It was sad to watch people pin their precarious financial hopes on a horse.

On Wall Street, seldom will a broker seek advice from the janitor, but at the track, even CEOs sought the help of exercise boys or grooms in the ironic hope someone making less than minimum wage might hold the key to a successful wager. Nicknames were commonplace — Fingers, the Mouth, the Greek, the Broom, the Printer . . . even I acquired a moniker: Bob the Cop!

I began the undercover assignment at Hollywood Park in Inglewood. I would walk down to the paddock before the race and observe the horses being readied. I listened as various gamblers commented on the mounts, usually unable to distinguish the subtleties they were observing. It didn't matter; I just wanted to learn the language and repeat it when I was around the targets. When I returned upstairs, I tried to remain within eyesight, if not hearing range, and would occasionally engage our targets in conversation about a particular race or horse. Typically, they blew me off, responding with a look or a grunt, or even more common, just ignoring me. It was no place for a fragile ego. After several weeks of just observing and then attempting to close on the subjects, I decided to make a move.

The Mouth, one of our prime targets, would put together a Pick Six wager every race day. He would often sell a piece of the ticket, asking trusted associates to contribute to the purchase price, allowing for a much larger Pick Six wager. The Mouth's Pick Six tickets were often in the hundreds of dollars and occasionally he wagered in the thousands. On at least two occasions when the Pick Six pari-mutuel pool was several hundred thousand dollars, I recall tickets costing more than ten thousand dollars. What I didn't realize at the time was that the Mouth held onto the losing tickets. They were gold at tax time, since winning wagers could be offset by losing bets. Even if the Mouth sold his entire ticket, he still kept the losing ticket to offset winnings. Events would subsequently prove that the Mouth's sophisticated tax fraud netted him hundreds of thousands of dollars in tax refunds each year.

On a Friday afternoon, I approached the Mouth as he stood near an usher. With the same brashness I saw in other gamblers, I introduced myself and asked if he was selling pieces of his Pick Six ticket.

"Who the hell are you?" he demanded. "What are you talking about? How do I know you're not an IRS agent?" He looked at the usher and jerked a thumb in my direction. "Do you know this guy?"

The usher said he'd seen me around.

As the Mouth continued with the tongue-lashing, I fished a wad of money from my pocket. As it turned out, green was his favorite color. He sold me a piece of his ticket, we hit five of six on the Pick Six wager that afternoon, and I won back all I wagered and then some. The Mouth and I became betting partners. From that day on, almost daily, I contributed some piece of a Pick Six ticket the Mouth wagered.

As the days and weeks progressed, I began to meet some of the Mouth's associates. Although I was never accepted as an equal, I could converse with them and occasionally bet with them on those days when the Mouth was absent from the track.

One associate had been gone for several months, recovering from knee surgery. When he returned, he questioned who I was and whether I was "a cop." In subsequent conversations, the Mouth and the others referred to me as "Bob, the guy Rene thinks is a cop." Soon the moniker was shortened and I became simply "Bob the Cop." Rather than hide, I played up the sobriquet. When the Mouth, who well deserved his handle, would refer to me in a loud voice as "Bob the Cop," I would ask him if he had purchased tickets to the policeman's ball. He'd laugh off the joke and we'd go about our business.

With the Mouth it was all business; he had little desire to socialize and our conversations were limited to track-related subjects. On one occasion, the Mouth introduced me to his associate, the Greek. The Mouth was going on vacation and introduced us so I could wager with the Greek, if I desired. When the Mouth referred to me as Bob the Cop, the Greek insisted I pull up my pants legs. I looked at him with obvious confusion. He repeated, "Pull up your pants legs. Show me your ankles."

I did as instructed. All he saw was socks and he was satisfied. The Greek said, "Undercover cops wear guns on their ankles." I was glad I left my gun in the car . . . but the Mouth went even further.

I was wearing a loose fitting sweatshirt and had not tucked it in. The Mouth grabbed the sweatshirt and pulled it up, exposing an elastic back brace I was wearing. The recording device was concealed in the front of the brace and wires ran up my chest to my nipples, where the microphones were taped. I quickly slapped the Mouth's hand, dislodging it from the shirt.

I then made a less-than-polite remark by way of letting him know what he could do with his hands.

He had seen the elastic band around my stomach. "What is that?"

"It's a back brace. I've got a bad back and standing around here on the concrete listening to your crap all day hurts my back. Now, who do you like in the first race?"

It was a close call. Had he pulled the sweatshirt any higher he would have seen the wires and the investigation would have ended in a New York minute. From that moment on, I tucked in my shirt.

One afternoon while at Santa Anita, some of the targets became suspicious of me for some unknown reason. The Mouth confronted me and demanded to see my wallet and identification. My hands shook as I pulled my undercover driver's license from my wallet. The Mouth noted the shaking, became agitated, and accused me of being a cop. I told him my hands always shake — which they often do, thus explaining my sometimes-poor shooting scores at the range — and told him to quit taking my money if he thought I was a cop. He seemed satisfied with my answer but the rest of them kept their distance throughout the remainder of the assignment.

San Diego, after the New York Conference
Following the New York conference, I had little communication with NAMBLA except for the occasional *Bulletin.* I was assigned full-time to a sensitive national security–related undercover operation and transferred to the San Diego office. I heard nothing further from NAMBLA on the privacy pamphlet, and maintained minimal correspondence with a few prisoners in the pen-pal program, primarily to maintain credibility in case Los Angeles desired my continued services on the pedophile case.

Once I settled into the San Diego office, I met with the Innocent Images National Initiative contact in the division. I explained to him in detail my membership in NAMBLA and the nature of my previous undercover activity. His enthusiasm was contagious and we clicked immediately. I sensed we could work well together and was hoping he might want to proceed. However, I left the decision up to him and his supervisor. They did not disappoint me: My new case agent contacted Los Angeles and got up to speed with the NAMBLA investigation.

In July, I received a handwritten letter

from Chris, the mop-haired socialist who had rambled almost incoherently at the conference. Chris was a member of the steering committee and was inquiring about my work on the privacy pamphlet. He said he was following up on the work I did and asked if I was interested in continuing on the project. Chris used the return address of PO Box 174, Midtown Station, New York, NY 10018, the address from which all the NAMBLA correspondence came. I assumed Chris was in New York and replied.

Chris,

I received your letter and am glad someone is taking charge of the pamphlet project. Thanks for doing that. Being in California makes everything so distant. You're lucky to be in New York and close to all the action.

I'm still interested in helping in whatever way I can. I do have some health problems so it isn't always easy to get too committed. Peter may have given you what I have already written on "Privacy." I submitted it to Peter and the others on the committee and never heard another word. . . .

As I told Peter, I have access to a hotel in San Diego where I booked an investment seminar. . . . If you were interested I could take advantage of this offer and we could maybe have the pamphlet people meet here for a weekend before the Membership Convention. Lots of young, tanned bodies in sunny Southern California. Something to think about. Just let me know.

About a week later, I received a letter from Peter, reminding me it was time to renew my membership. Had I truly been a boy lover, I'm not sure I would have expended the funds: the organization was of little benefit, as far as I could tell. I did not see it as "political" or "educational," as advertised in the statement of purpose. I was aware of no "spokespeople" who were raising "awareness in the media . . . and among the general public." Nor did I see any tangible effort whatsoever to modify age-of-consent laws. There was no lobbying at any level of government, no letters to the editors of major newspapers or magazines, no appearances on any media outlet. Support and comfort could just as easily come from going on the Internet and spending time in a chat room — without paying the membership dues. Whatever the membership numbers were, the organization's actual primary purpose, as I saw it, was to reinforce among members their destructive and criminal passions.

Kathy Baxter, the director of the San Francisco Child Abuse Counsel, accurately described the organization in the 1992 KRON-TV investigative report: "It is a group, in my opinion, of men primarily who get together to network with one another on where to find young boys, how to pick them up, how to get them involved, and how to feel good about what you're doing."

Nevertheless, I sent Peter a letter and a postal money order I know he gladly cashed. In August, I received my invitation to the November conference. My cover was still obviously intact.

The conference was being held in Miami, Florida. The invitation described Miami as a "delightful city . . . and November is a delightful time of the year to be there."

What followed was troubling: "We have reserved a block of rooms in a charming secluded inn at very reasonable rates. . . . The cost . . . will be $175. This low price is for double occupancy rooms."

Double occupancy! There was no way I was double-occupying any room with a NAMBLA member. For one thing, I needed some private space to store my surveillance equipment; a NAMBLA roomie wouldn't be very conducive to that. For another thing, I wasn't sleeping with one eye open for an entire weekend. No, double occupancy wasn't an option for me.

My San Diego case agent and I discussed the potential dilemma with his supervisor. Although both agreed a real undercover agent would take one for the team, they conceded that the Bureau would pony up enough funds to insure I got my own room, single occupancy.

I sent in my registration fee and began preparation for the Miami conference. On September 14 Chris sent his response, a handwritten note.

Robert:

Thanks for your efforts to get back to me. I can tell your [sic] busy! Thanks even more for your offer of a venue there [in San Diego]. It is too bad we couldn't swing it. Believe it or not with all the hurricanes, we plan to meet in Miami. I hope you can make it! Try to have in mind something you'd like to do, if you can think of something. It'll help. By the way, I don't live in the NYC area.

Meetings with the San Diego and Los

Angeles case agents, as well as communications with Headquarters and Miami, set the ground rules and expectations for my attendance at the conference. Since this would be my second time, I made all the agents aware that I thought I could be more open in my conversations with the various attendees at the meeting, inquiring more proactively for criminal admissions. We correctly assumed my credibility had been enhanced by my previous attendance and continued participation in the organization. We wanted to be prepared to handle any crime that might be discussed. In keeping with that concept, Los Angeles agreed to support the investigation by providing a Web site and posing as a travel agency.

Headquarters had already given its approval for such an operation. It was an arrow for my quiver, a tool that could be used should the topic of overseas sex tours be raised. I was also prepared to accept or purchase child pornography and enter into relationships where I would offer to exchange it when I returned to San Diego. I planned to remain flexible in Miami and aggressively pursue any investigative lead that might arise.

17
HALF-FULL OR HALF-EMPTY?

Los Angeles, 1996
Under IRS rules, any winning wager with the odds of 300-1 or greater require filling out certain tax forms in order to receive the winnings. At the track, the winning bet is called a "sign-up." One of the cottage industries that survive on the fringes of big-time gambling is made up of those who do sign-ups for others. They're called "signers" or "ten percenters" — a term derived from the fee the signer often charges the gambler.

In simple terms, if the wager pays $10,000, the track, before paying the winner, automatically deducts 28 percent in federal taxes. Thus the winner would only collect $7,200 from the window. He could offset the winnings with his losing wagers, but he would have to file a federal income tax return in order to collect the $2,800 withheld for taxes. Many gamblers don't wish to bother with the paperwork associated with gambling winnings and often don't want spouses to know where the additional income was derived. That's where the signers or ten percenters, come into play. For a fee, they will cash your ticket under their name, charging you ten percent of the winnings.

The Mouth, however, took signing to a new level. Rather than charge you for cashing your ticket, he would actually pay you for the opportunity to sign for your ticket. In other words, he might pay back half the withholdings. You would receive the $7,200 plus half of the $2,800 withheld by the IRS. You walk away with $8,600 ($7,200 plus $1,400). The IRS doesn't know you won the money and neither does your spouse.

When tax season rolled around, the Mouth would file his taxes, stating that he won the $10,000, but used the many losing Pick Six tickets he held on to, to offset his winnings, even though he may or may not have actually wagered the entire amount represented by the tickets. The IRS refunds the full $2,800 and the Mouth made $1,400 without doing any work other than filling out a few IRS forms on the day you placed the winning wager.

It was a sweet scheme. The track employees looked the other way because signers were viewed as providing a service to gamblers. The IRS had little interest in investigating the violation, and the Mouth was receiving annual refund checks in the hundreds of thousands of dollars. I came to grudgingly admire his initiative; he found a need and met it.

Once we figured out the scheme, it became incumbent on me to win some sign-up wagers — not an easy task. It was difficult enough picking a winning horse in one race, let alone an exotic wager with odds of 300-1 or greater. The track was unable to help, because they could not manufacture winning tickets, even if the FBI agreed to reimburse them. I began handicapping in earnest and eventually wagered and won three sign-ups. I hit the Pick Six twice and hit a triple that paid over $3,700. The Mouth signed for all three of my winning tickets.

Despite our best efforts, we were still no closer to identifying fixed races or implicating our targets in illegal race fixing. I learned that horses were being illegally drugged with clenbuterol, a performance-enhancing drug. I learned that certain trainers would instruct jockeys to hold a horse, preventing it from running to its potential, until the odds were more favorable. I learned that trainers would instruct jockeys to "just give the horse a workout, don't push it." I learned that jockeys were reporting to gamblers which horses were strong and which were injured. I learned that jockeys were betting on their own mounts and sometimes on other mounts in the races in which they were riding. All of these facts were unknown to the betting public, who relied only on information found in the *Daily Racing Form* or daily paper. But the fixed race still eluded us.

On January 28, 1996, I was at Santa Anita and had a Pick Six wager where I correctly selected the first five winners with one race to go. When I told the Mouth I was "still alive," he pulled me aside and said, "I could have gotten into the jockey's room and guaranteed this thing." It was the type of information we were seeking, but I could never get him to "guarantee" any race. I did manage to win the last race of the day and win the Pick Six wager. The Mouth did the sign-up.

With probable cause generated from the undercover operation, we were able to wiretap the Greek's phones. We developed evidence of illegal gambling and identified jockeys in almost daily contact with the Greek and the Mouth. But we never found the smoking gun. It was disappointing. My time at the track was not leading us in the direction we had hoped. Although the case agents and the office supported a six-month extension of the undercover operation, I told them I believed it was a waste of time. I did not think we were going to find sufficient evidence of race fixing. Even if we found a jockey taking payment to adversely influence the outcome of a race, we would still have to prove the horse could have won or should have won. After our experience with the steward at Los Alamitos, I wasn't sure we could ever get such an expert opinion to corroborate our allegation. It was time to take the investigation in another direction and salvage my six months undercover; it was time to go overt.

We reviewed every piece of evidence gathered and worked closely with two fine assistant United States attorneys, Ed Weiss and Jerry Friedberg, both of whom bucked the system and insured prosecutorial success. We decided to concentrate on the Mouth, the Greek, Fingers, and the jockey. When confronted with the evidence obtained through a wiretap on his home phone, the Greek agreed to plead guilty to federal gambling violations.

Fingers and the jockey proved more of a

challenge than the Greek. I took a run at both and the initial results were not positive. Without a confession, there was little chance of obtaining a conviction.

Because Fingers was banned from the track, I never met him while working undercover. We did pick him up while he was conversing with the Greek over the wiretapped phone. Informants provided details of his activities and we continued to seek evidence of his fixing the Los Alamitos races on September 28. I approached Fingers several times overtly as an FBI agent in an effort to elicit admissions from him. But each time, he gave a song and dance and we waltzed around the issue of race fixing. He was smart and provided a challenge. He was also engaging, which is why he was successful at convincing jockeys to risk their careers by accepting a few hundred dollars to hold a horse. He was a consummate con man. He had movie-star good looks and a boyish charm, but both were getting old as we played our cat-and-mouse game.

One afternoon, Fingers agreed to meet me for lunch at a hole-in-the-wall Chinese restaurant in downtown Los Angeles. We took our seats in the back and ordered. As I continued to press Fingers, insisting I was going to indict him for race fixing, he grabbed my water glass, which was half-full.

"Don't you understand?" he said. "Your glass is half-full. If you agree not to charge me, I'll cooperate and can give you all kinds of information about what goes on at the track. I can make your glass full." He poured the water from his glass into mine, filling my glass to the brim.

I leaned forward and spoke in a soft voice. "Several years ago I was working undercover in a drug investigation. The FBI pays me every other Thursday, right? One day, two drug dealers tried to kill me and I shot both of them. The next Thursday, I got my paycheck. It was exactly the same amount as I got the time before. I realized that I get the same amount of money every two weeks whether I shoot somebody or not." I picked up my now-full glass of water and dumped it over the remaining food on his plate.

"I don't care whether you cooperate or not, you're going to jail."

The possibility of conviction finally sank in. He agreed to accompany me to the FBI office and work out a deal.

Once we got into the FBI interrogation room, his bravado began to show once again and he hinted that he might not accept any deal. I was not going to let him get away. He suspected the jockey was cooperating because through informants we knew details Fingers believed only he and the jockey knew. I would never confirm the jockey's cooperation, but in fact he was not cooperating. But since Fingers believed the jockey was just as culpable as he and deserved equal punishment, he didn't want the jockey to receive a lesser sentence.

I played on this fear and his assumptions about the jockey. At one point, I feigned a phone call to the prosecutor. I knew Fingers could hear my side of the conversation. In hushed tones, I told the nonexistent party on the other end of the call to "prepare the same plea agreement we gave the jockey, including time off for cooperation."

When I returned to my conversation with Fingers, he told me how I "screwed up": he'd heard my conversation with the prosecutor and now he knew for certain the jockey was cooperating. He capitulated on the spot, afraid of being bested by the jockey. A short time later, Fingers pleaded guilty and was sentenced to prison.

I continued my attempts at cracking the jockey. The evidence was slim, but he knew what he had done. Eventually he succumbed and admitted to his transgressions. He refused, however, to cooperate by implicating others.

In July, 1997, the five-foot-two-inch, 115-pound jockey appeared before a federal judge. In an emotional hearing in which his wife cried throughout the forty-five-minute session, the jockey said, "I'm pleading guilty because I got involved with an unsavory person." He admitted to taking a $2,100 bribe for holding an even-money horse. The jockey also expressed fear for his safety and the safety of his family. Those fears were compounded by the news that someone broke into the house of the horse's owner, but were chased off by the owner's husband. Also, the owner of the other horse the jockey held back found a funeral wreath on his front lawn. Although we never found evidence of systematic fearmongering, the jockey was clearly reluctant to subject himself and his family to danger.

In October, the jockey was sentenced to three years' probation. At the sentencing the judge said, "You have dedicated your adult life to racing and worked hard to be a success. You worked fifteen years to achieve your goal, yet now you face a lifetime suspension from the California Horse Racing Board. You are a caring and sensitive young man, yet what you did has ruined a successful career."

The horse owner also spoke during the

sentencing.

This is a day when there are no winners. The Arabian racing and breeding business is the other victim. I've spent decades to build up my Arabian business and it took only one minute and twenty-one seconds — the time of the race — to tear all this apart. Integrity — you can't buy that, but you sure can give it away, can't you?

During the overt phase of the investigation, I received information that an out-of-town owner wanted his injured Thoroughbred horse killed so he could collect the insurance. After moving the horse to a safe location — a sort of a Witness Protection Program for animals — we sent the owner a telegram notifying him of the horse's death. I flew to Seattle and met with the owner, leading him to believe I was from the insurance company and wanted to settle the claim. After a few tearful moments during which he told me what a great heart the horse had, I informed him that the good news was the horse was alive, and the bad news was I was from the FBI and he was under arrest for mail fraud. "I've been deceived!" he shouted, his tears drying abruptly. I guess he never realized that was exactly what he was trying to do to the insurance company.

During the period I was undercover, I heard a great deal about the drugging of horses. Thanks to information our targets were receiving from trainers and others on the inside, we knew horses were being given a clenbuterol "milk shake" before the race. An appropriate wager usually resulted in cashing a winning ticket. The drug was difficult to detect with existing procedures, but thanks to our investigation, the CHRB changed the drug testing procedures, allowing for the identification of this illegal activity.

The Mouth was the last of our targets. He was charged in a seven-count indictment for his tax scheme that had netted him over a million dollars. He was found guilty and sentenced to federal prison.

So . . . although the results of the undercover operation — five convictions for a variety of offenses, as well as the modified testing procedures — were far less than we hoped when we began the investigation, we did experience limited success and I came home alive. So I guess it was a successful investigation.

18
THE MOST BIZARRE

Los Angeles, 2002
When asked to relate the most bizarre undercover case I ever worked, I never hesitate — one investigation immediately comes to mind.

In 1995, Congress passed the Federal Prohibition of Female Genital Mutilation Act. The congressional findings state, among other things, that "the practice of female genital mutilation is carried out by members of certain cultural and religious groups in the United States . . . and results in the occurrence of physical and psychological health effects that harm the women involved." The law makes it illegal to perform the surgery on a female under the age of eighteen except when done by a licensed medical professional "for the necessary health" of the child.

I was unfamiliar with this piece of legislation and had no idea the FBI investigated violations of the act. Although I had read about the practice and knew it to be more common among certain Islamic and African populations, I was unaware it was a major problem within the United States.

My knowledge of the problem was enhanced in the summer of 2002, when the Los Angeles office received a complaint from an advocacy group that an individual in the L.A. area was performing illegal circumcisions on underage females. The group received an anonymous e-mail describing how "Todd" performed the operation on a ten-year-old female who was severely injured as a result of the surgery. The case was assigned to the Sexual Assault Felony Enforcement (SAFE) team.

In short order, the case agent determined that Todd was not a Muslim or from Africa but was in fact, white and the self-described "world's premier body modification expert." He lived in Canyon Country, an upscale Los Angeles suburb north of the city, in a home valued in excess of $1.4 million. He was not what Congress had in mind when they passed the legislation, but he was suspected of violating a law that carried a minimum mandatory sentence of five years. If the anonymous tip were true, Todd needed to be investigated. The problem was in proving the violation, especially in light of the fact the victim never came forward or was identified.

Since the FBI had no evidence of a criminal violation, the female case agent, posing online as the father of two daughters, an eight-year-old and a twelve-year-old, posted in a chat room that espoused the virtues of female circumcision. She requested more information on the procedure. Todd was the only person to respond to the posting. The case agent and Todd traded a series of e-mails and eventually he requested that she call him in order to discuss the details of the procedure. With that as the backdrop, I was brought in to make the actual calls and any face-to-face meetings. At the time, I was working on a terrorism squad and welcomed the opportunity to work with the SAFE team.

On August 9, 2002, I called Todd at his residence and went into my undercover mode. I explained I was married to an Egyptian who had two daughters, my step-daughters. My wife's family had money, I said, and I managed their assets in the United States, so it was important for me to keep the family happy. I explained that my wife had the procedure done as a child and now wanted her daughters to participate in the same rite of passage. I told Todd I wanted to find someone who could perform the surgery in the U.S. and he never hesitated in answering my questions. He was very open in our conversation but explained that the procedure was "highly illegal" in the United States, carrying a five-year sentence, and that even if I took the girls out of the country to have it done, it was still illegal. He described the procedure in detail and claimed the surgery would enhance my stepdaughters' sexual experiences when they matured. He never hung up on me nor did he refuse to discuss the surgery, despite the acknowledged illegality of the act. In fact, Todd invited me and my wife to come to his house to further discuss the procedure.

I was excited about being invited for the face-to-face meeting, but that presented a problem: my nonexistent Egyptian wife. I wasn't willing to take in just anyone, especially some undercover agent who knew nothing about the procedure and who couldn't pass as Egyptian. My case agent went to work and finally, with the advocacy group's assistance, we found a Middle Eastern woman who actually had the procedure as a child and could speak knowledgeably about it.

Because it had taken us more than a month to find my "wife" and the clock was ticking, I couldn't be too particular about whether the two of us would appear compatible as a couple. I was, however, curious as to who would volunteer for such an unusual — to say the least — assignment and anxiously awaited our first meeting. Was I surprised!

My "wife" was beautiful, well educated, and articulate — so much so that, had I been the target, I would have questioned what she saw in me. In fact, I was concerned that she was so attractive Todd might balk at my request to perform the procedure, not believing my cover story.

My undercover wife and I met twice, putting together a game plan. It was important for both of us to have a certain level of confidence in each other. It was especially important for her to believe I held her safety as my paramount concern. I didn't really expect the meeting to be dangerous, but any undercover meeting can take a turn for the worse. When a target knows he is facing a minimum mandatory federal sentence, as Todd did, there is no telling what the reaction would be, should he suspect a law enforcement sting. Todd had a prior felony conviction and, based upon our investigation, had performed piercings and other more delicate body modification procedures on members of outlaw motorcycle gangs. As a result, we had no idea who else might be in the residence when we arrived, so safety was an obvious issue. My "wife" was satisfied with our preparation and confident I would protect her should matters head south. She was more than willing to assist in the investigation and go undercover with the FBI.

Los Angeles, 2001

This case wasn't my first time to work with the SAFE team. They introduced me to NAMBLA a year earlier. An FBI agent assigned to the SAFE team contacted me about an undercover assignment involving overseas sex tours. The topic intrigued me before I even heard the details.

The SAFE team operated out of the L.A. FBI office and consisted of representatives from various federal, state, and local law enforcement agencies. The task force had a great reputation and was highly successful in targeting online sexual predators. I welcomed the opportunity to work with them.

The Knoxville, Tennessee, FBI office obtained information during a search that a

Los Angeles–based travel agency catering to gays was arranging overseas tours affording opportunities for clients to have sexual contact with young boys. Representatives from the Justice Department and FBI agents from the Knoxville, Los Angeles, and Baltimore offices met in Knoxville and determined that Los Angeles would be tasked with opening an investigation on the travel agency.

By the time I joined the investigation, the Los Angeles case agent had already visited the travel agency's Web site and obtained general information about travel to Thailand. He also requested information about upcoming tours. With that as the basic background, I came on board to make the necessary phone contacts and the face-to-face meetings.

I knew convincing a gay travel agent I desired to have sex with adolescent boys was going to require a great deal of preparation on my part. I spent the next several days camped out at one of the office's covert computers, using my alias and accessing everything I could find on man/boy love. My knowledge of computers was very limited at that time, but I knew enough to fear that using my home computer would summon all kinds of unwanted cyber-junk mail into my living room. I was right. I am so glad I limited my Internet research on the topic to the covert computers. I was astounded and disgusted by the pop-ups and junk mail I began receiving in my undercover account.

I accessed a variety of Web sites and even entered a few "predicated chat rooms," sites the FBI identified as venues where Internet sexual predators roamed. Posing as "bobby13," I was quickly inundated by adults more than willing to engage me in sexual conversation. On more than one occasion, I was instructed on how to masturbate and was told by several that they were doing so as we chatted. The experience was as repulsive as it was enlightening.

Thanks to computer technology, child predators can find easy access to a network of support and comfort as well as opportunities to interact with teens and pre-teens. Web sites, chat rooms, forums, and postings are just a search engine away. My interest was man/boy love and there was no dearth of available information. Sometimes referring to their practices as Greek love, Internet authors went to great lengths to justify their pedophilic and pederast desires. Blaming centuries of repressive sexual mores, more than one writer claimed that true abuse was the by-product of limiting "intergenerational sex." Boy lovers claimed they hoped to build personal relationships that did not necessarily include — but certainly didn't exclude — sexual intimacy. They used words like "nourish," "growth," and "treasure." Abuse was alleged when a boy was prevented from experiencing a freely chosen, loving relationship that allowed him to develop his "unique personality and sexuality" — regardless of his age or the age of his adult partner. Prohibiting this experience was seen as an infringement of the child's natural rights.

Interestingly, girls are not given the same freedom in these contexts. The reasoning goes that boys by nature are "hunters," while girls are "nesters." Boys need to "explore" their sexuality and the boy lover is all too willing to participate in that exploration. I began to grasp the psychological and philosophical leanings of the BL.

I also came across the NAMBLA Web site. I was casually familiar with the organization but had never done any in-depth study of their philosophy. Now, though, I was interested. It wasn't immediately clear how large the organization was, but it appeared to be the largest organized group of boy lovers in the United States. I assumed that those who traveled with the Hollywood-based travel agency would or could be members; maybe the travel agent was a member. I decided that joining the organization would give me much-needed credibility. It would also put me on the mailing list for the NAMBLA *Bulletin,* their semiregular magazine, which I assumed would provide more insight into the boy-lover mindset.

I was working with Patti Donahue, the Assistant United States Attorney overseeing the Los Angeles aspect of the Innocent Images National Initiative, an FBI-sponsored program targeting online predators. Patti was a well-respected federal prosecutor and I welcomed her counsel. She approved my joining the organization.

On July 31, 2001, I sent a letter stating,

> I'm ready to join. Enclosed you'll find a money order for $35. I'm a little nervous about adding my name to your rolls. I don't trust the government but I just read where another coach was arrested for having consensual sex with a player. I'm tired of this.

I mailed the letter and money order to the San Francisco post office box listed on NAMBLA's Web site.

Within a few weeks, I received a form letter signed by "Peter Herman" from a Midtown Station post office box in New York City. My name was handwritten in the salutation, giving the impression this massive organization had little time to personalize its communications. I remained unimpressed. My letter, welcoming me to the organization, appeared almost to be an afterthought.

> Welcome to NAMBLA! We have received and processed your application. Thank you for joining us. You have taken a courageous step, and we congratulate you. . . .
> NAMBLA is a political and educational organization. We do not conduct, participate in, or support any illegal activity. We strongly condemn sexual abuse and all forms of coercion, while making a distinction between coercive and consensual activities. We expect all of our members to be aware of this. . . .
> Membership and participation in NAMBLA are your right under the U.S. Constitution's First Amendment and the Bill of Rights. . . .
> Congratulations on your decision to join us and take part in an historic

campaign to defend personal freedom in America.

Joining the organization was as simple as that. I was hoping to at least receive a membership card to flaunt at my fellow undercover agents, but I had to make do with a letter praising my "courageous step."

I began to contact the travel agent. Believing the e-mail communications he had with the case agent were from me, the travel agent spoke with me at length in one of our early conversations of my interest in an upcoming trip and my desire for a younger "clientele." He mentioned an opening on an October excursion. I specifically told him of my desire for "a ten-year-old mocha teddy bear." He balked at that comment and strongly cautioned me about talking so openly on the phone. However, he didn't hang up. We continued the conversation, and he instructed me to mail the application and deposit with a copy of my passport, which I told him had expired and I was getting renewed.

On August 13, I sent a four-hundred-dollar postal money order and the following letter:

Here's my deposit and application. . . .

You're right about the phone. Sorry, if I talked too much. It's just sometimes I get depressed and need somebody to talk with. I guess 10 is unrealistic but I hope 12–14 years old won't be a problem. I just want my boys young and "mocha." If it's a problem I'll understand. Just return the money, no "hard" feelings. Thanks for being so understanding. . . .

I was surprised when on August 23 the travel agent returned the $400 money order, tour application, and letter. He had underlined in red "10 is unrealistic" and "12–14 years old" and added the following notation: "This would be a problem. Sorry, but I did not realize you were looking in that neighborhood. . . . We cannot [help]."

I assumed our case was dead and that, for one of the few times in my career, I had lost. I pushed too hard on the phone and was over the top with the written letter.

I would soon discover, however, that this case was far from over.

19
Rub-a-Dub-Dub

In October 2002, as the time drew near for our first face-to-face meeting with the "world's premier body modification expert," the case agent and I did run into one administrative hurdle, clearly form over substance. The case agent administratively opened a file and classified my undercover wife as an informant. At that time, the FBI had two designations for what some departments categorized as a single classification. An informant was someone who provided information to the FBI without ever revealing that fact to the outside world. A cooperating witness, on the other hand, was an individual who sought to hide his or her identity during the course of an investigation, but was willing to come forward and testify should testimony be required. As the case agent and I were meeting with the SAFE Team supervisor and the FBI Assistant Special Agent in Charge, the ASAC balked at using my undercover wife in such a potentially dangerous situation, exposing the Bureau to potential liability should something go wrong. I could not understand his reluctance as he reviewed the written plan. I explained that throughout my career I often worked with CWs — cooperating witnesses — in more dangerous situations. But my UC wife was not a CW, he explained, she was an informant. With the stroke of a pen and some additional paperwork, we converted my wife from an informant to a cooperating witness. She was unaware of the modification to her status — again, form over substance. But the ASAC was satisfied and the operation was approved.

On October 10, two months after the initial telephone call, my "wife" and I made our way to Todd's estate, a beautiful home set on a large piece of land surrounded by the houses of actors and professional athletes. I had my wife stay in the car as I approached the residence. I politely knocked on the door several times with no response. I then pounded. As I began to question whether the target suspected an undercover sting and decided to cancel our meeting, the door opened.

Before me, stood a five-foot-eight-inch,

forty-year-old man with a protruding paunch. He was barefoot, shirtless, and sported earrings, pierced nipples, and tattoos. Todd wasn't exactly the picture of professional competence I might have expected should I truly be seeking someone to perform such a delicate procedure on my daughters.

It was late in the afternoon and he excused his appearance by stating that he had performed a procedure that lasted all night and was just now awakening. I signaled for my wife to join us and we followed Todd into his expansive kitchen, almost as large as my first house. As the three of us sat at the kitchen table, a female who appeared to be in her early twenties entered the kitchen and stood by the refrigerator, almost at a parade-rest position, her arms folded behind her back. She was extremely thin but reminded me of the actress Jennifer Garner.

Todd was not the least bit hesitant in discussing his activities and readily answered our questions. My biggest problem was controlling my wife, who peppered him with queries, often interrupting him as he was about to make incriminating statements. She was a perfect undercover wife, and her sincere inquiries added to our overall credibility. However, I needed evidence: verbal admissions that he performed the procedures in the past and was willing to perform them on our underage daughters. Todd, however, was careful and skated around the law in his explanation of the procedures he performed. He agreed to do the procedures on our daughters but would not acknowledge having done them on juveniles in the past.

I was shocked when Todd interrupted one of my questions by loudly snapping his fingers and demanding a soft drink. Robyn, the pretty female standing near the refrigerator, grabbed a can of soda and marched over to the table. She squatted down, kissed the can, and ceremoniously presented the can to him using both hands. She then rose, took one step backward, executed an about-face, and returned to her position guarding the refrigerator.

Did I just see what I thought I saw? I wanted to snap my fingers and see if I could instigate a repeat performance, but I was too stunned to move.

Within a few minutes, Todd demanded that Robyn "bring the notebooks." She returned with four huge notebooks crammed with hundreds of eight-by-ten photos of procedures he had done, including male and female circumcisions, piercings, and genital modifications. Every photo was of an adult and Todd, who only admitted to "dabbling in college" and didn't claim to be a licensed medical professional, was not violating federal law by performing the procedures. His patients were consenting adults and the FBI had no desire to legislate morality. Had he refused to perform the surgery on our "daughters," we would have thanked him and moved on — but the afternoon was far from over.

I expressed concern for my daughters' safety, trying to elicit an admission that he had safely performed surgery on underage females in the past. I even suggested a child's anatomy was different from an adult's. Todd skillfully avoided answering the question with any criminal admission and once again emphasized the illegality of the procedure. He assured us, however, that his methods were safe. To reinforce his emphasis that no harm would come to our daughters, he asked us to accompany him to the downstairs bedroom. As the three of us got up, Robyn meekly asked permission to sit at the kitchen table, now that we were leaving. He granted her request. But the theater of the absurd was only beginning.

Todd walked us toward a large bedroom with a king-size, four-poster bed. He matter-of-factly explained that this was where he performed his procedures. He tied patients to each of the four posters, restraining them as he operated. He then escorted us into the bathroom. On the bathroom vanity, I immediately noticed several sanitary napkins soaked in blood, but as I turned the corner I was confronted by a scene few would ever believe: two people sitting naked in a bathtub of bloody water!

I had no idea how to react and there is no way any undercover school could have ever prepared me for such a sight. Before me was a large white woman in her late thirties wearing glasses. She had purple hair, the largest breasts I have ever seen — not intended as a compliment, by the way — and both her nipples were pierced. The other person was a thin white man in his mid-thirties, tapping away on his laptop computer.

I managed to hang on to my composure as Todd explained that he had performed procedures on both of them throughout the night. They were sitting in an herbal preparation that encouraged rapid healing. Rather than bandaging the incisions, his patients were allowed to bleed into the herbal bath. By now my curiosity took over and I inquired about what procedures were performed. The female had circumcision, the same procedure I wanted for my daughters, he said, and the male had his urethra rerouted so he could urinate out an opening in his scrotum. The naked male, calmly working on his laptop computer while bathing in blood, told us he reasoned that if sperm and urine came out of the same orifice, the sperm might be contaminated, thus creating the possibility of diseased or disabled children.

I am not making this up.

The fact that men have been siring children since Cain and Abel by means of a single, multipurpose opening didn't seem to enter his calculations. I suppose the moral of the tableau is that a fool and his money are, indeed, soon parted.

As our meeting ended, I thanked Todd for his hospitality and promised him my wife and I would discuss everything. I told him I was certain we would be speaking again. After all, who knew what sort of sideshow he might provide next time around?

After my initial, failed overture to the gay travel agency in 2001, I decided to make one more try. I called the travel agent and apologized for the misunderstanding. We spoke briefly and apparently my mea culpa worked. I must have come across as a naïve pedophile. By the end of the conversation, he said he could "satisfy" all my needs, but I could not talk about such matters over the phone or put my requests in writing. Such statements became evidence for inquiring law enforcement officials, he warned. We agreed to meet in the near future.

He had plans for the next week or so, and although I couldn't say anything, I anticipated being tied up in court on the Eddie Nash case. I was the FBI representative on a four-person task force that spent years investigating Nash, an infamous Los Angeles criminal who made Hollywood fame when his story was depicted in the movies *Boogie Nights* and *Wonderland.* Nash surprised us all, however, when he pleaded guilty to violating the RICO Act on September 10, 2001. His unexpected action freed me up to concentrate on the travel agency investigation. Unfortunately, though, the next day was September 11, the day our world changed forever.

As I was heading into the office on 9/11, a call came over the Bureau radio, directing all agents to report to a secret location designated for times of national emergencies. I quickly tuned to the "happy-time" radio and learned of the attacks on the

World Trade Center and Pentagon.

The next several days were nonstop as we covered leads our office developed as well as those sent by other offices. No one got a lot of sleep. It was the FBI at its best, operating in crisis mode. It was an exciting time, but our other investigations didn't just disappear.

In between covering national security leads, I found a quiet room and called my travel agent target; I feared any delay in our communications might arouse suspicion. The October trip was still a go, he told me, and even questioned why I would assume it would be canceled. He had little concern for the events happening on the other coast, he said. He viewed the attacks as an annoyance that might inconvenience his future travel plans. His cavalier attitude made it easier for me to operate. There is always a personal as well as a bureaucratic fear that undercover agents will get too close to a target. Personal feelings could interfere with effective undercover dealings; sometimes, an agent might choose to cross that thin line separating us from them. My new friend made it easy, though. Our nation was at war with terrorism, and he considered himself unaffected. I vowed to make the time to continue my contacts.

On Saturday, September 15, as the rest of the office continued working around the clock covering thousands of leads following 9/11, I had my first face-to-face meeting with the travel agent.

I had no idea what to expect and feared it was going to be difficult to pull off the boy-lover role. I thought hard, trying to come up with an appropriate cover and some type of gimmick that might throw off my target. For limited roles in the past, I have used my Hollywood makeup contacts to produce unsightly scars across my face, temporary tattoos in highly visible places, or long, greasy hair. None of these ruses seemed appropriate for this assignment, however.

An idea came to me that seemed to have at least a reasonable chance of success: I would be handicapped. A five-dollar wooden walking stick purchased at the Salvation Army store provided the perfect crutch — and a handy weapon should I need it. Add to that a few effeminate gestures and I thought I would be ready for my grand entrance. Surely no one would suspect a fifty-year-old with an exaggerated limp of being an FBI undercover agent. To complete my outfit for the day, I wore sandals, cotton shorts, a T-shirt, and no underwear.

The travel agency was located in a 1950s-vintage apartment complex just off Hollywood Boulevard. The faded stucco exterior was in need of repair and the "security" gate at the vine-covered archway was broken. As I walked down the courtyard toward the unit at the end of the complex, I noticed that families, most of whom were Hispanic, occupied the majority of the units. Children were everywhere. It made me uncomfortable having so many innocent kids in such close proximity to an establishment I suspected of catering to pedophiles.

I knocked on the wrought iron security door several times before the travel agent answered. A gray-haired, white male, tall and thin, warmly welcomed me. With all the deliberation my cover identity demanded, I made my way into the dingy, one-bedroom apartment. I did my best to make it obvious that walking was a painful activity. The apartment was being used to house his travel agency and an adult pornography distribution business. A computer was set up in the dining room area and gay porn was stacked from the floor to the ceiling. A few posters of Thailand served as the only wall decorations.

He offered me a seat in the cramped living room. The furnishings consisted of a dirty loveseat, a chair, and a glass-topped coffee table. I awkwardly made my way past the stacks of videos. It was hardly a menacing environment but neither did I find it comfortable. Of course, my cover personality never let on.

As we made small talk, I learned the travel agent would also be the host for the October 15 trip. He described himself as a gay porn actor and producer, a veteran of over five hundred films. I didn't attempt to pretend I was familiar with his work and was glad he didn't ask. I realized he was noticing my lack of underwear, which served to solidify my cover, but made me a bit nervous in other ways. In retrospect, my "exposure" may not have been a wise tactic, given the sexual orientation of my target, but I guessed it was distracting, lessening his chances of thinking that I could be other than who I said I was.

Still, one concern any undercover agent has is sexual advances and especially avoidance of situations that could compromise the investigation. Women are no more than a commodity with many criminals, and their offers to set up the agent with prostitutes, girlfriends, daughters, and even wives constitute an issue requiring advance preparation. On a good day I'm a three-and-a-half out of a possible ten, so when women have come on to me, their ulterior motives seem obvious. When the situation has called for it, I have been fortunate enough to find skilled and attractive female undercover agents who were willing to humble themselves enough to accompany me as my girlfriend.

But that sort of "protection" wouldn't work on my travel agent friend. With this assignment, I had been concerned that appearing gay might place me in the position of being offered sex or having to fend off undesirable advances from my male target. At this point, my research on NAMBLA paid off. I was not gay; I was, instead, a "boy lover." Body hair "turned me off" and I had no desire to engage in any sexual tryst with anyone past adolescence. Another benefit of this cover was that should the travel agent offer me a boy for sex, I would arrest him on the spot. Case closed, situation resolved. I doubted, however, he would be so bold, at least this early in our relationship.

20
ENOUGH TO GO ON?

When my undercover wife and I left Todd's house that day, we returned to the staging area to debrief with the rest of the team. I could hardly wait to tell the other agents about the weird bathtub scene we witnessed inside the house, but each attempt met with complaints. The agents had a long drive back to the office and clearly weren't interested in the gory details of our experience inside Todd's House of Pain. A head start on the commute home trumped the bloody bathtub story.

I returned my wife to her residence. She and I, at least, were able to laugh together and decompress from the surreal experience.

I realized as I reviewed the evidence that although I witnessed a most peculiar situation, there was no recorded evidence of my observations. The meeting was recorded, but my conversation did not include a detailed description of what I was observing. Even though I did not see evidence of a federal crime, I assumed at the very least that Todd was practicing medicine without a license, which was a violation of state law. I needed some confirmation of what I had seen.

I cleared that up with my next call. In a recorded conversation with Todd, I explained that my wife and I discussed the procedure and wanted to go forward. He emphasized the need for secrecy and expressed concern that "if the little girls have a problem and they go to the doctor, then they're gonna have a big problem." He bragged that he was the most qualified person outside Egypt to perform the procedure, but would only consent to doing the operation if we agreed to follow the healing process he prescribed. Todd said his bathtub visitors would have to sit in the herbal bath for at least two weeks while their genitals healed. He had employed the healing process for years without any problems, he told me.

I then proceeded to recap the bathroom scene and told him how my wife was initially taken aback by what she observed. Todd acknowledged that two naked people in a bathtub of blood might be upsetting to the uninitiated — the understatement of the week — but it was part of his protocol. Todd told me his price to perform the procedure on both of our girls was eight thousand dollars — discounted from his usual fee. I guess he was running a two-for-one special.

Unfortunately, in all his rambling, Todd had still not admitted to performing the procedure on underage females. In a series of subsequent phones calls and e-mails, he provided references from adult patients and referred me to testimonials on his Web site. One such testimonial came from Robyn, whom Todd described as his "sex slave." In her testimonial, she stated Todd performed her circumcision.

Todd insisted on meeting my daughters and wanted to discuss the procedure with them to insure they were mature enough to understand the need for secrecy. Todd continued the refrain that the procedure was illegal and should the girls mention to their playmates what happened we would all be arrested and sentenced to at least five years.

Todd's description of Robyn as a sex slave raised an issue as to whether she was being held against her will. While I was at the residence she appeared free to come and go, but his comments concerned me and I decided Robyn's status needed to be explored.

On December 4, 2002, I returned to the residence, this time without my wife, whom I claimed was ill. Todd welcomed me back into his home. Robyn brought both of us soft drinks but only Todd received his in a ceremonial fashion. After she presented Todd his drink, she kneeled down and remained at his side. Todd admitted to performing numerous illegal surgical procedures on men and women, but refused to confirm performing any of them on underage females.

Todd told me he performed the surgeries in the nude and Robyn assisted him. When I expressed concern that his nudity might be upsetting to the girls, he repeated his need to meet them to make sure they were mature enough to understand the procedure.

There was no way we were going to introduce two children into this undercover sting operation and I needed to gain criminal admissions without perpetuating the investigation beyond my meeting with Todd and Robyn. I was not sure I would ever get him to admit he performed the surgery on the anonymous ten-year-old, but he certainly was willing to enter into conspiratorial talks about performing the illegal procedure on my nonexistent stepdaughters.

Robyn was wearing a pair of very skimpy shorts and I observed a strange mark on her hip. It wasn't a tattoo but it appeared to be a six- or eight-inch double *S* with an intertwined rose. When I commented on the mark, Todd said that it was a "brand" and that the *S*'s stood for "sex slave."

At one point during the afternoon, Todd excused himself to make a phone call. I used that opportunity to speak with Robyn. I asked if she voluntarily entered this relationship and she assured me she had. She even remarked that she was seeking a "sex slave sister." She and Todd had interviewed several girls, but as she explained, it took a certain type of person to be willing to submit to such a relationship and it was difficult finding the appropriate companion. I couldn't argue with her on that point.

Todd took me on a tour of his home, pointing out the room where he performed the piercings, a different location than where he performed the other procedures. He also showed me his office.

Next, he told me he owned the house on the next lot and offered to show me that residence. I agreed to accompany him, but before we left, he called for Robyn. When she entered the room, he informed her we were leaving and ordered her to "say goodbye." She knelt down in front of him, kissed both his feet, then looked up as he bent over and kissed her on the lips — quite a ceremony for a trip of less than a quarter mile.

As we walked to the residence next door, I asked Todd where he found a sex slave and he said Robyn responded to his posting on the Internet. She willingly sought the role and I could find one, too, he assured me, if I knew where to look.

The residence next door was massive. He claimed it was seven thousand square feet of living space and I had no reason to doubt. What I also found was Todd's wife! She lived in the large house and Robyn lived in the smaller residence. Each knew of the other and, according to Todd, both were content with the arrangement. When I inquired as to where he spent most of his time, he smiled. "Where do you think?" Robyn, apparently, was the object of most of his attention. I never got the chance to ask his wife how she felt about that.

Since Todd insisted the girls would have to sit in the herbal baths for two to three weeks following the procedure, we set up the surgery for the upcoming Christmas vacation, less than a month away. I left Todd and Robyn that afternoon, again stunned by what I observed, wondering if the residents of this neighborhood of multimillion-dollar estates had any idea who their neighbors were.

The next day, I called the residence, knowing Todd would not be home. I wanted to speak with Robyn and gain more criminal admissions from her. Robyn, who admitted to being twenty-three, told me she enjoyed assisting Todd with the procedures. When I asked the extent of her medical training, she replied, "Nursing assistant, certified care giver for the elderly, went to college for medical transcription, and part of the course is learning exactly what a doctor does, learning the names of the tools." She might as well have told me she stayed once at a Holiday Inn Express; that would have been just as reassuring. When I inquired about the most bizarre experience she had assisting Todd, she responded that the most "intense" was her own circumcision, because she did not use any anesthetics. Throughout the conversation she referred to Todd as "Master" and never answered my question about whether he ever performed this procedure on minors.

Knowing we had taken this about as far as we could from an undercover perspective, the case agent prepared to execute a search warrant on the residence. On December 19, a team of FBI agents and members of the Medical Board of California conducted a search. After entering the residence, Robyn, the docile sex slave, got downright hostile. She demanded an attorney and told Todd not to speak with the agents.

The search was most successful. The agents found numerous weapons — all illegally possessed, since Todd had a felony conviction. They also discovered child pornography on the computer.

The subsequent federal prosecution of Todd and Robyn took place only because of the diligence of Mark Aveis, one of the finest Assistant United States Attorneys I ever met. Initially, the U.S. Attorney's office rejected the case, referring it to the state for prosecution. The state also declined to prosecute. I had done some undercover work on a case Mark successfully prosecuted and when I described the details of the circumcision investigation, he agreed to take a second look. Thanks to the hard work of the case agent and Mark, the government pursued the matter and the result of their labors was the first arrest, indictment, and subsequent conviction for a violation of the

1995 Federal Prohibition of Female Genital Mutilation Act. Todd and Robyn both pleaded guilty and received federal prison sentences, and for my mental scrapbook I received souvenirs of the weirdest case I ever worked.

In my September 2001 meeting with the travel agent, I spoke of my desire to travel to a "safe haven" and about my lack of overseas travel experiences due to my medical condition. He warned me I had to be very careful talking about my pedophilia because, even in the gay community, it was not always an acceptable orientation. He assured me he wasn't judgmental and welcomed me on the trip.

He was gay, but denied being a boy lover. He enthusiastically spoke of the "magical beauty" of Thailand, the joy of interacting with the Thai people, and his ability to fulfill all my specific needs. He went into great detail of how we would travel to the various tourist sites during the day and then visit the gay "scene" in the evening.

He painted a very vivid picture of the towns of Pattaya and Phuket, including the boy bars where a "bar fee" to the proper person would provide the results I was seeking. In Thailand, he told me, I could experience temples, festivals, and markets by day, and receive sexual fulfillment at night.

As clearly as I could, I spoke of my desire for prepubescent boys. Although it was important from a prosecutorial standpoint that he agree to provide boys under eighteen, it was very awkward as an undercover boy lover to ask for a specific age. After all, I was supposed to be fulfilling a fantasy; so long as the boys looked like juveniles, what difference did an actual age make? But without that specific commitment on his part, successful prosecution was going to be difficult.

During our conversations, I spoke of how "pubic hair really turned me off." He responded, "Just give 'em a razor and have 'em shave." It wasn't the answer my prosecutor would want to hear. My target was extremely careful and refused to incriminate himself. He was smart; he knew the law, even admitting to knowledge of specific statutes.

He promised to set me up with a contact in Thailand whose name he provided. My guide was familiar with the night scene, he said, and I could tell him of my particular desires. What I did on my own time after daytime sightseeing was up to me. I pushed for specifics but his response was calculated:

"Trust me, you won't be disappointed."

He handed me a travel package containing a variety of documents for the trip: travel brochures, maps, luggage tags, tour itinerary, and a list of travel dos and don'ts. He also gave me a bill for the balance due of $1,790 and said he needed the money as soon as possible. More significantly, he provided a passenger manifest naming those going on the trip. I was shocked to receive such a document. I looked at him with deep sad, soulful eyes and asked — almost begged — him to tell me which passengers were also boy lovers so I could communicate openly and honestly with my travel partners. With some hesitation, he took the list and put marks beside three of the names. All of them were "into boys," he said.

Inside, I was bursting with satisfaction. This, in my mind, was the smoking gun. He was providing travel opportunities overseas for men he knew to be boy lovers and had even given me the name of someone who could insure that my desires would be met once I landed in Thailand. I had him! Rack up a conviction — or at least so I thought.

When the meeting was over, I rushed to LAX, where my case agent was assigned for post-9/11 duties. We both agreed the meeting was a success, and it was just a matter of time before we could stick a fork in the travel agent — he was done.

Our celebration was premature, to say the least. The prosecutor listened to the tape. The magic words were never said. The travel agent carefully couched his sales pitch in a way that did not implicate him in criminal wrongdoing. He merely set up the trip. What the traveler did once he arrived in Thailand was a matter for the individual's conscience. We didn't have enough to indict.

The wheels of justice move slowly. We were awaiting clarification by the prosecutor and Headquarters as to what course of action we could take to further the investigation. The case agent and I were both continuing our post-9/11 responsibilities and were still debating how we could get the travel agent to incriminate himself.

On September 28, I spoke again with the target. His previous pleasant demeanor changed, and in less-than-friendly terms, he said that he needed the balance due on the October 15 trip. If I didn't have the money to him by noon, I would forfeit the deposit and lose my reservation. We had already received permission from Headquarters to pay for the trip, so I rushed to the bank, withdrew the cash, and raced over to the travel agency to make payment. I made it by noon and maintained my reserved spot for the trip, but my attempts to guide conversation in a profitable direction went the way of the previous meeting: "Trust me, you won't be disappointed."

For reasons based primarily on post-9/11 travel restrictions and the failure of the travel agent to incriminate himself, Headquarters had not yet approved my travel overseas, even though we paid for the trip. A few days prior to my scheduled departure, HQ called, announcing that any travel plans were canceled. They went so far as to order the Special Agent in Charge to take custody of my passport to prevent me from traveling. Maybe my passion for the case was evident. It may have also had to do with the fact that I had a reputation for finding ways to maneuver around Headquarters' mandates. I never did surrender my passport . . . but neither did I make the trip.

Since the travel agent identified several boy lovers going on the trip and we already paid for it, it only made sense I should at least fly with the group to see if I could get the BLs to engage me in incriminating conversation. If they admitted to traveling for the purpose of having sex with underage boys, they would be in violation of federal law and could be arrested before setting foot in Thailand.

But Headquarters wouldn't buy our argument. The case was dead. There was little else we could do except bow out gracefully from the trip.

I concocted a plan that seemed stupid on its surface but actually worked. The day before my scheduled trip to Thailand, I went into the FBI garage, turned on the siren of a Bureau car, and called the travel agent. In a weakened voice, with the siren blaring in the background, I told him I thought I was having a heart attack. "An ambulance is on the way, and I'm just not sure I can make the trip." Like I said, it was stupid but it was all I could think of at the time. He had his money and didn't really care. I never made the trip and he never suspected my "heart attack" was staged.

About a month later, I called him. We spoke of the trip and renegotiated for a January date, hoping Headquarters would come around to our position. They never did. The FBI executed search warrants on the travel agent, but no incriminating evidence was found. The case was administratively closed.

I never discussed NAMBLA in my conversations with the travel agent, but at the very least, I had sold myself as a boy lover, even if my target professed not to be one. I was confident I could continue the role and decided to maintain my NAMBLA membership should other opportunities arise.

21
NAMBLA Pen Pals

In late November, after receiving the letter from NAMBLA congratulating me on taking my "courageous step" into membership, I received an e-mail from Peter Herman asking me to participate in their politically correct "holiday card program."

Each Christmas season, NAMBLA members were asked to send cards to incarcerated boy lovers as a means of providing moral support. Peter asked that I provide a number and he would send me mailing labels for the prisoners.

This was one of three programs NAMBLA established for incarcerated members, the others being the *Prisoner's Letter,* edited by Rock Thatcher, and the pen-pal program. As stated on their Web site, NAMBLA recognizes that in prison, boy lovers "experience a harsh and exceptionally hostile environment which undermines their self-concepts and self-respect." Correspondence and communication from the outside world can provide a "lifeline" and "much-needed social and psychological support for inmates facing an arbitrary and often brutal prison system."

I discussed the holiday card program with the prosecutor, Patti Donahue. She supported my involvement as a way of attempting to learn more about overseas child-sex venues. Remember this was not an investigation into NAMBLA, per se, but an attempt to learn more about criminal travel. It was hoped that those incarcerated could provide valuable intelligence as to the who, what, when, and where. When the issue came up later in the investigation about whether the FBI illegally infiltrated the organization, Assistant United States Attorney Michael Wheat in San Diego said it best: "NAMBLA can best be described as barnyard defecation. We aren't interested in the defecation, but the flies surrounding it." We were hoping the imprisoned flies might help in our investigation.

I responded to Peter Herman's e-mail, saying I could send fifteen cards that Christmas. Over the course of my three-and-a-half-year membership in the organization, I received the names of over 165 prisoners participating in the NAMBLA prison program. I assumed all to be NAMBLA members.

With the concurrence of Patti Donahue, I sent a card to each prisoner on my list, with an accompanying letter. Over the course of my membership, I kept my Christmas correspondence generic. A sample letter reads,

> I am a member of the association that puts out *THE BULLETIN* (I think you know who we are) and was given your name as part of the holiday card project. I just want you to know that there are people outside thinking of you.
>
> Most of us have done what you have done, only you were unfortunate enough to get caught. Maybe someday, society will wake up and realize that intergenerational love is natural and normal. It was good enough for the ancient Greeks, so why not us?
>
> I plan to have a boyful Christmas. Here's wishing you a Merry Christmas and a better New Year.

This aspect of the investigation was one of the most difficult, and became even more difficult when I received the responses to the cards. Initially, I hated the thought of giving aid and comfort to those incarcerated. For some reason, dealing face-to-face with the membership, knowing that possible incarceration loomed in the future, was easier than offering support to those now in prison. But the responses I received in return were also troubling, for a variety of reasons.

I received everything from carefully considered letters by those seeking forgiveness to missives from unrepentant sexual predators who described their actions in graphic detail. I heard from born-again Christians, praying for me because of my "tendencies," and others requesting I not contact them again because they were trying to put the thoughts and deeds behind them. One member even forwarded my name to a prison ministry group and I began to receive their literature in my undercover name.

As a Christian, I wanted to reach out to some of them and offer hope — but, of course, that was impossible without compromising my investigation. For others, I wanted to find a way to insure they would never see daylight again.

We terminated communication with those seeking forgiveness and not offering up sordid details of their lives. To the others, I responded.

Thanks for writing back. This was the first time I participated in the Christmas card project and wasn't sure how my cards would be received. I was also afraid to say too much in the card for fear I might cause you some problems.

I guess we're the lucky ones on the outside because all of us out here are probably doing the same thing but you were the unfortunate one and got caught . . . thanks to archaic laws and a close-minded society. . . .

I'm single and unattached right now but am always looking for a "special" friend. Before my medical condition got worse I coached baseball and soccer. My last coaching job was at a private school but an incident happened and I had to move. It was all hush-hush and no one got hurt. I love coaching boys and still get to the parks on weekends when I can, just to watch them play (and maybe do a little scouting!)

In October I was planning a "special" trip to Thailand but the day before I was scheduled to leave I had what I thought was a heart attack. . . .

I know there are lots of "special" boys in Thailand who are supposed to be accommodating. I was looking forward to the trip. Did you ever travel? Know any good "travel agents" or people who can really help us enjoy ourselves?

I'd appreciate any help. I just want to go somewhere where WE can be safe. . . .

Well, better go. Great talking to you. Be safe.

The responses I received were enlightening — and disturbing. They came from inmates claiming to be from all walks of life: businessmen, pilots, professors, investigators, foster parents, blue-collar workers . . . from the barely literate to MENSA members . . . gay, "straight," and bisexual. As I would find when dealing with the offenders face-to-face, they were rarely stupid. Many may have displayed obsessive, self-delusional qualities, but most I encountered were college-educated, several with advanced degrees. The responses answered some of our questions about overseas travel, allowed us to assist in keeping at least two inmates from being released from a civil commitment facility, and provided insight on the mindset of the boy lover few have ever seen.

Their own words provided a glimpse into their mind and emotions — what drove them, how they operated, how they succeeded, and how they failed. I was amazed so many readily shared their exploits, often in graphic detail.

I was and always will be a BL. . . . I was 21 when I got locked away for a very long sentence. Two life terms for having been involved with four boys ranging in age from 7 to 11. . . . I'll never know the pleasure of holding a boy and smelling that little-boy scent or tasting every part of them.

Boys . . . are to be cherished and loved and protected. . . . With the right kind of lucky little boy you can share a deeply intimate physical connection. . . . I've always dreamed of having sons of my own to raise and make into good people and whom I could teach the wonderful mysteries of the body to, in my own special way.

I'm doing 10 years on a 20-year sentence for forcible rape of a 9-year-old.

I am serving 51 months for possession of child pornography. Prior to my arrest I was a professor at a large Midwestern state university. . . . Like many boy-lovers I lived a closeted existence. I was even married and in fact my wife discovered what I had and turned me in. . . . I now realize how badly we must all hang together and look forward to being able to support the organization when I get out.

Hey Robert, are you hetero or homo or bisexual w/ a little boy-love in ya? Cause I was gonna ask you if you could go online and copy some photos of some sweet little asses.

First, I am 95% boy lover and 5% girl lover. No, I've never [had sex with] any girl, but I have had some good times with 2 in my life, but I've had 10 tons of boys, some just once or twice then others for 2 or 3 years.

As for why I'm here . . . so-called none concede sex with a miner [*sic*] a.k.a. rape. It was not, the boy wanted it, he was 11 and in ohio they say he is not old anuff to say he wanted to.

[A juvenile male] started to write to me while I was in prison through a pen-pal club. [His mother] wanted an older man for her son to communicate with and now they both want me to come down whenever I can get the bus fare and a little spending money together. . . . No, I don't have any nude pictures of him, not yet anyhow. I'm working on it though. Hopefully when I go down I can get him to shed his shorts for me.

I've had sexual encounters with boys of all ages, up to puberty, and some were very young, being 5 and 6 or so.

My tastes are in pubescent boys and young men, say 12 years or older. I'm not really into pre-pubes. Although many of those are cute and beautiful, I prefer boys who can actually have an orgasm and give me a physical and/or emotional response. . . . My ideal situation would be to have a lover who is old enough to [reach orgasm] but never has. Then I could be his first experience, the first to introduce him to joys of sex.

Basically, I am a straight acting bisexual/homosexual. I say bi- because my main interest is pre-pube girls, but I enjoy boys also and adult men. I have enjoyed sexual encounters with all of the above. I am very open-minded as far as age limits also. Nothing turns me on more than a nude child's body, except intercourse with the child.

What's your age range? Mine's 3–13. You see, I was sexually, physically, and emotionally abused starting at age 4 by some of my most trusted friends and family and even though I'm working through all that to become a survivor, my attractions for children will always be there.

Do you think you could go online and find me a minor pen-pal, a boy of course, about 12 to 14?

None of my true foster boys ever turned on me, in all my going and doing I got to say only 2 or 3 ever did, I'd say most of them was [*sic*] happy to have someone that really cared for them and looked after them.

She left her husband and wanted to live a little. Her son and I got along real well and she asked if I'd be interested in spending time with him. It was love at first sight and our friendship was even stronger.

Although I shall always be attracted to pubescent males I have enough control to avoid and not fall for one. . . . There are rational, logical and reasonable reasons to avoid sexualizing young boys, particularly to same-sex experiences. True, many will find their way there anyway, but why take the chance of steering a young lad into homosexuality or later pedophilia or sexual confusion or exposure to the trauma, public exposure, interrogation, humiliation, and embarrassment?

I am doing two life sentences because I made a mistake and grew up loving boys. The circumstances are a bit complicated but not all the boys turned on me. In fact only five were involved out of the several dozen I've known and had relationships with.

My personal favorite age ranges are from 11 years old to 14 1/2. I can go down to 10 year olds with exceptions. My favorite phase of their lives is at the cusp of puberty. Also I am starstruck/vixened by angelically cute to supercute looking, charming, intelligent and mature acting . . . whom I call "cuties" or "supercuties." . . . I write "cuties" as "Q.T.s" and "supercuties" as "super Q.T.s." . . . I am only gay/bisexual with Q.T.s and super Q.T.s. I am fluently heterosexual with adults. . . . I'd love to be able to have a great relationship with a tall, attractive, physically fit, intelligent, passionate, sociable woman who shares in our mutual interests.

As I've said before, the toughest part of this assignment, especially as the months and years wore on, was thinking of people like my prison correspondents and "fellow" NAMBLA members existing in the same world as my son and other innocent young boys I cared about — that and resisting the near-constant urge to single-handedly, suddenly, and violently remove them from the face of the earth. I comforted myself with the knowledge that if I did my job properly and remained patient and attentive, the courts would handle the situation. At least, that was what I hoped.

22
THE MIAMI
NAMBLA
CONFERENCE

My San Diego case agent and I arrived in Miami on Thursday, November 11, for the NAMBLA conference. We flew separately; I traveled in my undercover identity. He brought all the recording equipment, since he could get it through airport security without any questions.

When I arrived at the airport, I was disappointed that the Ford Mustang I'd reserved was not available. I thought the car would add to my boy-lover flare and it upset me that going into the conference I was already making adjustments. The pressures were starting to mount and I didn't need a rental car problem.

The solution from the rental agency was to provide me a Dodge minivan.

That's right, the limited availability of cars put me behind the wheel of a soccer mom's ride. It wasn't the image I was going for, but it eventually worked to my benefit.

I spent Thursday night at an area hotel not far from the conference site. But while checking in I ran into another problem. I had two undercover credit cards and was using one exclusively for the international weapons case I was also working at the time, thus simplifying expense records for that case agent and his auditors. I hadn't even brought that card with me, just to make sure I avoided charging on the wrong card. When the hotel clerk ran the card I did bring, we discovered that the credit card company had flagged this account for some unknown reason. I was stuck. I had insufficient cash and no other cards. I couldn't check in but I wasn't about to sleep in the street.

I called the company remaining in my undercover persona and spent what seemed like hours on the phone. My blood pressure was rising, as was my anxiety. Posing as a boy lover among "experts" was stressful enough without having to worry about how I was going to pay for my room and board. I was supposed to be living off my private family foundation, for crying out loud!

I eventually straightened out the misunderstanding but not without doing a song and dance for the credit card security department. The rental car issue was resolved but upsetting. Now the credit card fiasco had me climbing the walls. I eventually relaxed and settled into a room.

After I unpacked, I decided to find the "charming secluded inn" that was hosting the conference, and set out for a late night drive through Miami. I'm sure the local residents find Miami easy to navigate, but I got lost, perhaps because my senses were already jangled by the rental car and credit card experiences. I eventually located the Miami River Inn at 118 SW South River Drive, but by accident rather than navigational skill. Located in an older section of town, the inn was nestled among mature trees behind a tall, wrought iron fence. The fence may have been more for protection than beauty: because of the hour, the streets were hardly crowded, but those few denizens I did observe appeared as though they could easily have sported felony rap sheets. I headed back to the hotel, hoping to get a solid night's sleep in anticipation of the next day's preparations with my case agent and the surveillance team, followed by my arrival at the NAMBLA conference.

For much of the next day, I made preparations for the weekend. I assumed my contact with my case agent would be minimal once the conference began, and I wanted to insure we had all the bases covered. Around three in the afternoon, I met with the Miami surveillance agents who would be covering me that evening and throughout the weekend, if necessary. As I have found in almost every city I have worked, the agents were great. They were most helpful and looked as if they would fit in with the surroundings. FBI agents discarded the white, button-down collar shirts long ago and these guys presented the right Miami image. Nothing spells stress to an undercover agent like surveillance agents that reek of J. Edgar Hoover's FBI.

With the briefing complete, I suited up, strapped on the recording equipment, grabbed my crutch, and headed toward my secluded rendezvous. Once again my navigational skills failed me, and I circled the area several times before stumbling onto the inn.

Billed as Miami's only bed and breakfast, the inn was built almost a century ago and is listed on the National Register of Historic Places. A member of the International Gay and Lesbian Travel Association, the complex is located just west of the Miami River. The inn has four cottages with a total of forty rooms. Although management describes each room as "uniquely decorated with antiques and period pieces" many of the furnishings appeared to be Salvation Army thrift store chic. The "lush tropical garden" was overgrown and "the manicured croquet green" needed mowing. But this was business, not pleasure.

I pulled into the parking lot, and as I exited the Dodge Caravan, Mike from Cleveland parked next to me. His was a familiar face from the New York conference the year before, and together we made our way to the registration desk, hidden toward the rear of the complex.

After registering as part of the Wallace Hamilton Press group, Mike and I were escorted back to a secluded, three-story cottage. The building had a large sitting room and two bedrooms on the first floor, with bedrooms on the second and third floors. Because of my "handicap," I never got beyond the first floor and can only assume the rooms housed one or two people. My room was just off the sitting room, conveniently located so I could slip in and out of conversations taking place when the members gathered. The room was cramped but I greatly preferred that over a spacious one with a roommate, so I had no complaints.

After putting my things away and secreting the five recording devices I brought for the conference, I walked outside and ran into Peter Herman, who was being followed by David Mayer. Peter introduced us. We chatted briefly and made our way back toward the cottage as others began to arrive.

I was in the sitting room greeting the members when David Mayer came down from his bedroom. We quickly struck up a conversation. He said he was an international flight attendant from Chicago for American Airlines. Within an hour of arriving at the conference and less than ten minutes after I met David, he kindled my investigative interest to a warm glow.

David: Do you travel a lot?

Me: You know, not internationally. I'll fly back and forth to . . . Atlantic City.

David: [I've been to] Thailand three or four times. . . . Costs me next to nothing.

Me: Yeah. I bet Thailand's special.

David: They're fun. It's hit and miss, not consistent. You've got to get out of Bangkok and again it depends what your taste is. The youngest that I've seen is five.

Me: Really?

David: Usually by thirteen, fourteen, they're old and they're done. Acapulco is another fine place. If you ever get a chance go down to Acapulco, the beach, the gay beach.

Me: Pretty easy pickings?

David: Yeah, real easy. Again, though, not consistent. You know, I've been there when it's been like, you know, being a kid in a candy store, and I've been there when it's like, basically, nothing going on. Very inconsistent, but when it's good, it's great!

I couldn't believe his boldness. The New York conference experience was disappointing from an investigative standpoint: Jeff Devore was the only one who discussed his criminal ventures. I hoped to be more assertive this weekend, but David made it easy by initiating the criminal conversation. Within the first hour of our weekend investigation, he ratified the theme we were expecting to find: sexual predators who gathered annually to network with other predators, openly discussing criminal dreams. We found our first nugget in what would prove to be a gold mine.

I was disappointed to learn from Peter that only about seventeen members were coming to the conference. Since this was an annual gathering, I assumed that everyone from New York and possibly more would travel to Miami.

That evening, several members joined me in the minivan as we made our way over to a Brazilian all-you-can-eat buffet on SE First Avenue where Peter arranged for us to eat. When we arrived, I assumed we would have our own room, but there was no private banquet area and as more members arrived they merely pulled up chairs in a crowded, noisy setting. Much of my recording from the restaurant was inaudible.

Ten attendees went to the restaurant. Peter Herman, Mike from Cleveland, and Floyd from San Francisco were people I'd met at the New York conference. My "new friends" included David Mayer from Chicago, Tim from Michigan, Sam Lindblad from New Mexico, James from Miami, and Dick Stutsman from South Carolina. Also at the restaurant, but not joining us at the table, were Paul Zipszer and Brian. The conversation that evening was light. I sat between David and Sam and when I said I lived off a trust account, both offered to marry me. My private room was looking better by the minute.

Sam, a former schoolteacher and three-time convicted sex offender, had a very gentle nature. The balding, fifty-seven-year-old with a thin build readily spoke of his conviction, and I was interested in learning more about him as the weekend progressed.

James sat across from me. His handsome features and youthful appearance betrayed his age and his sexual desires. Neatly dressed and wearing a tie, he appeared to be a young account executive. I wasn't too far off in my initial assessment; he said he worked for a downtown Miami law firm. He looked much younger than his true age, forty-six. Legally trained overseas, he was unable to take the bar in the United States. He settled for working as a paralegal. Although articulate and personable, this was his first conference and, at least for the evening, he was understandably reserved.

Tim was intriguing. I guessed him to be in his mid-forties. Close to six feet in height, thinly built, with close-cropped, dark hair, he claimed to work at a juvenile detention facility in Michigan. He had a melodic voice that reminded me of one of my favorite ESPN sportscasters, Dave Campbell. But Tim was guarded. He seldom responded to direct questions, and as David Mayer learned later, "Tim" may not have been his true name. I had little contact with him during the weekend so I had no idea if he was really from Michigan or where he actually worked. His fears stemmed from an earlier infiltration of the group when, as he said, the "FBI came knocking on my door." That visit scared Tim and he was reluctant to disclose too much information about himself. I realized I still needed to be cautious about probing too deeply, so I spent almost no time speaking with him.

Dick from South Carolina was a talker. Although he had gray hair and a short, gray beard, he appeared to be in great shape for his age.

Following a dinner that lasted several hours, we all returned to the inn.

23
RELAXING WITH
PREDATORS

The lounge outside my room was comfortable, and I gathered there with those who rode in the van with me as we waited for the others to arrive. Someone brought a large bottle of cheap whiskey and someone else found paper cups. I nursed my drink throughout the evening as the bottle emptied. I hoped the demon drink would loosen tongues.

I slumped into a soft easy chair, preferring to limit my interaction with the others and just allow my friends to incriminate themselves with their conversation, if possible. My personal safety was not a major concern, and I believed my credibility within the organization was intact, but the less I talked, the less opportunity I had to misstate some time-honored BL line of thought and possibly arouse suspicion.

David's sense of humor was evident throughout the evening, as was Tim's paranoia. The issue of sexuality dominated much of the conversation. The underlying theme was that the age-of-consent laws were "the arbitrary impositions of a repressive society." I had little interest in their opinions on the topic, but tried to appear as though I was participating, giving the occasional nod or grunt.

Tim observed, "Repressed sexuality is such a taboo subject that we don't sell anatomically correct dolls. Can you image selling a doll without a head or an arm?" He also blamed the industrial revolution for bringing about the extension of childhood.

James concluded that "youth aren't even the owners of their own sexuality. . . . We've extended childhood beyond its natural boundaries. . . . In the agrarian society people are adults at thirteen, fourteen."

"Because of medical breakthroughs, children are reaching puberty faster," claimed Floyd, the father of four.

Chris, the mop-haired socialist from Illinois "lived on the streets in San Francisco for a year and a half," which apparently made him an expert on everything.

The screen door sprung open and Todd Calvin, the divorced dentist from Dallas, entered, breaking up the conversation. Working the room, glad-handing the attendees, he quickly won over David and the others with his warm personality.

When Todd mentioned he flew to the conference in his privately owned single-engine Beechcraft Bonanza, he and James had an immediate connection. James knew a great deal about planes, and that topic began to dominate the conversation. For me, though, it was another subject in which I had little knowledge or interest.

Todd incurred the wrath of some in the room when the conversation turned to politics, and he apologetically admitted to voting for President Bush, the only member to have done so. That announcement turned heads and several times throughout the weekend David, a "dyed-in-the-wool Democrat," brought up the topic.

The evening's entertainment arrived when Paul Zipszer and his friend Brian entered. Both had been at the Brazilian buffet but were afraid to join us. Paul, a body builder in his late thirties, was shy about outing himself and even debated coming to the inn following dinner. Brian, his crutch, provided the necessary courage.

Paul introduced himself and took his belongings up to his room. Brian stayed behind and entertained the troops. In his late thirties or early forties, the blond Brian was not a NAMBLA member, a fact that would cause Peter much consternation when he learned Paul brought a nonmember friend. Described by Paul as manic-depressive, Brian was definitely manic tonight. "I'm married for seventeen years and it's over, okay. Now I'm living with a man for a year and a half . . . but I'm not one of you all."

When someone asked whether he was gay, he replied, "I'm bisexual because I just had sex with a female about four days ago." David shivered and drew a loud laugh when he said, "That's weird sex!"

Brian said he was "aspiring to find a rich old man who is gay." A huge smile came across David's face, and he turned toward me and said, "I've already found one."

Brian went around the room asking us what we did and where we lived. His boldness made my job easier. I merely had to sit there and let the recorder run. When the conversation turned to David, we learned he had a doctorate in economics, master's degrees in psychology and social work, and had once been recruited by the CIA.

Todd's eyes opened wide. "Really! Are you working for the government right now? Is there a representative from the government here in this room?"

Before I could answer, Brian chimed in: "Yeah, I just came from the welfare office." No sense both of us admitting we were government agents, so I kept quiet.

Brian complained that his wife, an exotic dancer who had had various plastic surgeries to enhance her appearance, engaged in sex with other women for pay, but objected to Brian having a homosexual relationship; she caught him with another man when she came home early one evening. A spirited discussion developed about the double standard existing between lesbian affairs versus male homosexual affairs.

Todd turned the discussion back to a more serious topic among BLs: the issue of talking openly with someone having like desires and needs. He asked, "How many in this room have friends who know what they like?"

"Why?" Brian asked.

"Because it would be great to be able to talk [with others] about things we're talking about," Todd said. "This is my third NAMBLA meeting to come to, and aside from this I've never knowingly had contact."

James tried to explain the issue to Brian: "That's one of the purposes of the organization . . . contact with like-minded individuals. . . . That's one of the reasons that the organization subjects itself to being attacked by groups that would like to see an end to it. They believe that such an organization actually engenders a greater proliferation of that kind of thinking. They don't want organizations like this to exist."

Brian said, "But you know what? The way I look at it, blacks were looked down upon, okay? Gays — looked down upon. You all are certainly looked down upon, right? Fifty-nine years from now, it'll be all right."

"Hey, great!" Todd said. "We'll be dead and gone. I'll be eighty. Where's the Cialis? We'll need it then." Todd went on to say it was so difficult to even chance a discussion with someone about the topic. He had so much to lose if it were discovered he was a BL and a member of NAMBLA. "Because of what I do for a living, I have everything to lose."

Maybe I had more in common with the attendees than I thought: we were all living multiple lives. I was an FBI agent posing as a pedophile one day and an international weapons dealer the next, while others were predators attempting to hide their secret from the outside world. I learned to lie to further my assigned undercover investigative tasks, yet they had been lying just as long to survive in a society that hated what they espoused. We were all practiced liars; that made detection more difficult — for both sides.

Floyd, an elder statesman in the group, saw it differently. "I don't have those issues. I've spent most of my life very open and direct about what I do and what I don't do. . . . If you try to hide it, it comes out in most unexpected ways."

Brian observed, "The secret best kept is the one told."

I wasn't ready to tell my secret — at least, not yet. In a few months though, I would tell all — hopefully to a jury in a courtroom, with these guys sitting at the table of the accused. I grabbed my crutch and ambled to my room, hoping to sleep and ready myself for a new adventure the next day.

Saturday marked the beginning of the conference meetings. I awoke refreshed and excited about the possibilities for the upcoming day. I could feel the adrenaline rush as I dressed. I slept well, which for me was unusual. I'm often restless the night before an undercover meet, mulling over in my mind any of a hundred scenarios that might confront me during the assignment.

As I reflected on what I knew so far, I realized David's opening salvo the day before about his overseas adventures boded well for a day of successful information gathering. I looked forward to pursuing that topic with him. It was important that David raised the travel issue, since that would negate an entrapment argument in court. It also paved the way for me to explore the subject in further detail. I strapped on my recording equipment — for the first several hours, a concealed camera — and made my way toward the garden area, where a continental breakfast was being served. Many had gathered, including guests who were not part of NAMBLA.

The weather was perfect. Some even suggested we conduct part of the meeting outside, but security concerns prevailed. We spent every session inside the conference room.

As I joined my NAMBLA "friends" around a wrought iron patio table for some easy conversation prior to commencement of the conference, Todd was in the middle of a story about his motorcycle adventure in the Turks and Caicos Islands in the Bahamas. While vacationing with a group called Flying Dentists in February 2002, he decided to rent a motorcycle and tour the island, including a visit to a conch farm.

This was his first time on a bike this size

and he was unfamiliar with the toe brakes. Riding by himself, he lost control on a back road straightaway and crashed. The results were a broken collarbone, four broken ribs, and a broken hip. The injuries and the resulting seven missed weeks of work were devastating. But according to Todd, the most embarrassing part was he was rescued by seven carloads of Girl Scouts and their mothers. David never missed a beat: "Too bad it wasn't Boy Scouts."

"That would have made it all worthwhile," Todd said sincerely.

When David Mayer briefly left the table, he was the topic of conversation. All we knew about him from the night before was that he had a doctorate in economics, master's degrees in social work and psychology, and worked for over twenty years as an international flight attendant. It appeared he was not using his education to its fullest. Todd said David admitted to talking with a CIA recruiter when he was in graduate school. David's CIA "contacts" would reemerge as the investigation progressed.

We made our way to the building that housed the conference room, just off the pool and garden. Compared to last year's facilities in New York, these accommodations were quite an improvement, though the hardwood floors were a bit worn. Still, there was a kitchenette, and turn-of-the-century photos of the greater Miami area adorned the walls. The chairs were set up in a semicircle and the attendees took their seats.

24
LEADERLESS, SHIRTLESS, CLUELESS

Peter welcomed us.

> This group is unique. It's membership-based. You are responsible as to how we move from here. . . . Even the European groups — they may hold work meetings, but the largest group that we know of is Martangue in the Netherlands and I think basically they just send out a magazine like we do and have a steering committee, but I don't think they hold general membership meetings. But this general membership meeting really guides what NAMBLA will do for the rest of the year.

Chris spoke next, asking for a wider participation in NAMBLA's work by the attendees. Chris referred to this small gathering of seventeen men as the organization's "core group."

311

Peter asked each of us to introduce ourselves, if we were comfortable doing so, and to answer the questions "What do we want?" and "What are our aspirations?" The responses were interesting: No one admitted coming for any of the organization's stated purposes as outlined in the NAMBLA policy statement. The primary theme of their comments, as the FBI suspected all along, was "networking."

Sam Lindblad began. The Albuquerque resident readily admitted to being "a year and a few months out of prison, where I put in seven years." He came seeking "camaraderie and a common soul."

Tim from Michigan said,

I live pretty much in isolation from other BLs. . . . Part of my interest in coming here this weekend is meeting other BLs and begin[ning] to develop a community of people [for] exchange . . . and . . . support. I don't really see this as a time in this country where we can go out and be, like, real vocal and active in the sense of carrying signs. . . . I think the focus for us, as a group, is to try to reach out among ourselves and provide more support than maybe we're doing right now. I see this as kind of being dark times and if we don't support each other, I don't know who is going to.

Someone followed with an "amen."

David Mayer came for the networking; Mike from Cleveland wanted "to develop a better networking community of other guys that have the same feelings as myself."

John from San Francisco identified himself as a "gaytheist" who had "been in jail twice and any commitment to anyone might facilitate my way back into jail." Decrying his plight as a boy lover, John admitted to being "out as a gay" and "out as an atheist" but "those things are different. You go around saying you like to run your hands through a boy's hair, or you like to kiss him or do other things like that, it doesn't get the same reaction."

Substitute teacher Dick Stutsman, fifty-nine, from a small town in South Carolina, said he loved boys: "I admire them; they're beautiful creatures." He had lived in South Carolina for over a year, having come from Atlanta, where he was a mentor in a middle school. Dick described himself in reassuring terms: "I think I'm not a sociopath. . . . In my twenties and thirties there might have been cases where I seduced, inappropriately, people who were naïve . . . I am fearless to a fault . . . open to a fault, and I don't want to be a danger to this organization."

Paul Zipszer, from the Orlando area, was attending his first conference. "Basically, the reason I came was to see what's going on."

Todd Calvin from Dallas was attending his third consecutive conference and spoke passionately when he said he came for "the camaraderie, for actually being able to be yourself and having nothing to hide because we've all been hiding a whole lot for a long time. We don't have to do that here."

Steve Irvin from Pittsburgh was "active in eighty-eight and the nineties, met a lot of nice people, then got busy and paranoid and drifted away . . . so I came just hoping to meet some new people."

Chris read several disjointed quotes that had nothing to do with the introductions. He quoted Tim Reed who wrote about pre-1994 Kandahar, Afghanistan, "where the streets were filled with teenagers and their sugar daddies flaunting their relationships." He quoted foreign politicians and national writers. He quoted a writer who said NAMBLA was into "transnational prostitution" and "kidnapping." Finally, Peter and others called him on his rambling, and we moved on to David R. Busby.

David R. got a big laugh when he explained he "first found out about this organization somewhere around 1989 or '90. Since I was a kid into a young adult, I was very active in the Boy Scouts. I got to go to this national meeting. . . . The then chief executive of the Boy Scouts of America, his name was Ben Love, told us about this incredible organization that he thought was so horrible, called NAMBLA. And from that point on I was a member. I didn't have any idea that you existed, but thanks to the Boy Scouts, I now know."

David R., who described himself as "not gay because I like what I like," spoke with used-car-salesman zeal: "I truly believe that, probably in my lifetime, people will come to think of people like us the way they think of homosexuals. . . . [It's] good to get together with people who like what you like and believe what you believe, so I really like being here." David R. also admitted to being a nudist. Soon after that, Mike from Cleveland took off his shirt and remained shirtless throughout the day. David R. told me more than I actually wanted to know, and I was hoping Mike didn't take David R.'s encouragement any further.

As the pointless oration droned on, I allowed my mind to go on a little R&R —

while keeping enough of an ear on the proceedings to maintain the appearance of engagement in the discussion. I looked around at the guys in the room and tried to imagine them sitting in prison cells. I didn't know for sure how the arrests would go down in this case if we were successful enough to reach that point, but fantasizing about taking these guys down — hard — helped me stay sane during the emotional wear and tear of my time as a "BL."

Thinking about their arrests took me back to my very first collar as a new agent. "Every Marine is a rifleman." It's an adage all Marines know. Even though I was a judge advocate in the Corps, I attended both the ten-week Officer Candidate School and the six-month officer basic school (known as TBS, The Basic School) at Quantico, Virginia. Upon graduation I was qualified to lead a rifle platoon into combat. Instead I was assigned to the Naval Justice School in Newport, Rhode Island, and then to the Marine Corps base at Camp Pendleton, California. I never saw combat in the Marines, so I never really knew how I would respond to that first real moment of truth. I believed in my Marine Corps combat training but never put it to use. The four-month training at the FBI Academy prepared me for a different kind of combat. But I wondered how I would respond to that first "fight or flight" incident. Once I reported to the San Diego office of the FBI it wasn't long before I was tested.

My first squad assignment included fugitives, which meant we were tasked with tracking down those charged with "unlawful flight to avoid prosecution": UFAP, in its inevitable governmental acronym form. We were following up leads on a fugitive who was wanted for robbery, kidnapping, and attempted murder. Our subject knocked over a jewelry store, then grabbed the owner and dragged her away as a hostage, subsequently tossing her off a seventy-foot cliff in an apparent effort to eliminate her as a witness. Unfortunately for him, she survived the fall and identified him. He vowed never to be taken alive and crossed state lines to elude capture, which is where the FBI came in.

One night my partner and I were working late on some information linking the fugitive to an apartment complex in the Mission Beach section of San Diego. We managed to hop the security fence and approached the apartment in question. As I stepped forward to knock on the door, I landed in fresh cement — making a large footprint outside the door to the apartment. Since I had already messed up somebody's handiwork I knocked on the door but there was no answer. My partner and I laughed off my gaff and planned our return the next day.

It was early the next afternoon when we approached the apartment a second time. A handyman was on his hands and knees smoothing out my mistake from the night before. He resorted to language I was all too familiar with from the Marines when, with a cherublike face, I inquired about what happened. Before I could even offer an apology — which I had no intention of doing — the fugitive opened the door preparing to leave his apartment. He looked down at the handyman and looked at us. We were dressed in "soft clothes" and appeared to be with the handyman. It was obvious he couldn't step through the wet cement, and we assumed he was retreating to the back door. The handyman told us the apartment had a back door that led to an underground parking garage.

We sprinted toward the garage tunnel and arrived there just as the large, cast-iron door was opening. Without much thought — as will soon become obvious — I planted myself in the center of the drive and pointed my .38 at the fugitive bearing down on me in his car. I hollered out commands with Marine Corps authority. For reasons I will never understand — but attribute to God's care for his foolish children — the suspect obeyed me. Instead of turning me into road-kill, this fugitive, who vowed never to be taken alive, stopped the car, turned off the engine, and threw his keys on the sidewalk. I rushed up to the car and stuck my .38 in his left ear, deep into the ear canal. My adrenaline was pulsating at near lethal levels and my hand was shaking, as was the barrel of the .38 lodged inside his ear. My partner and I pulled the now shaken captured fugitive out of the car, cuffed him, and waited for the A-Team to show up.

When our more experienced squad members arrived they weren't real happy we captured an important fugitive without their assistance, but they took him into his apartment and began questioning him. Within a few minutes I walked in, and as I approached the still-cuffed fugitive, he nodded with his head toward me and said with a quaking voice, "Th-th-that's the son of a bitch who almost killed me." I know I flashed an ear-to-ear grin. I faced the enemy and won. I belonged in the FBI.

■ ■ ■ ■

Sitting in the conference room in Miami, I wished I could jam a .38 in a few pedophiles' ears as I read them their rights, but for now I had to remain patient. I had to smile and nod and invite them to tell me their darkest fantasies, hoping to elicit the magic words or actions that would allow the justice system to prevent them from harming any boys for a long time.

By this time, Floyd was speaking. He had senior status in the organization, having been a member since 1981. His current responsibilities included working on the *Bulletin,* the Web site, and the steering committee. He said that over the years, he had been a member of the New York, San Francisco, and Los Angeles chapters and "appreciated the diversity that you find among boy lovers, all shapes and sizes, all kinds of tendencies. We need to respect that and not try to force everyone into a mold." Boy lovers did come in many "flavors," as Bob from Atlanta liked to say. By this time, I realized it was wrong to assume that BLs always had effeminate mannerisms. They came in every sort of package, from every economic stratum. Some were openly gay, some liked adult women *and* eight-year-old boys, and some, like David R. Busby, were only attracted to boys.

Floyd professed a desire to gain a "greater sense of the boy lover movement in other times and other places. We're not the first and we won't be the last." *So,* I thought, *a history buff.* Of course, BLs were constantly playing on the theme of the ancient Greeks and their reported propensity for homosexual liaisons, some of which, presumably, were between older men and younger boys. Floyd's interest in the supposed "history" of boy lovers had some context.

James heard about NAMBLA over twenty years ago, he said, but it took him "nearly twenty years to join." He spoke cautiously and was one of the few not to mention interacting with other BLs as a motivating factor for attending the conference. His reason was quite pragmatic. He was "attending this conference to have an impact in the organization." Then, he warned the attendees, that it is "healthy to be fearful of society and reticent to be too open about yourselves to people you don't know. I'm sure prisons are full of people that didn't intend to get there." I, of course, hoped a few more ended up that way.

When it was my turn to speak, there was

no need for tears this year. I was accepted and as comfortable in this setting as my mission and training could make me. I said I came for the "fellowship" and, referencing Chris's earlier remarks, I joked I was "in charge of NAMBLA's transnational prostitution ring." Before I could complete the thought, Peter pounced, immediately chastising me. Bob from Atlanta interrupted Peter and said, "I'm Robert and I'm in charge."

The interchange drew laughs, but Peter continued: "The problem is, I don't think there are any bugs here, but that's exactly the sort of thing that's hostile to us. . . . It's not a good idea to say things in jest." Peter was right on both counts. Even things said in jest might be taken literally, and there were definitely "bugs." I would be wearing one throughout the conference.

Bob, the attorney, wrapped up the introductions. "I'm Bob and I live in Atlanta. I was born in New York, but I live in Atlanta now. . . . I'd like to see the *Bulletin* have fewer pictures of eight-year-olds and more pictures of fifteen-year-olds."

That drew a chorus of "boos" from some of the others.

"Everybody has his own tastes, you know," Bob said. And then he returned to the oft-stated theme of most BLs:

I love the *Bulletin.* I love the pictures. I'm sorry that we can't have sexier pictures like we used to have. I like to come here just to hang around with other boy lovers, just to juice up my engines. I was out of the closet thirty years ago, and I started getting more comfortable with liking boys about twenty or twenty-five years ago.

Following the introductions and Peter's safety lecture, we began a discussion to determine the agenda. The conference was to last two days, and most of the morning session would be taken up discussing what we would be discussing.

Had I really been interested in advancing the stated goals of this association, I would have been frustrated by its lack of organization. Since my interests lay strictly in the criminal conduct of its members, however, I merely sat there attempting to look engaged.

The air was thick with ideas being batted around with no apparent rhyme or reason. Dick Stutsman wanted to know, "What are the ways to change society's opinions?" His question was never addressed.

Chris, my socialist comrade, advanced the

idea of regional meetings for those of us who attended conferences, to handle the neglected "social aspects."

Others threw out other notions, but no one was taking notes, and Peter was having trouble keeping the discussion flowing smoothly. When James brought up Robert's Rules of Order and suggested the "meetings could be structured in such a way to more easily obtain the goals of the conference," he was drafted to chair the proceedings.

It was James's first conference and within an hour he held the gavel: a born leader. Sam assumed the role of secretary and began taking notes. To everyone's relief, James and Sam quickly got the meeting on track.

Tim observed that the organization was being held together by two or three people and that more leaders were needed.

I thought to myself, *Same song, four hundredth verse.*

25
CRIMINAL ADMISSIONS

The first break would be a most welcome respite. The discussion during the session was of little value for my mission, and I hoped break time conversations would lead me in the right direction. Just before the break, I realized the recording time on my concealed camera had expired. Saying I needed to take some of my medication, I excused myself from the meeting and hobbled to my room. I took off the peephole camera strapped to my chest and replaced it with a digital audio recorder that was easier to conceal.

David Mayer and I sat at poolside. Within seconds, he complained about the pace and structure of the meeting. I rolled my eyes and agreed. I told him it was similar to last year. "That's why I just came for the fellowship." Todd joined us. The conversation began angling in promising directions.

David: I agree. I mean, I would just come to socialize. . . . This is worthless. Bob [the Atlanta attorney] is right. I'd have a much better day walking the beach looking at boys with a couple of you . . . going, "Yum, yum cute . . . yum, yum cute," letting my imagination go.

Todd: Do politics a little bit and celebrate what we love the rest of the time!

I brought up the issue of travel with Todd, but before he could answer, David said that he, Todd, and Paul Zipszer talked about travel last night after I went to bed.

David: Where's the travel bureau? When we were talking about it last night, we know that someone knows. So, give us that information. . . . I don't know who's lying to who. . . . They're lying to themselves. Like, "This is all political, this is all to change society . . ." Bullshit. Like, bring on the boys!

Throughout this conversation, David kept referring to Paul Zipszer as "the guy with all the muscles." Twice he said, "I gotta play with his chest!" The exchange was humorous, but in a few seconds, as David was talking, he stood up, circled around me, and began rubbing my chest, demonstrating

326

what he desired to do to Paul. Had I still been wearing the camera, he would have easily found the device. It might have been a challenge to explain the wires running up my stomach, my multiple "nipples," and a pinhole camera taped to the front of my ribcage. It's unfair to say I dodged anything like a real bullet, but the discovery would have ended the investigation much sooner than anyone in the FBI desired.

Todd said he traveled a lot but was unsuccessful at finding boys. "I have good 'gaydar' for many adults who are gay, or at least I think I do, but for kids, I just don't." I had to conceal a smile; apparently, his gaydar wasn't working as well as he thought.

A few moments later, I continued the conversation about travel just as Dick Stutsman joined us poolside. Trying to elicit criminal admissions, I said Jeff Devore had mentioned a place in Mexico and I also heard about a place in Costa Rica. Todd immediately said he remembered Jeff, "the minister." And David said he was aware of a place in Costa Rica called Big Ruby's and, since American Airlines flew there, he could get "twenty-four passes a year."

Even as Jeff's name was leaving my lips, I realized that in my haste to discuss travel, I made a major undercover blunder: I lied in such a way that I could be caught. Undercover agents lie often and lie well, but this was not a good lie, since my story could be checked out if one of my hearers was so inclined. I mentioned Jeff's name, and to my knowledge, Jeff never traveled to Mexico. Certainly, he had not told me about any such venue. Todd knew Jeff and might have even had a contact number for him.

As all these thoughts ran through my head, I realized I should have corrected myself on the spot, or at least hedged, saying I thought it was Jeff who had told me. The moment passed, though, and I decided to let it ride. Interestingly, Jeff's name never came up again. No one caught me in the lie or the subsequent inconsistency. As the investigation progressed, I was able to attribute all my travel details to an imaginary friend. Another bullet dodged, even if it was one of my own making.

When Dick joined the conversation, I asked him if he traveled. He told us of the only two trips he ever made overseas in nauseating detail.

Well, I found . . . a so-called House of Boys in Amsterdam, not too far from the train station. There's just a door on the street. It actually said "House of Boys" on the door. You ring the doorbell. Someone — a boy — comes in. You go upstairs and it's a little bar with two or three bedrooms and a lounge.

Dick then continued the torture by detailing another success.

There was one, in what country was that? It was a brown-skin country. Turkey or something . . . yeah, Turkey. I think he was around eleven. Then there was someone in France. But they were peak experiences. . . . I gave my partners as much pleasure as I had. . . . Sure, they're supposed to pretend, but I really truly think this kid had never had his armpits licked, and for some reason, I suddenly thought this would be a great thing to do. You know, it turned me on, but it turned him on, too. Anyway, I had success!

David shared his experiences on the gay beaches of Mexico and in Thailand, a topic he would repeat several times during the investigation. He said he "virtually never" did anything in the United States.

The break-time conversation was a gold mine of admissions, but was unfortunately interrupted by Peter's call to return to the matters at hand. Groaning inwardly, I raised myself off the lounge chair and headed inside with the others.

The Saturday afternoon session was no more thrilling than the morning. James, the newly anointed moderator, noted that Chris did a lot of "thoughtful research and was a repository of information about political, legal, and social events related to us in the press." David looked at me and rolled his eyes and I had to agree with his assessment. I never claimed to be the brightest bulb on the tree, but I'm not sure I was ever able to follow any line of reasoning Chris proffered. If he was the best hope for the next socialist uprising, I was putting my money on capitalism.

At one point during the discussion, Chris enlightened us with the fact that Israeli intelligence determined Yasser Arafat was having sex with the Palestinian boys who threw rocks at Israeli tanks. Peter, who is Jewish, smiled. "Oh, is that so? Now I'm changing my mind about him."

Peter spoke of commissioning a former member who was a talented cartoonist to depict the boy-lover struggle in an art form readily understood by millions. Peter wanted the cartoon, consisting of several panels, to depict how society was led to hate Jews, blacks, gays, and BLs. Yet society had been proven wrong, he said; many great people from these groups contributed so much to the world. Peter wanted the final panel of the cartoon to show NAMBLA and what contributions its members made. He never actually filled us in on the identities of the great, influential members of NAMBLA and their world-changing contributions. I guess we'll have to wait for the cartoon.

James suggested the theme of this conference should be reenergizing the membership and getting more involvement from those in attendance. From my perspective, he had a point: three or four people were doing 95 percent of the work. Peter Herman, aka Peter Melzer, age sixty-five, served in a CEO-like capacity. Floyd, age sixty-eight, was the "filter and censor" for the NAMBLA Web site and, along with Joe P. from California, performed most of the editorial duties for the *Bulletin.* The situation was ripe for an ambitious undercover agent to assume management responsibilities and wreak havoc on the organization. But, as I said often and under oath, the scope of our mission was to identify the criminal activities of those networking at the NAMBLA conference, not to target the organization as such. It was for this reason I kept my involvement at a minimum.

Peter worked hard to garner support and encourage attendees to contribute beyond the payment of the annual dues, but most of his lobbying efforts were wasted. I almost felt sorry for him as he floated projects and ideas and continually failed to find takers. Peter admitted that last year his goal was to issue a press release about NAMBLA's twenty-fifth anniversary, an opportunity to let the world know NAMBLA was alive and well. Celebrating twenty-five years as a "liberation" movement was an achievement worthy of attention, he said. But the press release never materialized. As the discussion languished, Peter asked James to write an article for the *Bulletin* about seeking more involvement from the membership. James reluctantly said he would get with Sam to discuss it. The next two issues of the *Bulletin* failed to sound the call. The organization was big on plans and poor on follow-through — perhaps because its members were primarily focused on networking and justifying their sexual agendas.

During an afternoon break Bob, the Atlanta attorney, lashed out at the gay community and its supposed hypocrisy.

They don't like us. They don't want our publications even to exist. They don't want to even afford us the opportunity to speak out in discourse in an attempt to convince people. . . . We were part of the gay liberation movement . . . a different flavor of gay. . . . The irony is that they tried to sweep us off the table to make one closer to the center more palatable and they haven't succeeded. . . . The same kind of people who will go to the Supreme Court to protect the right of the fifteen-year-old girl to abort her fetus without having to tell her parents don't want to allow that fifteen-year-old to choose her own sex partner. . . . We support the right of kids to have self-determination. You want to choose the partner of the same sex, that's great. You want to choose a partner in the same grade, that's great. All of a sudden, you want to choose a partner who's twice your age — can't have it!

Bob was on a roll and somehow the issue of consent was broached. Needless to say, he had an opinion.

There's a lot of boys and girls over the years who said yes at the time, and who

333

claim to have been molested sometime later, when it was found out. . . . I think the question is really whether there was consent. . . . I still say if they want to put an age off-limits, let them put it off-limits . . . let it be like you sold alcohol to an underage person. . . . The kid is punished for going after the booze and the cigarette. The merchant is punished for giving it to him, but there's no suggestion that there wasn't consent.

During a break in which Bob was pontificating on the life of the BL, I spoke briefly with Steve Irvin, a tall, thin special education teacher in his mid-forties, from Pittsburgh. Steve said he attended the 1988 conference in Baltimore. He met Bob Rhodes there and they went down to Santo Domingo for a week and "had a great time." Steve admitted that one of the reasons he came this year was because he wanted to travel again, and hoped he would meet someone who could provide information on where to go and where to stay. I suggested Steve check with David, since "he's thinking about trying to put something together in Costa Rica . . . a less restricted environment down there." In our brief conversation, Steve said his age of preference was "eleven or twelve."

Peter set up a table with various publications available through NAMBLA. During the afternoon break, I purchased two: *Diary of a Pedophile* by D. J. Davis and a magazine called *Made in the USA*. The magazine had disturbing photos of boys in various poses, displaying full-frontal nudity. I bought it, hoping its distribution by Peter would be a violation of child porn laws. Later, however, one of our analysts reviewed the magazine and declared the pictures "erotica," but not federally prosecutable images rising to the level of child pornography under the current state of the law. I still think most Americans would find it pornographic.

26
JUST BECAUSE YOU'RE PARANOID DOESN'T MEAN I'M NOT OUT TO GET YOU

Much of the remainder of the day's discussion revolved in some way around NAMBLA members' frustrations and fears — frustrations over the organization's lack of social cohesiveness and opportunities, and fears about being infiltrated or otherwise sanctioned by the authorities or society at large.

Following the break, Peter spoke of the holiday card program and asked that attendees volunteer to send cards for the coming holiday season. Almost everyone agreed to participate except John, the "gaythiest." His reasoning made sense: a twice-convicted sex offender cannot afford to have his name on any prison mailing list, especially one linking him to other convicted sex offenders. Peter and others tried to reassure him no one had ever been "outed" for participating in the program. But John's concerns went deeper than the potential social stigma, apparently. Frustrated, Peter finally asked James to move on to the next item on the agenda.

James suggested taking a page from other liberation movements by developing a theme and sticking with it throughout the entire conference. I'm sure several assented to this noble idea, but my BL buddies had a persistent habit of straying off the beaten path into various philosophical, social, and cultural thickets. I'm certain that for the guys who really just wanted to talk about having sex with boys, it was especially maddening.

This conflicting need may have been what prompted Chris, the resident philosopher, to launch into a monologue about some information he turned up about the sexual practices of certain primates that somehow was supposed to lend credibility to the BL lifestyle. James, who previously referenced his respect for the odd ideas bouncing around in Chris's fuzzy head, suggested that such "research" could be used to refute the findings of such anti-BL groups as the American Family Council. I'm surprised Peter didn't call for a committee to draft a pamphlet on the topic. After all, monkey sex seems like a great justification for the BL's proclivities.

Some discussion began about reviving the regional meetings. The topic would be explored on Sunday as an actual agenda item, but the issue ignited a great deal of discussion on Saturday as well.

Chris advocated social support groups at some sort of regional level. He complained, "We talk at these national meetings about everything but sex. I mean everything but sex." Chris wanted to start the regional support groups with "people we have here or people from last year. Not people I don't know."

Quickly, however, the theme of unsuccessful experiences in the past arose. Such negative events generated apprehension in some longtime members. They cautioned that each chapter would have to have a leader who could be counted on to screen the list of invitees to the regional chapter meetings.

David R. Busby said, "Peter can vouch for everyone here," but with local chapters we would have to count on the local leader to be an extension of Peter Herman. "Peter has a handle on who's here," he said, and the chapter president would then have to have a handle on who was there. Peter, David, and the others would eventually learn, however, that Peter's screening process wasn't as foolproof as they thought.

Peter said that years ago people came to the conferences whom NAMBLA knew little about. He advocated learning more about all members, including where they lived and where they worked. "We should know everything about you."

"I agree," I shouted. Hey, I had to maintain my camouflage, right? Besides, it well suited my fine sense of irony.

Peter believed anyone who was going to be an activist should agree to that kind of scrutiny.

We're not worried about police and such because at none of these meetings do we do anything illegal, and they would be wasting their time coming here. What we're worried about is people who do stupid things, and there are people with emotional problems that can, you know, do stupid things and betray everything.

I also didn't miss Peter's oblique reference to "people who do stupid things" — people like Jeffrey Curley's murderers.

Chris even suggested patting down attendees, like the government does at the airport. This was actually the most practical thing I remember hearing him say.

Peter said he was "upset by Paul [Zipszer]

bringing a friend [Brian]. We don't know who that guy is. I hope you are aware of that. . . . Paul brought a friend, and that person was not one of us. . . . Even if he knows somebody for twenty years and is totally confident, you never know."

I couldn't have agreed more.

James added, "This is why we don't have chapters today and it needs to be thought through if it's going to happen at all."

Peter interrupted, saying he wasn't dismissing the idea of regional meetings; he just wanted to insure that anyone invited to a regional meeting was carefully screened. Peter considered participation in the holiday card program, where a member had to have a return address, as a critical component. From there, Peter believed in a "slow buildup," lessening the vulnerability of the organization to an infiltrator. Once again, my credentials were passing muster with the "brains" of the outfit; I was golden, as far as Peter Herman was concerned.

Apparently, though, my reputation as an upstanding BL didn't give me carte blanche. When I suggested a regional social meeting limited to those who had been members for several years, Peter said prior to doing that "we must set up protocols." As David R. Busby pointed out, even with rules in place, problems could occur.

James waxed passionate.

This is an organization with its own
peculiar difficulties, and setting up
regional things of any kind is going to
be difficult . . . because, like Chris was
saying, we talk about the business of
philosophy and politics, but we don't
talk about sex. This organization doesn't
exist to be a network of child molesters;
that's not why we're together. And that's
why people would want to take this
organization down, for that very reason.

Clearly, James's caution had not been
diminished by the allure of warm-and-fuzzy
regional gatherings where pedophiles could
just be themselves.

Peter recommended that David R. Busby
and James meet to set up a protocol and
guidelines for establishing regional groups.
Once it was set in place, then Peter would
set up groups in Southern California and
the Chicago area. Peter asked me if that was
acceptable. As the facilitator of a Southern
California regional chapter, I would have
had a tremendous opportunity to gather
information on the membership in that part
of the country and a potential means to

destroy the organization . . . but that was not my mission. Had it been, we should have put the investigation of the various members on hold and waited for the implementation of the regional chapters. But there was never any thought to slowing down our investigation — the FBI was interested in catching criminals, not in social engineering.

As a housekeeping matter before breaking for the day, Peter warned us management knew we were NAMBLA; we were not allowed to have boys in the room. Even at a hotel that catered to the gay trade, it seemed, NAMBLA's reputation preceded it.

After the Saturday session was over, several of us waited in the sitting area of our "chateau" as we determined dinner plans for the evening. David, Peter, James, and Tim joined me for casual conversation.

Discussing the membership rolls, Peter said NAMBLA had a mailing list of 6,000 and at one time had about 1,200 members. He put the current membership numbers at approximately 250, a reduction of approximately 100 since the New York conference. It would have been reasonable to attribute the declining numbers to the Jeffrey Curley lawsuit, but Peter refused to minimize the actual number of boy lovers. He believed the numbers were growing and would continue to grow in an "enlightened society."

I brought up the topic of the Jeffrey Curley wrongful-death lawsuit. Peter said, "The thing is, I sleep comfortably at night when I think about it. . . . You know, I mean, working your whole life and then having everything you work for pulled out from under you . . ."

I asked him whether the two who killed the ten-year-old were NAMBLA members. Peter seemed confused about the facts.

[They were] members in the sense that they sent in thirty-five bucks. The one who actually killed the kid wasn't a member. We believe that the guy who was . . . the member was a real decent person who somehow got, you know, hooked up with this strange guy. . . . [Charles Jaynes, the NAMBLA member] was kind of fat, a mulatto, you know, sort of black and white, you know . . . and somehow got in with this idiot.

It had perhaps slipped Peter's mind that, by all accounts, Jaynes, the NAMBLA member, sat on ten-year-old Jeffrey Curley, shoved a gasoline-soaked rag into his mouth, killed the child, sexually assaulted the deceased youngster, stuffed the dead body into a garbage can, poured lime in the can to speed up the decomposition, then dumped the body over a bridge into the river. Yet, according to one of the most prominent leaders of NAMBLA, he was "a real decent guy."

About this time, we made our way to the parking lot, waiting for everyone to assemble. James, the local resident, was offering suggestions for where we could go.

Someone noticed an older man, poorly dressed, sitting on a bench near the pool, and questioned whether he was part of our group. He wasn't, but someone else suggested he might be on surveillance and joked that he was talking into his wristwatch. I said, "It could be; it's always the one you least suspect."

After some abortive discussion and very little initiative demonstrated by anyone, Coconut Grove won by default as our dinner destination.

We divided up into the several cars available. At this point, I was glad my slick, boy-magnet Dodge Caravan was part of the transportation inventory. I would not have been able to fit David Mayer, Todd Calvin,

David R. Busby, and Sam from Miami in the Mustang I reserved and failed to get.

Sam from Miami rode shotgun, as I followed Paul Zipszer and his friend Brian, who were in a Corvette. We headed south on Route 1 toward the Miami suburb of Coconut Grove, described as the "oldest and most important settlement in Florida."

27
SIX-PACK ABS
AND A KEY OF COKE

Riding along in the Caravan behind Paul and Brian in their Corvette, I kept thinking about that morning's conversation, and David's wish to play with Paul's muscular chest. Again, I was relieved I'd removed the camera before David's impromptu fondling.

Paul reminded me of another fine physical specimen from my earlier FBI days. His name was Eric, and he occasioned one of the more humorous moments I was able to provide for my surveillance team.

Eric was truly chiseled; he had rippling abs, bulging biceps and pecs — and a preference for other men. He was a model and actor, appearing in everything from body-building magazines to *Vanity Fair.* The women in our office, not knowing of his sexual orientation, used to swoon when his picture was passed around during the course of our investigation.

He became of interest to the FBI for

reasons that ultimately had little to do with the outcome of the investigation: he purchased a restaurant from a guy I'd been watching for a while, a suspected member of the Sicilian Mafia. When Eric purchased the property, we assumed he had mob ties as well, though any such relationship would soon prove to be tenuous, at best. Through an informant, however, I learned Eric was selling coke, so I decided to keep him on my radar screen.

Not that selling coke made Eric unique: in the L.A. of the early '90s, providing cocaine for recreational users was a growth industry. Still, I convinced my supervisor to let me take a run at Eric. This would be my first undercover assignment since the parking lot shooting incident less than a year earlier, and it was important for me to prove to myself I could still operate in a UC setting.

Like the women in the office, I didn't know about Eric's sexual preference until I had already sold the investigation to my supervisor and couldn't back out. Not that I'm homophobic, but I admit to being a bit anxious when the informant, after telling me Eric was gay, further explained that the former restaurant was now a gay nightclub featuring male exotic dancers. One night each week was designated as "underwear night," when the usual ten-dollar cover charge was halved for anyone who showed up in his skivvies. Knowing the Bureau's penchant for economy, I was having uncomfortable visions of evenings spent at Eric's club wearing nothing but my BVDs. I needed a good cover story.

Fortunately, I had the use of a limo, and the informant agreed to introduce me as his straight friend who had no place to hang out after dropping off his Hollywood clients for their outings. I really didn't mind being at Eric's under this assumption, and the scenario worked well, especially since "my clients liked to party," and I was able to tell Eric I often supplied their cocaine needs.

Eric and I hit it off. I introduced another undercover police officer who occasionally accompanied me to the nightclub. Often, I just went by myself for a few hours until it was time to pick up "my client." The nightclub was doing well, by all appearances. The male exotic dancers drew large crowds and seemed to enjoy entertaining. Eric was open about his tastes and experiences . . . and his drug dealings. It wasn't long before we were negotiating for a one-kilo purchase: a thousand grams of nose candy, so popular with the Hollywood types in those days.

Eric set up the first deal for late in the evening on Super Bowl Sunday, not a date that pleased my surveillance team, but they agreed to cover me. The negotiated price was seventeen thousand dollars. We had permission from HQ to let the money walk. Our purpose was to use this kilo buy to set up a much larger purchase, where we would seize a sizeable quantity of drugs plus Eric's assets. Since the buy money came from the federal drug Superfund, there was always a sense of satisfaction, knowing that other drug dealers were paying for us to investigate their colleagues.

That evening I prepared for the deal. I recorded the serial numbers of each bill that would be used to purchase the cocaine, strapped on a recorder and a transmitter, and stuffed the $17,000 down the front of my pants.

The sun had already set as I marched into the nightclub prepared to do business. Eric greeted me immediately and escorted me over to a table near the dancers. He seated me with my back to the front door. Playing the ever-cautious crook, I stood up and grabbed a seat that put my back to the wall and allowed me to see the front door. Eric looked at me quizzically. Before he could ask the question, I said, "I've got $17,000 strapped to my privates and I wanna see that front door. If someone doesn't come struttin' in here like Zorro, the Gay Blade, then I know they're a cop. I wanna protect my back."

Without even hesitating, Eric smiled and said, "We noticed that bulge in your pants when you walked in and the only thing you have to protect is your ass."

I learned later that evening that when the surveillance team heard that, they practically fell out of their cars laughing. Most of the evening's subsequent radio traffic involved speculation on how far they should let me go before bailing me out. From then on, I always seemed to get Cheshire cat grins from members of the surveillance team.

In typical drug-dealer fashion, Eric's supplier couldn't deliver that evening, but the deal wasn't dead yet. We agreed to postpone the transaction to later in the week.

Within a few days we were back in business. I picked up Eric in the limo and he directed me to his supplier, who lived in Hollywood, just off Sunset Boulevard. On the way, Eric lifted his shirt and showed me not only his ripped six-pack abs but a 9 millimeter. My cover boy/muscleman was taking this business seriously. Use of a firearm in a drug transaction upped the ante on sentencing, but it also ratcheted up the tension. At least he showed me the weapon; if something started to hit the fan, I knew where to direct my attention.

Eric surprised me when he took me directly to his supplier. Most middlemen aren't that accommodating because it means they could get cut out of the next deal. Apparently, Eric had full confidence in me and his supplier. We hiked up the steps to the supplier's condo and entered.

Eric introduced me to Craig, who was short and thin — too thin. The living room was well decorated, but my eyes were immediately drawn to a man covered with blankets, asleep on the couch. Next to the sleeping man was a coffee table crowded with bottles of medication. Craig whispered throughout our conversation. His friend, he explained, was dying of AIDS. Craig was also infected and was using the profits from his cocaine sales to pay for all kinds of experimental medications. Craig had buried more than fifty friends over the last several years, he said, and his friend would be dead within a few weeks. As we sat at the dining room table counting out the $17,000 and finalizing our negotiations, his friend lay dying. I had trouble concentrating on the business at hand.

After Craig counted the money, he made a phone call. It turned out Craig wasn't the source, but a conduit for a Mexican supplier. Shortly after the call, Caesar arrived with the kilo of white powder. Through some quick maneuvers, I was able to meet Caesar as well. The conspiracy was growing.

We consummated the transaction without a hitch and everyone was satisfied with the completed sale. The product wasn't the highest quality I had ever purchased, but the law is more concerned with quantity than quality. It weighed out at a thousand grams, roughly 2.2 pounds, and that's all that concerned the prosecutors. Had I been a real coke dealer, I might have complained, but I could plausibly argue that I could "step on the key a couple of times" and make a sizeable profit.

As Eric and I resumed our negotiations for a larger transaction, the figure of fifty kilos continued to arise. Eric claimed he was capable of delivering that amount and we were hoping he could produce. But as we talked, Eric kept delaying and reducing the amount. It was obvious Craig and Caesar were either uncomfortable or unable to produce such quantity. We eventually settled on five kilos, small by *Miami Vice* standards.

I picked the day this time. I don't think Eric, Craig, or Caesar ever realized that Wednesday, the day my "money man" would be ready, was actually April Fools' Day. There was usually a method to my madness.

Thanks to my stupidity, though, it almost never happened. Cell phones were coming into vogue and not everyone had one. Today, school children and grandmothers carry one, but it wasn't the must-have item in the early '90s, even for a drug dealer. The day of the buy, however, I was given a recently seized cell phone to use. Since rain was in the forecast, we figured the cell phone was better than standing in a down-pour while using a pay phone, should I need to make a call. None of our other targets carried one, so it was somewhat of a novelty. I was given a thirty-second primer on how to use the brick-sized phone. I'm not a tech wizard, but figured I could handle a phone. How difficult could it be?

Once again, the time for the deal came and went — no drugs. I was dealing directly with Eric and kept pressing him to put it together. Eric laid the blame on Craig, who, according to Eric, was having trouble connecting with Caesar. It was frustrating. I had a number of agents tied up, and as the sun was setting, they were getting a little annoyed. Besides, the rain made for less-than-ideal conditions to sit in a car while waiting for the go sign. For those in the surveillance van outside Eric's Wilshire-area residence, it was especially uncomfortable.

Finally, I had waited long enough. I called Eric and ranted at his ineffectiveness. I was irritated and let him know it. In frustration, he told me to call Craig directly and gave me Craig's number. Thinking Eric had hung up, I immediately dialed Craig. I was recording the call and put a quick preamble on it, giving the date and time and announcing I was calling Craig at the number Eric provided.

What I didn't realize was that I had forgotten to push the end button on the phone. Eric was still on the line and heard my abbreviated preamble. He immediately called my informant.

I spoke with Craig, who explained the delay and promised the coke would arrive within the hour. As soon as I hung up the phone, the informant called. "You blew it," he said. "It's over. Eric thinks you're a cop. He heard what you said before you called Craig."

The informant was right: I did blow it. My patience had worn thin, and I stepped out of character without thinking. To recover, I went on the offensive. I turned on the recorder and immediately called Eric. Practically screaming at him, I asked what the problem was. He repeated verbatim exactly what he heard me say. I then said, "What time is it?" He told me the time. I said, "Yeah, and a few minutes ago I did exactly what you said. I looked at my watch and was griping about the time and repeated the number as I dialed Craig. Just like you told me!" Then I told him I spoke with Craig, and the coke would be delivered within the hour. If he wanted out, then he should step out now, I told him, because once I did the deal with Craig, I wasn't cutting him in for a piece. The offensive strategy worked and greed overcame common sense, as it does so often. Eric invited me over to his place to wait for the cocaine. I breathed a long sigh of relief.

When Eric answered the door, paranoia suddenly consumed him. He pointed to a van parked in front of his residence most of the day. He still contemplated calling off the deal. His instincts were correct but he had the wrong van; ours was parked just up the street, capturing in a photo him referencing the suspicious, but innocent, vehicle.

Shortly after I got over to Eric's, Craig arrived. Caesar came a short time later with the five keys I ordered. I did a quick examination of the product and was satisfied. I told the three the money was in my car and left Eric's, heading toward the sidewalk. Once outside the residence, I gave the sign and the arrest team moved in.

They quickly took Craig and Caesar into custody and seized the five kilos. Eric decided to play desperado and rushed into his bedroom, concealing himself behind his bed with his 9 millimeter locked and loaded. But within a few minutes, he came to his senses and surrendered.

We worked through the night and into the next day, arresting two others who supplied Caesar. All five eventually pleaded guilty in federal court to various narcotics conspiracy counts.

Following the Corvette out to Coconut Grove, I wondered if Paul Zipszer ever owned a nightclub.

28

Predators Out
on the Town

Sam from Miami, who had been a NAM-BLA member since the early eighties, had debilitating arthritis and walked with a cane. A Navy veteran from World War II, he was a retired schoolteacher. He taught in North Carolina and Florida and proudly stated that one of his students was the first female Supreme Court justice in North Carolina.

In an effort to make conversation, Sam asked, "Are you into the performing arts?" I lied and said yes. He then went on to explain that the local boys' choir was far better than even the Vienna Boys' Choir. He enjoyed watching them perform: "all those young prepubescent boys." And I thought he went for the music.

As we rode along in my rented Dodge partymobile, I wished I had brought one of the CDs I used to provide my own personal soundtrack for investigations. Even if nobody but me got to enjoy the irony, I loved nothing better than to have Elvis's "Jail-house Rock" blasting when a suspect was riding with me. I remember on at least one occasion when two subjects were literally dancing in their seats as I cranked up the King to full volume. His "Suspicious Minds" lyrics also played well: "We're caught in a trap. . . ." Of course, the late, great Johnny Cash's "Folsom Prison Blues" was another song I enjoyed humming as a target sat in my passenger seat.

Since I'm a big country and western fan, Charlie Daniels provided some great lines for my personal musical score. While targeting a Vietnamese gang member who rode in my car several times, Daniels's "Still in Saigon" was frequently on my stereo. For one target I often cued Daniels's song "Uneasy Rider" to a particular line. Every time the subject entered my car and I turned on the engine, the first line he heard was, "He's an undercover agent for the FBI." My favorite accompaniment, though, was during the purchase of two kilograms of high-quality crystal methamphetamine, when Harold Melvin and the Blue Notes softly serenaded us with "If you don't know me by now. . . ."

Probably my best hint was actually a Christmas card picture, which went to my

NAMBLA correspondents. The photograph showed me, "Robert from California," seated in a chair with a blanket across my lap. I was smiling at the camera, sending out holiday greetings to all my pedophile buddies. When I showed the picture to my FBI colleagues, they roared with laughter.

The blanket had an emblem in the center, folded in half across my lap: the FBI seal. But because it was folded in half, or maybe because I was so handsome, none of my NAMBLA pals ever realized I was flashing my government credentials at them in my Christmas card photo.

I once joked with a prosecutor that I gave clues to my true identity in nearly every meeting with a target. I'm confident that had the higher-ups in Washington or the shrinks who evaluated me every six months learned of my flirtations with discovery, they would have pulled me from the assignment or at the very least strongly counseled me toward a wiser path. I don't know, I guess it was a combination of ego and my constant search for the next adrenaline rush. I wanted to make the job a little harder, maybe — increase the "degree of difficulty," just to see if I could still pull it off. No doubt, I'd be an analyst's dream — grist for several articles in some headshrinker journal.

We arrived at Coconut Grove, parked in a lot several blocks from the center of town, and made our way to the preplanned meeting spot, the Coco Walk Mall. It was a clear night and the warm breeze blowing off the Atlantic made for a perfect evening.

The streets were crowded with the beautiful people of South Florida. As we gathered near the mall, I was faced with one of the tougher aspects of this assignment from an undercover perspective. I am an unabashedly heterosexual male — happily and faithfully married for many years, but nonetheless a healthy heterosexual. The women parading up and down Grand Avenue were gorgeous! Or, at least, I think they were. Many appeared to be celebrating the unusually warm evening by wearing provocative clothing designed more for a beach volleyball tournament. It was a major chore to keep from staring. It took every bit of discipline I learned in the Marine Corps to keep my eyes front and center, maintaining eye contact with whatever boy lover friend was attempting to engage me in conversation.

As we waited for the others, David Mayer and David R. Busby engaged in their own version of *The Dating Game.* Two preteen boys crossed our paths and the men immediately chose their imaginary dates for the evening. "Do you like solids or stripes?" The choice was based upon the shirts the boys were wearing. The game went on throughout the night. As one of the BLs spotted a youngster, the call would go out: "Oh, look at the kid in the number thirty-two jersey!" "Look, look, the striped shirt at three o'clock." They were like high school sophomores sneaking a peek at cheerleader tryouts.

In between the voyeurism, other topics included David R. Busby's discourse on an area resident who was caught in an online sting operation. He also spoke about Sam Lindblad being caught in some type of undercover snare.

With "Jailhouse Rock" racketing inside my head, I suggested that if I hosted next year's conference I would like to invite an FBI agent to speak to the group about how the Bureau captures online predators. I said we should all dress up like Boy Scout leaders and convince the agent we have the boys' best interests at heart. I also suggested we each bring a prosecutable image of child pornography with us and as soon as the FBI agent turned his head we would swap it right under his nose. My suggestion drew a big laugh, but Todd agreed we could learn a lot with such a presentation by the Bureau.

In typical NAMBLA fashion, our gathering — even for a meal — featured a debate. No one exercised any type of decisive leadership in selecting a restaurant. I nominated Hooters, reasoning that no law enforcement official would ever look for a gathering of BLs there. No one seemed enthusiastic about my choice or my logic.

David Mayer finally suggested that Todd, David R. Busby, and I join him at Johnny Rockets, across the street, while the others found another eating establishment inside the mall. I concurred, viewing this as another opportunity to discuss sex tourism, a prosecutable offense, with those who had already expressed interest in it. As I have mentioned before, had I been targeting the organization as such, or had my mission been to disrupt NAMBLA, it would have made more sense to join Peter, Floyd, and Chris — all steering committee members — for dinner. Instead, criminal prosecution of the members, not the dismantling of the organization, was the goal. If the dismantling or disruption came about because of the criminal prosecution, it would be an added bonus, but that was not my assignment.

The four of us made our way across the

street and found an outdoor table on the sidewalk. Johnny Rockets is a fifties-style diner. Bobby-soxer waitresses, jukeboxes, chrome countertops, and red vinyl counter stools created a *Happy Days* atmosphere. We ordered as my tablemates drooled — but they were looking at a different menu.

As with the Times Square Toys "R" Us visit the previous year, Johnny Rockets provided the eye candy my BL friends desired. David R. Busby seemed to always be the first to point out a viewing target. Heads quickly turned. It was difficult not to react to their leering; I very much wanted to reach across the table and strangle whichever of the three was commenting on each boy who passed by our table.

Finally, though, when David R. Busby announced he had a foot fetish, and even provided a Web site address that featured pictures of little boys' feet, I had to excuse myself from the table. I did not know his criminal history; I didn't even know if his name was, in fact, David R. Busby. But what I did know was he was a sexual predator, a boy lover who was fixated only on prepubescent boys as his sexual object of choice. I could guarantee he offended in the past, and that he would offend again.

After I returned, Busby treated us to a magic trick he used to entertain boys he was grooming. Taking a plastic straw and folding it in a prescribed manner, he then snapped it, causing a loud pop, just the type of tactic that would capture the interest of his preferred quarry.

Todd renewed an earlier conversation about gaydar, a topic of a recent *20/20* broadcast. Todd said they proved it existed. Both David Mayer and Todd said they had "nearly 100 percent gaydar in the United States" but admitted that outside the U.S. it was a more difficult assessment because of cultural differences. David, with advanced degrees in social work and psychology, said that he had also been observing the body language of those attending the conference and had drawn some interesting conclusions.

That comment caught my attention: had he made observations that might allow him to expose me? My apparent interest, posture, and relaxed manner during the meeting times must have fooled him; he had no evaluation for me. Instead he assessed Chris, the socialist from Chicago, Mike from Cleveland, and John, the "gaythiest," as suffering from various psychological problems. I was relieved to know I passed his psychological profile.

We talked of traveling outside the U.S. for sexual gratification and exchanged e-mail addresses. David Mayer spoke of Big Ruby's and the gay beaches of Costa Rica and Mexico. He regaled us with stories of the "boy bars" of Thailand. Todd told of a near-death experience in Jamaica when he paid to have sex with an eleven-year-old boy but was unsuccessful. All these were stories they would later repeat on videotape. We all agreed a "safe haven" was our mutual goal.

The conversation also had its lighter moments, especially when David Mayer suggested that James was the heir apparent to the throne and crowned him the "future first lady." With the Mohawk hairdo, David referred to John the gaythiest as "Chief" or "Schmohawk," and Paul's friend, Brian, was given the moniker "Trixie." David's humor and Todd's warm personality at least made the table talk tolerable.

I have often told younger agents interested in undercover work that unlike many in their agent peer group, a successful undercover agent must see the "gray." The UC world is no longer black and white. I advised them to find qualities of the target with which they could identify, latch on to those qualities, and proceed. Hatred of the person or the crime may be a strong motivator, but most criminals can easily detect hatred. After all, a big part of their survival depends on being suspicious of almost everybody. For the undercover agent, hatred of the target may be difficult to conceal, but to be successful, it is necessary. I had to keep reminding myself of my own advice as I sat at the table with these pedophiles. That was why any scrap of honest amusement was a welcome relief from the almost constant revulsion I experienced when I had to listen to their fantasies about the boys around us.

I knew at some point my recorder would run out of time, but I wasn't sure when that moment would come. I had no way of reviewing the recordings while at the conference, so I only hoped I could get my targets to rehash their experiences and desires at a later date. Our comfort level with each other was high, so I had little fear of being able to induce them to recap much of our discussion sometime in the future.

Dinner concluded and we made our way across the street to the mall, joined the others, and returned to the inn. Worried I was running out of recording time since I only had one device left, once we returned I decided to head for bed, attempt to get a good night's sleep, and prepare for Sunday's meeting.

29
LEGOLAND MAKES
IT UNANIMOUS

The next morning, as I made my way to the courtyard where the continental breakfast was being served, Mike from Cleveland, who described himself as being well versed in computers, was discussing Internet safety with several members. Privacy was a concern — especially for BLs — and Mike was explaining spyware detection and other techniques for insuring that files were not accessible to inquiring law enforcement officers who might be online. Certainly, this discussion was not illegal, but it emphasized to me once again that the purpose of these meetings went beyond advocacy and age-of-consent discussions. The break-time conversations dealt more with the issues that truly concerned the membership: travel to safe havens, ways to avoid law enforcement detection, and the acquisition of underage sex objects.

I ate and ambled over to the conference

room. Tim and I spent a few minutes alone, discussing "the state of NAMBLA." He described the organization as the weakest he had seen it during his twelve-year membership. Referring to these as "dark times," and admitting the membership rolls were shrinking, he had no solution for increasing the base. Tim, who professed the most paranoia of all the attendees, wanted to increase membership, but was unwilling to even acknowledge his membership apart from those at the conference — not exactly a good prospect for becoming a NAMBLA missionary. In fact, Tim would not even acknowledge his true name. Reenergizing the membership and the organization was the same theme discussed at last year's conference, with no resolution or visible results. But unless members were willing to go public or the organization was willing to take a more public stance, how could it ever expect to increase the support base? Few members were willing to go public. Most sought to conceal their membership, as well as their proclivities — unless they were among those who shared their tastes.

John, the gaythiest, walked in, and we spoke briefly before others joined us. Short and stocky, he definitely would catch your eye if he were walking down the street.

Heavyset, in his late fifties, with his Mohawk hairstyle, earrings, shorts, and black support stockings, John had my vote for the *Bulletin* centerfold. He was a twice-convicted sex offender who went on two state-imposed vacations while living in Illinois. The first was for two years, three months, and the second was for two years, nine months. Both counted as strikes in California, and he feared a third conviction would result in life in prison. John admitted he left Illinois after being caught a third time with a juvenile. When questioned, however, the boy refused to cooperate, and John left the state as quickly as possible. He lived on the streets of Miami for a few years and then moved to San Francisco where, he said, the public assistance was more lucrative.

After the members assembled, the morning session began.

The topic of next year's conference topped the morning agenda. I offered to host the conference in San Diego. Chris offered Chicago. November in San Diego versus November in Chicago seemed like a no-brainer. In keeping with my mandate not to attempt to disrupt this vaunted organization, I argued that I was concerned about the declining membership and suggested that in order to encourage more participation we should have the next conference in whatever region had the greatest proportion of the membership. But — with touching humility, I thought — I offered that if the steering committee or the membership chose San Diego, I would be honored to host the conference.

Sam Lindblad inquired as to whether the host hotel in San Diego would know we were NAMBLA. There was some concern that, even after the fact, the hotel might co-operate with authorities if it learned NAM-BLA held their annual conference in "America's Finest City." I assured them that would not be a problem because of San Diego's openness to the gay community. Peter acknowledged that the Miami River Inn knew us to be NAMBLA. When the confer-ence was held there six years previously, it was done so under the NAMBLA banner. Sam, however, was deeply concerned that my hotel management contacts in San Diego might be "Bush supporters" who would "kowtow" to law enforcement pres-sure. Peter was not worried that any mem-bers invited to the convention would act in such a way as to draw law enforcement at-tention to the organization. He mentioned that in a meeting a few years earlier in New York, several members were talking in a manner that "made the manager uncomfortable," but Peter assured him "everything was on the up and up."

And, then, the clincher: Bob from Atlanta reminded the membership that San Diego had Legoland. With that all-important piece of intel before the voters, San Diego received a unanimous favorable vote. Democracy in action.

I'd like to say my humble act was what won the day. However, it was pretty clear the siren call of Legoland did it. Not that I was incapable of rendering the appropriate dramatic flourish when needed; obviously, my soulful, tear-drenched tell-all at the New York conference helped put me across as a true-blue, card-carrying NAMBLA stalwart, but I could play the full spectrum, even a tough guy when I had to.

I remember one especially memorable performance, when my audience was actually a Mafia leg-breaker. The beginnings of my participation in this little drama were unusual, in that I got involved with the case through one of the most hated assignments in the Bureau: complaint duty.

Complaint duty consists of assisting walk-ins and taking phone calls from those who have an issue — real or imagined — for or with the Bureau. In an average-sized Bureau office, each agent can expect to draw this duty about once a month. The problem with it is there is absolutely no prescreening process; you have to talk to any crank who ambles in off the street or picks up a phone and dials the number. As you can imagine, many of the complaints registered by these folks are spurious, at best. Nights with full moons are always the worst.

For example, every time I drew complaint duty, Joan would dial up and tell me the Russians were beaming microwaves into her apartment and burning her retinas. She forcefully and repeatedly requested I activate the "heat shield" the FBI apparently controlled; which would provide her with at least minimal protection against the attack.

Another guy, whom we dubbed "Harmonica Joe," called about as frequently as Joan and, with a booming bass voice, would announce he intended to serenade me with a harmonica solo. If I wanted a few minutes of music while logging in the other callers, I would put him on the speakerphone; Joe actually wasn't bad.

Other callers could be belligerent and abusive, often blaming the Bureau for some perceived misstep by the federal government. We were a convenient target and most phone books had our number listed on the front page. Seldom, if ever, did the callers have a complaint over which the FBI had jurisdiction, and if we did have the investigative responsibility, I usually had little knowledge of the statute governing the matter. I'm sure it was as frustrating for the caller as it was for me. I can count on one hand the number of calls that led to the opening of an investigation.

Once, though, I got that rarest of all opportunities: a complaint call that actually made sense. I had the Sunday duty and had been receiving my quota of nut calls. I was looking forward to the end of the shift when the phone rang for the umpteenth time. The caller clearly identified himself and came to the point, after apologizing for interrupting my Sunday afternoon. I liked him already.

He was a television producer who ran into some problems with a business associate on the East Coast, he told me. The associate claimed the producer owed him ninety thousand dollars, a claim the producer denied. Rather than looking to the courts for redress, the associate engaged some New Jersey mobsters to collect. The producer had just received a call informing him a collector was coming to L.A. the next day. The collector expected payment in full, he said, or Hollywood would be reading the producer's obituary in the *Los Angeles Times.*

I was liking this call more and more. I obtained as much information as I could and agreed to meet with the producer after my shift so he could fill me in on all the details. What I liked most about the producer was his refusal to be bullied; he was not going to pay and was willing to testify. That evening we worked out a scenario for the next day, and I spent most of the evening getting all my ducks in a row.

The Los Angeles FBI offices are just off the 405 freeway on Wilshire Boulevard in West Los Angeles. We are directly across the street from the Los Angeles National Cemetery, where fourteen Medal of Honor recipients are buried, and within walking distance of Westwood Village, the home of UCLA. The producer lived in nearby Westwood, and to make it even more convenient, we set up the meeting with the New Jersey mobster at a restaurant in the Village. The mobster was actually staying at a motel just a few blocks from our office and was going to walk to the restaurant.

I contacted a prosecutor from the Organized Crime Strike Force and he approved the plan, which was pretty simple. We would have two agents inside the restaurant watching our producer, who would be wearing a transmitter, capturing on tape each extortionate threat. I also asked another agent to assist me on a quick-hit undercover assignment. The agent I asked was relatively new to the office and nicknamed Hard Body: he was a former college linebacker and maintained his playing weight. He was my muscle, and I'd do all the talking. This was going to be fun!

The next day, everyone was in place. Our producer was seated in the rear of this upscale restaurant. Sitting a few tables away were two agents. Hard Body, the prosecutor, and I were a block away in a Bureau car, preparing for our respective roles.

As soon as the mob guy showed up he introduced himself as Anthony — a perfect name for a nice Italian boy. Once we knew Anthony was in the restaurant, Hard Body drove the Bureau car into the parking lot behind the restaurant. This would put us closer to the action and would allow for better reception of the transmitter. The prosecutor was in the backseat listening intently to the conversation. Once Anthony said all the magic words and we had our violation, Hard Body and I were to spring into action.

I was relaxed and looking forward to the next few minutes, sitting in the front passenger seat as Hard Body pulled into the lot. I crossed my legs, and immediately a siren started going off. Were we being arrested? Was this some kind of reverse sting? Did Hard Body commit a traffic violation as he turned into the lot?

We looked around, and then I looked down. While crossing my legs I had inadvertently hit the siren toggle for the Bureau car. All three of us burst out in laughter as I shut off the siren: "Your highly trained FBI in action . . ."

But had Anthony heard the noise? Would he have second thoughts about his extortion mission? We listened intently for a few seconds and it became obvious Anthony was oblivious to my faux pas. As we listened to the transmitted conversation, he threatened to break the producer's legs. Then he threatened to break the producer's arms. Finally, he threatened to run the producer over with a car. It was perfect. Anthony said all the right words and was burying himself deeper with each tirade. John Gotti would have been proud. Our prosecutor was more than satisfied, so Hard Body and I went to work.

We walked into the back of the restaurant and quickly found the producer. Anthony was sitting across from him. The wise guy was in his late forties, heavyset, and looked like a character out of *The Sopranos;* he had obviously done some mileage for the mob. I understood why my producer was intimidated.

I pulled up a chair and turned it around, straddling it as I positioned myself a few inches from Anthony's face. His hands were on the table, and I kept them in my peripheral vision. Hard Body stood off to the side, ready to rumble. We were both packing and weren't going to take any chances. If Anthony made any sudden moves, we were ready. Anthony was the real deal, or at least so we assumed.

"Who gave you permission to come into this town?" I asked him, looking him in the eye.

Anthony balked.

I repeated the question, only louder. "I said, who gave you permission to come into this town? We're with Pete Milano, and this man" — I indicated the producer — "is with us. Nobody, I repeat, nobody leans on him without our say-so."

Pete Milano ran the L.A. Mafia family and was the target of one of my earlier undercovers. At the time of my meeting with Anthony, Pete was in federal prison, along with fourteen of his mob associates, all as the result of our investigation. But Pete's name still carried weight in Los Angeles. It remained his town, at least from a mafioso's point of view.

Anthony made a big mistake: he looked down, showing weakness. Now, I admit Hard Body gave me some much-needed credibility. He was a heavyweight; I was a middleweight at best. At the time I was about 155 pounds, ran five miles every day, and boxed several times a week, but I was a little guy compared to Anthony and Hard Body. One-on-one, the mobster from New Jersey would have given me a tough fight. But he looked down — and I pounced.

"Who gave you permission to walk my streets? I want a name and I want it now. You never go into another man's town without permission. Where are you from?"

I kept pummeling him with questions. I was seriously getting into my role. Even Hard Body was smiling, enjoying the performance.

Anthony answered each question. Then I demanded he get his boss on the phone. We walked over to a pay phone near the restrooms, and Anthony dialed a number, spoke briefly, and handed me the phone. I repeated my questions and demands, giving the guy on the other end of the phone little time to respond. When he said he was from Fort Lee, New Jersey, I said, "Fort Lee? What's that? What am I supposed to call you — 'General'? I want your man to apologize to our guy. You guys better straighten this out now. Anthony isn't going anywhere until this is straightened out. Do you understand me?" I handed the phone back to Anthony.

We returned to the table and I demanded that Anthony apologize.

"I'm sorry I threatened to break your legs," he said to the producer.

"And . . . ?" I said.

"I'm sorry I threatened to break your arms."

"And . . . ?"

"I'm sorry I threatened to run you over with a car."

With the apology accepted, I instructed the producer to leave the table and he quickly obliged, practically running out of the restaurant.

I turned my attention to Anthony and apologized for being so hard on him, but explained that I had to show the producer I meant business, because I knew he would tell Pete. "He's an earner for us and we have to protect him. Nothing personal."

Anthony smiled with relief. He said he thought everything had been cleared through his New Jersey people and admitted he had no right to come into L.A. without permission of the boss. Then he said, "I should have known better. I just got out of the joint. I did a dime for the same thing."

Apparently, this extortion job was one of Anthony's first paying gigs since spending ten years in prison. The penal system's rehabilitation efforts obviously failed, but we were going to see he got another shot. We all started to walk out of the restaurant and Anthony invited us to join him for drinks. When I told him we still had a problem, he said, "What? We can work anything out."

I pulled out my FBI credentials and identified myself as an agent. He looked at me, closed his eyes, looked toward heaven, and said, "I am so stupid."

What could I say?

I would have loved to have been able to stage a reprise of my role as a wise guy for a few of my BL friends. I thought about how great it would be to get up in Peter Herman's face, with Hard Body looming over my shoulder, and rip him a new one. But this was a different role, and called for a different approach. If things went well, though, I could hope for a similar result.

30
AGE OF
CONSENT: ZERO

NAMBLA policy was the next item on the agenda and age of consent dominated that discussion. As an organization, NAMBLA has consistently refused to advocate a particular age of consent even though some members have called for a lowering of the age rather than its outright abolition. The position would not be modified in this conference. In fact, Peter stated that designating a specific age of consent would be "disastrous" and not result in any greater support among the general population.

Peter drew an analogy between baseball and sex. "When someone says, 'Baseball for kids,' everyone says, 'Oh yes.' But what kind of baseball is given to a four- or five-year-old? What is given must be age appropriate, or it can be very dangerous in both situations." I'm not quite sure what point Peter was trying to make, but the T-ball example was apparently an attempt to present certain sexual acts — oral sex, presumably — as more "age appropriate" than, say, anal penetration. One was okay for young boys, apparently, and the other should be reserved for later ages.

I knew from reading past issues of the *Bulletin* that age of consent was a topic being debated continually among the membership. In the May 2004 issue, "John" urged the membership not to modify its position on this issue, claiming that any modification would amount to a "dilution of our principle. Please, let us not compromise our ideals in a quest to appear more 'reasonable' or 'mainstream' to the world at large."

In an accompanying article, John quoted art historian and social activist Camille Paglia.

I fail to see what is wrong with erotic fondling with any age. I would really want to push the issue of what is wrong with anything which gives pleasure. What is wrong with it, even if it does involve fondling the genitals?

John then argued,

Even a newborn baby fresh out of his or her mother's womb instinctively and neurologically can discern the difference between a "good touch" (such as a gentle stroking) and a "bad touch" (such as a slap from the attending doctor). As the child begins to grow, parents and teachers instill in the youngster THEIR concepts of "good touch" and "bad touch" (with anything involving the genitals inevitably constituting a "bad touch"). Yet, if such contact is (as the anti-sex crowd claims) intrinsically harmful to an undeveloped or developing person, why the need to teach them these feelings? Maturity is NOT a prerequisite to physical enjoyment; in fact, judging by the uptight attitudes held by many adults in this world, it would seem the reverse is true! Perhaps this world would be a much better place if adults would perceive sexual activity in a more juvenile way!

John further stated,

The argument that older people should not pursue younger partners because the older person has an unfair psychological advantage is blatantly ridiculous. Does a man with a handsome face and muscular body cover himself up when he's around the fairer sex so as to not take advantage of his good looks? Does a woman with long blonde hair and large breasts hide under a hat and baggy clothing so as to not upstage women not so blessed with these attributes desired by most men? The idea that "all is fair in love and war" applies to intergenerational courting as well!

Finally, John concluded, "I firmly believe that there can be only one 'age of consent': zero."

I found this to be typical of NAMBLA reasoning. They would frequently start with principles of human development anyone could agree with, then at some point in the discussion, they would make an illogical leap to get on the track to their destination: justification of making sex objects of under-age children. John's argument, for example, started with what is demonstrably true: babies react differently to gentle touch versus harsh touch. However, he seems to suggest eroticized touch is in the same category as a parent's caress and shouldn't be differentiated from it in any way. Does that prove eroticized touching of children isn't detrimental to their development of healthy self-concepts as adults? I can find truckloads of child development experts who would instantly refute such a notion. And yet, in the black-is-white world of NAMBLA, John's line of reasoning is seen as valid.

Attorney Bob brought before the conference that the law should be amended so sex between an adult and a child "could be validated" by proving it was consensual. Under the current law, sex with a twelve-year-old "is criminal because consent is not an issue. . . . The law presumes rape." Bob argued it should be a "rebuttable presumption": that the charged party could prove sex was consensual on the part of the juvenile. In other words, infants who enjoy the "good touch" as defined by John's letter in the *Bulletin* would be free, under Bob's notion of the law, to engage in sex with him without the law presuming they were raped.

One member mentioned he knew of gay men who claim to have engaged in sexual experimentation at the ages of four, five, and six. It was something they sought, they said, and had no regrets. Yet, he knows of some who now claim to feel remorse for having the experience at such a young age. Others at the conference immediately challenged that position because it was believed those holding it were unduly influenced by a "moralistic society."

Some brought up anecdotal evidence they supposedly located, such as aboriginal peoples who engaged in oral sex on infants for purposes such as pacifying and soothing the boys. This, of course, was readily accepted by the attendees as valid and proper behavior in an "enlightened" society. In this manner, the discussion wandered to and fro, with no discernable action being taken and no particular resolution being passed. Everyone got a chance to have his sexual preference affirmed and validated, and NAMBLA's age-of-consent position remained unchanged.

What interested me about this agenda item was the fact that there was no discussion of efforts the organization might be planning to abolish or even modify the age-of-consent laws. The organization may "advocate repeal" of laws that "criminalize sexual relationships that are loving and fully consensual," but there was no dialogue about plans to lobby any legislator at any level of government for relief from the supposed criminalizing and repugnant statutes.

Next, the discussion returned to the previous day's hotly debated topic of regional meetings. Fear remained the central theme of this spirited exchange — fear of infiltration and fear that rogue individuals within the group might bring unwarranted law enforcement attention.

As with most issues broached at the conference, the debate was disjointed. Confusion reigned as various attendees contributed to the discourse.

Attorney Bob viewed the problem from a legal perspective: "History is full of situations where somebody commits a crime and sells out the entire chain or even people who are entirely innocent."

James added, "There are people who will set up anybody . . . if they think they can sell it to the prosecution and get a lighter sentence."

Peter came up with an idea. "Okay, how about this? NAMBLA doesn't facilitate the contact between people; however, when we're at the conference there is contact. People are free agents and they can exchange addresses and get together. [But] isn't that also difficult to defend if they do something stupid?"

Peter understood exactly our argument for infiltrating the organization. It was not the FBI's intent to silence NAMBLA, as repugnant as their conversation was. Our intent was to determine those members who were doing "something stupid." The difference was the Bureau had a very specific and functional definition of "stupid," found in the federal criminal code.

James interrupted Peter with what struck me as a significant indicator of the real purpose of NAMBLA's "advocacy" position. James countered Peter's question likening "stupid" actions at the national conference versus those that might occur among regional chapters. "It's a possibility, but at least [national meetings are] a further step removed from having a structure that is a social contact. That's why the whole thing has to be structured around the work project. We can't say that we're a social club. This opens up the door that the advocacy is just pretext."

Bingo.

The question that should be posed, is whether it is realistic to advocate the complete abolition of age-of-consent laws. In truth, isn't NAMBLA's untenable position merely a ploy to drape their sexual proclivities under the banner of the First Amendment? Isn't NAMBLA's real purpose to allow the networking of men who desire sex with underage boys? The conference is a way to meet others with like interests but cloak the networking process under constitutional protections. Every attendee knew the real purpose for these conventions. Each stated his purpose for attending during the previous day's introductions; nobody said "advocacy."

The opinions of Floyd and Peter almost always received deference from the members. Floyd's position on regional meetings was clear:

> The risks are enormous. We had a regional meeting in Dallas, Texas. . . . Against my recommendation, the steering committee authorized . . . a regional meeting and they had met not once but several times. But during the course of their meetings they got into a petty disagreement among the people there. The person who organized this group then went to the police department and provided them with a list of names and addresses. . . . You can't do this kind of thing without adequate safeguards.

So, it would seem, networking is what everybody wants — as long as nobody gets caught.

Later in the discussion, Floyd indicated a lack of sufficient quality leadership to handle regional chapters. He cited the Los Angeles situation: L.A. had a chapter that drew people from Arizona and throughout Southern California. There were no problems for ten years. Then, when the facilitator tired and handed off the responsibilities to another person, "within a very short time big trouble happened." Floyd opined that the Dallas problems occurred early in the formation of the chapter, because the facilitator "did not have the skill or the will to guard the interests of the members."

Peter defended his earlier position. "That's what I was proposing and I was proposing to do it very incrementally. Not . . . a call for regional meetings. That wasn't the model I proposed." But Peter understood the importance of seeking new avenues to reenergize the membership: "I like people to realize that unless we develop a mechanism for increasing participation, I don't see any hope for this organization continuing much longer."

Others argued convincingly that unless there was some vehicle for getting together, nothing would ever be accomplished. NAMBLA could never move forward without greater participation, and that would not occur as long as the organization only convened once a year, they said. Regional meetings seemed to hold the answer, but no one could devise a protocol to eliminate risk. Some suggested Peter could screen those invited to attend the regional gatherings just as he screened those invited to the national conferences. Others suggested regional meetings only be hosted by steering committee members. Chris even suggested new invitees be interviewed at a neutral site, so as not to identify the city from which the screener came.

As a way of "incrementally" moving toward regional meetings, Sam Lindblad proposed I have a working group assigned to help me plan the San Diego conference. My resulting hopes of identifying San Diego–area members were dashed when David R. Busby interrupted, stating I could accomplish the task by myself. I tried to avoid involvement in policy decisions and did not speak up in my defense. Sam's idea received little subsequent support and was dropped.

As the debate raged — or should I say meandered? — on, I wondered if any other organization claiming to be founded under First Amendment principles refused to allow its members to meet in a less formal setting for fear those members would commit a criminal act. This entire argument demonstrated to me the real intent of the membership of this organization was not that which was articulated inside the cover of every issue of its official publication. Those in leadership clearly understood the real motive of the majority of its members in joining this august body — a motive that was not pure.

The vote was not unanimous, but a motion passed to begin working on a protocol for "regional work groups." David R. Busby, James, and Sam from Florida, all Miami-area residents, were selected to draft the guidelines and report to the annual conference next year.

Then we had a dust-up over when to break for lunch. The chaos that accompanied almost every suggestion and discussion would make a sane boy lover question why he would even attend any NAMBLA function — except to network with other BLs.

Prior to breaking for lunch, James made a very astute observation, questioning any organization that would place a first-time attendee in the position of chairing the annual meeting: an excellent point, I thought.

Peter was taken aback by James's comment. After all, he had judged James by his appearance and pronounced him fit for service. But since James raised the issue, Peter said, "Well, let me ask you, are you a charming sociopath?" Without skipping a beat, James replied, with only a slight smile, "I'm not charming." Peter's response may have been more telling; he was not concerned about James being a sociopath as long as he "put together an acceptable protocol" for regional working groups. Even though I was a trained investigator, James fooled me. I saw little in his actions or mannerisms that would have alerted me to the fact that he was a boy lover. His public persona did not reflect his private deeds. Maybe he *was* a sociopath.

Peter's frustration was beginning to show, and he raised his voice. "I personally am not willing to continue if we have an organization that does not have the . . . internal resources to regenerate itself." Peter came to the conference seeking new blood to assume organizational responsibility, but so far, few stepped forward, and the one who had been "anointed" by the conference to chair the proceedings was indicting himself as unfit.

I almost felt sorry for Peter. The reason few stepped forward was clear to me: the majority of the attendees came for networking, not protocols; fellowship, not politics. As David Mayer said, "Bring on the boys."

In an effort to understand who the leadership was and what the leadership did, Peter talked to the attendees about the steering committee. Via conference call, the committee met every month. Peter complained that the calls were usually on Sunday evening, interfering with his viewing of *Malcolm in the Middle.*

Before leaving the meeting to fly home, I said my good-byes to David and Todd, confident we would continue to communicate. Sam Lindblad and I exchanged e-mail addresses, and I wished the others well.

Peter walked with me as I exited the conference room. We spoke briefly about next year's conference that I would be hosting. When I suggested opening the conference to all the members, Peter balked, and replied, "We're as open as we can be without being foolish."

I would soon discover that the seeds planted about a sex trip were taking root. David Mayer gave the opening signal on Friday afternoon in Miami before the NAMBLA conference even began, when he initiated the discussion about traveling overseas to have sex with boys. Soon after the conference, he fired the next salvo.

On November 15, the day after the conference ended, he e-mailed Todd and me:

Dear Robert & Todd,

Hope you both had safe uneventful trips home. I got to the airport early enough that I was able to get an earlier flight home. The good thing about that is that I did not have to sit next to Chris!

I am sending both of you some web sites that you might find interesting & helpful.

Best wishes,
David

The Web sites were for Big Ruby's/La Plantacion in Costa Rica and Acapulco's gay guesthouse resort accommodations.

To borrow a line from Sherlock Holmes, the game was still afoot.

31
TROLLING FOR A THREE-TIME OFFENDER

Big Ruby's described itself as one of the world's foremost gay hotels. The photos featured on the Web site were beautiful. As part of a "tropical paradise" overlooking the ocean adjacent to the rain forest of Costa Rica's Manuel Antonio National Park, the twenty-four luxury rooms appeared most intriguing. The Acapulco gay guesthouse guide was equally inviting, offering accommodations near the "magnificent Condesa Beach and Beto's Beach Club where the beach boys are waiting to get to know you." David's selections certainly catered to a gay clientele, but my interest centered on determining his intention, if any, to travel in order seek sex with underage boys.

I waited a day to reply to David and Todd. In keeping with the style and content of our conversations in Miami, I wanted to keep my responses light but with a sense of concern.

Hi guys,

This past weekend was great! I really appreciate your friendship and look forward to a trip to a real safe paradise. I know it will be fabulous. I'll check all the websites David (if that's his real name) is recommending and I'll check with my friend from last year. I know he said he found a safe haven. Safety should be our concern, right Todd (if that's your real name)? . . . I think we should invite Chief and Cleveland Mike as well as Chris to go with us. Of course don't forget to copy Peter with everything.

Please take care and be safe. Just so you know, I only use the PC at KINKOS, just to be safe, so it will usually be a day or two before I respond.

Again, thanks for a great time.

Robert (if that's my real name)

At the conference, Peter cautioned us about even joking about any kind of criminal activity. I wanted to capitalize on the incipient disdain my targets expressed toward Peter's "overly cautious" attitude, so, tongue-in-cheek, I suggested we copy him with every communication. What I didn't know at the time of my e-mail was that Peter had, in fact, heard that several of us were planning a trip and tried to intervene.

Todd e-mailed David that on November 16 Peter called and said he heard "through the grapevine" about the trip. Peter warned Todd, "Don't do it." As to the trip, Todd told David, "I still very much want to, though cautiously, of course." I also learned Peter contacted David, as well. Yet Peter never called me. Did he know I was an undercover agent and saw no need to warn me?

Peter could have sabotaged the entire investigation by his calls. But in reality, he helped. Todd and David were clearly warned but chose to go forward. If the case got to trial, this would tend to defeat entrapment arguments by demonstrating their desires to go even after our "secret" journey to paradise was exposed.

Part of the thrill and the challenge of working undercover is posing as a bad guy but staying within certain boundaries in dealing with the criminal element. As a NAMBLA member and a BL, I should have been outraged that Peter was interfering with what we wanted to do. Who was he to tell us not to travel? Based upon his admissions to an undercover officer years ago, he traveled to the Philippines for sex. Why couldn't we? And who is his "grapevine"?

Does this "libertarian, humanistic" organization sanction the use of snitches within its ranks to report on the activities of others? My e-mail to Todd and David expressed my supposed outrage and frustration.

Hi kids,

Got each of your emails and glad I checked them today. I'm a little pissed. What does Peter mean, he heard it thru the grapevine? Who is he, Gladys Knight? I think I know his grapevine and it sounds like the other David. Maybe I'm wrong because I thought David was cool and wanted to join us, but do you think he told Peter? I don't think I told anyone other than the ones sitting at Johnny Rocket's. Todd, when did Peter call you? Were you still at the conference or was this since we came home? That said . . . what is he, a virgin? You mean he never traveled or had a special friendship? Makes me mad that someone would try to interfere with what we know to be a safe trip. Just because other guys are impotent is no reason to stifle our fun. All I can say is my friend went and returned. He's not in jail and he loved it!!!! Maybe I'm getting paranoid but I tried to email Sam to the address he gave me and it never got through. Have you guys heard from anyone else? Did anyone try to email the other David? It doesn't matter what others say, I'm a BIG GO after the first of the year. I'll let you know after Turkey Day what my friend says.

Daddy

David's response was classic, demonstrating the humor that, while admittedly twisted, made our relationship tolerable.

OOOOOOOOOOOOOOOOOOOOOOOh Daddddddddddddy!

I just love it when you get all butch and angry! However, I agree 100% with what you said about Peter. I got a call from him around 10 p.m. CST two (?) days after we got home. He left a very cryptic message stating that he had to speak to me ASAP. Needless to say I was already searching for my passport and wondering if I was too old to speak Spanish (I figure I might as well go to a country where I could have some fun!). I literally did not sleep that evening. When I finally got his email, I was lectured about traveling. I was pissed!

My thought was that the "mole" was

"Tim" (not his real name from "Michigan"). More a gut feeling with little to back it up, other than I saw the two of them huddling together. My feeling is that David would never pass up the chance. . . .

I am going to email Big Ruby's and ask for a brochure, rates, and availability. Will keep you posted.

Hope you are both well and I miss the camaraderie, along with the laughs.

Best wishes,
David

PS Robert: if you get the correct email for Sam please forward it. Thanks.

The three of us continued to trade e-mails, with me promising to learn more after Thanksgiving from "my friend" about his trip to the alleged safe haven in Mexico. At this point I had no such friend and didn't have a particular safe haven in mind. But I wasn't worried about creating my fictionalized paradise. There was no real reason to put off telling them details of the trip, other than I was waiting to get everything in place with Los Angeles and the U.S. Attorney's office in San Diego. There was no immediate need for us to provide details unless Todd or David came up with their own locale that would actually put boys in danger.

My only real concern was the fact that David seemed so anxious to travel. Knowing that as a flight attendant he could travel at will, I was fearful he might want to fly into San Diego some weekend and expect me to entertain him or join him in a quick trip to Mexico. For that reason, I wanted to set up the trip as soon as practical after the first of the year.

The two members in whom I had the most interest following the Miami conference were David Mayer and Sam Lindblad. Come to think of it, they both proposed marriage to me, but that had zero to do with my interest. David Mayer admitted to traveling overseas for the purpose of engaging in sex with boys, and Sam Lindblad was a three-time convicted sex offender.

With the e-mail traffic occurring shortly after my return from Miami, we were well on our way to developing a prosecutable case against David Mayer. It was now time to turn my attention toward Sam. At five feet eleven inches, 165 pounds, the balding, blue-eyed, fifty-seven-year-old hardly looked menacing. His actions, however, proved otherwise.

Upon Sam Lindblad's release from prison

in Colorado and his subsequent move to Albuquerque, New Mexico, the Bernalillo County sheriff's office notified the Albuquerque FBI. According to the information provided to the FBI, when arrested in Colorado, Lindblad admitted to fondling thirty boys and targeting an additional two hundred. He told arresting officers he could not control his impulses, yet actively sought employment in areas where he would have access to boys. Investigators also discovered a tunnel under his Grand Junction, Colorado, home. They speculated that Lindblad intended to use the tunnel as a body disposal site. Although there was no evidence of such activity, New Mexico law enforcement had a well-founded interest in Lindblad.

Within a month of settling in his Albuquerque apartment, Lindblad posted a notice in the laundry room of the complex, offering to tutor children with their homework. A search of his trash found apparent coded messages. When investigators pieced together shredded correspondence, they found notations such as, "Played with a little sidewinder this afternoon. He was four feet long," and, in reference to a boy, [he was] "twelve meters tall." Investigators could only speculate as to the meaning of the letters, but possible interpretations included Lindblad noting contact with a boy who was four feet tall and twelve years old. Even though he had no school-age children, his trash revealed sales tags cut from new boy's clothing and crayon drawings made by a boy. Once Lindblad learned that his trash was being recovered and searched by law enforcement, he began waiting until the trash trucks came to the curb so he could place his garbage directly in the truck. Lindblad also volunteered to be a docent at the Albuquerque Aquarium. Among his responsibilities, if he was given the position, would have been directing tours for school-age boys.

Even his driving tactics gave rise to the belief he was engaged in some type of criminal activity. On more than one occasion, Lindblad was observed driving erratically, making U-turns, stopping in the middle of traffic, parking at the side of the road for a short time, observing passing vehicles, and then reentering traffic. Lindblad's actions begged further investigation.

He mimicked a great deal of what I read in my correspondence with incarcerated NAMBLA members. He practiced textbook "grooming," using every opportunity to "court" any boy he met. The Albuquerque

FBI learned that Lindblad visited a community youth co-op and chatted with a ten-year-old boy about computers. After returning home, Lindblad wrote the boy a letter, sending it directly to the co-op and addressing the youngster as "Master." Complimenting him on his computer knowledge and thanking him for his assistance, Lindblad provided the ten-year-old with an e-mail address. Although the letter contained no sexual references, knowing Lindblad's criminal history, it was an obvious grooming tactic and an apparent attempt to circumvent the parents.

Investigators in Colorado learned that, prior to the arrest that led to his 1996 conviction, Lindblad maintained contact with numerous boys after meeting them. He would send letters or birthday cards in an effort to enhance a relationship. Lindblad would cautiously include statements such as "you can ask me anything you want." Although not sexual in nature, it was part of his grooming process.

Lindblad, like most NAMBLA members I encountered at the conferences, was a persuasion predator. He obtained his victims through seduction and trust rather than abduction and force. His grooming and subsequent bonding with a victim was his foreplay, a precursor to "consensual" sex.

At the conference, I had established with him the fact that I wrote for the *Bulletin* and I expressed an interest in Sam's prison experience. I decided to approach him on a project for the *Bulletin* discussing his struggle with the law. I wanted to make clear to him that this would be a joint project, rather than just me writing an article for the *Bulletin.* I believed the wording of my request would be important to avoid potential charges that I somehow infringed upon a First Amendment right.

On November 18, I sent my first e-mail to Sam.

Just wanted to say it was great meeting you this past weekend. I had to leave early to catch a plane but I understand you were selected for the steering committee. I think that's great. . . .

Let me know if there are some ways I can help you with your responsibilities. I want to see this thing work. I just know how lonely it gets. . . .

As I mentioned at the conference, I've written several articles for the *Bulletin.* Maybe you might consider letting me interview you about your experiences. . . . I think a lot of our readers would like to hear what it was like in the trenches. Maybe, though, you don't want to talk about it. I would understand that as well. Think about it.

If I don't get back to you before turkey day have a great Thanksgiving. Be safe.

Robert

Shortly after sending the e-mail I received a notice that it was "undeliverable." I checked the e-mail address again and feared Sam had given me a bad address at the conference to avoid further contact. The next day I re-sent the e-mail and it went through. I said a quick little prayer of thanks. If Sam Lindblad was stalking boys in Albuquerque or anywhere else, I sincerely wanted him caught and punished, and any sort of helpful intervention, especially the divine variety, would be appreciated.

32
BAITING THE HOOK

As with the others with whom I traded e-mail addresses at the conference, I also wanted to maintain the connection with David R. Busby. He was a potential traveler and proven pervert. His foot fetish and comments at Johnny Rockets were disturbing. I was sure there was much more to him than he revealed in Miami. On November 19, I sent the following e-mail:

> Just wanted to say it was great spending time with you this past weekend. It really is one of the few times I feel like I can relax and be myself. It can get so lonely the rest of the year and I'm not much of a chat room type of guy. . . .
>
> In a few months I'll be picking your brain about how to put this thing together for next year. I'm already getting excited. Almost as much as I do when I watch SILVER SPOONS!!

Hope you can join us for a trip after the first of the year. I'm meeting with my friend after turkey day and will get all the details.

Be safe.

David R. Busby did not immediately respond to that e-mail.

David Mayer sent Todd and me an e-mail wishing us a happy Thanksgiving and stating he was "looking forward to hearing about our travel adventure from Daaaaaaaaaaaddddy after the holiday."

It took more than a week for Sam Lindblad to respond to my communication, but his response was priceless: he e-mailed the minutes of the Miami conference and asked me to review them and comment. In fact, he e-mailed me the minutes before he sent them to Peter. All in all, he did an admirable job of following and documenting what was actually a very disjointed and disorganized set of proceedings. I was especially proud of an entry in the section concerning Saturday's discussion of regional meetings and the need for care in communications with persons not well known to the membership: "It was agreed that infiltration of the steering committee and general membership can happen, but it is unlikely because of apprenticeships and the vigilance of the current leadership."

On December 1, Sam e-mailed me agreeing to be "interviewed for whatever I can do to support others that struggle with being a BL."

I responded two days later.

Sam,

So glad to hear from you and that you had a great Thanksgiving. Thanks so much for the minutes. . . . I really believe the organization needs the leadership that you can provide. I actually thought of letting my membership lapse but now am so glad I went to Miami. . . .

Let me put together some questions and maybe after the first of the year I can mix business with pleasure and stop off in Albuquerque for lunch or dinner and we can work out an article. Of course I would let you approve anything I write before I submit it for publication but I think you have a story that needs to be told. And I think our readers/members would love to hear personal interest escapades.

I will chat at you later. Be safe!!!!

Robert

I previously told David and Todd I was hoping to contact Sam Lindblad, the NAM-BLA secretary, to discuss writing an article in the *Bulletin* about his story. David also e-mailed me about having trouble contacting Todd. With those two subjects in mind on December 4, I again tossed my line overboard and began trolling the waters for boy lovers willing to take the bait.

First, I sent an e-mail to David and Todd.

Hi kids,

Got lots to talk about today. Todd, glad to hear from you. David and I were getting a little worried but I'm glad you're back in the fold. I finally heard from Secretary Sam but no one else. He's doing well and has agreed to let me interview him for an article for the *Bulletin.* So, we'll see how that goes. No one else has replied to any of my e-mails except my two loving sons, who are so devoted to DADDY.

The BIG news is I met with my friend last night and I have what I think to be GREAT news!! He has traveled twice with this outfit and wants to go again. It is very discreet and he said well worth the expense, which I think is pretty reasonable. Here's the deal. You travel by boat from the U.S. to just below Ensenada. The facility is a bed and breakfast and they have four- or seven-day packages. He's only been on the four-day package. The cost is well under $800 and that includes the boat trip, four days and nights, breakfast, lunch, and dinner, plus use of the boat. More importantly, it includes the "special friends." Honest to goodness! You provide the age range and they provide the entertainment. He said if you aren't satisfied you can ask for a new friend, even multiple friends. But no one he traveled with had any complaints whatsoever except that it rained one day. Big deal! Stay in bed with your friend. What's the problem? He said the only extra expenses were gratuities and meals if you didn't want to eat at the house. We can use the boat for whale watching and fishing. The "friends" love to do that. You can take pictures and even videos if you want. He said just throw the "friends" a little extra. Everyone was MOST accommodating!!! David, I know you traveled down there so you can tell Todd how great the "friends" are.

Ensenada is about 70 miles south of San Diego and is Mexico's wine country.

Everyone speaks English and the locals take American dollars. We can pick up the boat in LA or San Diego. That makes this extra special because no one knows we went to Mexico. There is no paper trail. It's safe and the local Mexican authorities really don't care as long as you aren't abusive. Like I said, he has been twice and can't wait to hop aboard the "love train" again.

There is one down side to this: You need a minimum six people for the trip. I'd rather not go with strangers. So can we come up with six? My friend will go so that makes four. Can we come up with two more? Do you think davidrbusby will come out here, or Muscleman? I'm open to suggestions. I guess we don't ask Peter or Tim (that's not his real name). We could always ask Chief but I think you have to bathe in order to get on the boat. I would rather not take a chance going with strangers just in case, safety must be our number one priority. (By the way, they can accommodate ten, so there are discounts for eight or ten travelers, respectively. Can we get that many?)

I checked the website and it said under construction, but my friend said that's just part of their being discreet.

What do you guys think? Both of you have traveled. David, you've been successful. Todd, you almost got killed. This is safe, affordable and recommended. I'm in. I'm thinking mid- to late January. My schedule is flexible but I don't know David's flight plans or Todd's practice restrictions. Assuming they have availability we can do a long weekend or during the week. My friend said they can work around our scheduling needs as well.

Let me know. This sounds better than Costa Rica but he told me about a place down there as well. If we don't want this I can check into that.

While I was writing the text of the e-mail, David instant messaged me. Although not life threatening, the IM threw me into somewhat of a panic. My computer skills are weak, at best, and every communication with the targets had to be preserved. I had no clue how to save the IM chat and preserve the evidence. I called a member of the L.A. FBI's SAFE team from the Kinko's where I was using the computer. He walked me through the process, but it was cumbersome. With the other undercover case I was working at the time, I had in excess of one thousand recordings and didn't need the additional paperwork. Trading e-mails with the subjects, on the other hand, was easy. My San Diego case agent eased that administrative burden, but David was creating another evidentiary headache. I dropped out of the chat, preserved the evidence, completed the e-mail, and pushed "send."

Within the hour, David responded in big bold print: "SIGN ME UP! . . . YEAH!" He suggested inviting James, whom he called "the future first lady," or Paul, whom he called "Muscleman." He assumed Sam Lindblad would not be able to go because of his status as a convicted sex offender and thought that David R. Busby couldn't afford the package.

Todd responded the next day with, "WOW! I agree. That is GREAT news!! The whole thing sounds fabulous, almost too good to be true. I'm so excited." Todd said that the second or fourth weekends of February worked best for him. He and David had spoken by phone about financially assisting someone like Paul and offered to chip in for "soap and laundry detergent" for Chief. Todd did say he knew of no one outside of NAMBLA to invite and hoped David or I could find "two more people

417

wanting some quality time with 'special friends.' This new info has certainly got me all fired up inside. Let's do it!"

David was working hard to make this trip happen. On December 5, he e-mailed Todd and me, writing that he found "Paul, the massive chest's, phone number" and thought of two other non-NAMBLA members who might be interested in going, but questioned whether he should contact them at that time or after we had more details.

I replied to both David and Todd on December 6.

Kids,

I'm so EXCITED that you're excited. I think we have the beginning of a wonderful relationship. (Was that a line from *Casablanca*?) We should probably be looking for the first week in Feb. since that's Todd's choice. Like I said, I'm flexible.

Let me apologize and explain a few things. Because of my condition, it's hard for me to type very fast, so it's really tough to do the IM. David, DADDY wasn't mad when he dropped off on Sat. Now, the other thing: My mother lives with me and so does my ex-sister-in-law (I'm not sure for how long). It's a long story but sometimes it's hard for me to talk at the condo. So, that's why I didn't return your call. Still love me? But that's one reason I go to Kinko's. Hope you understand.

Now, back to the trip. David, I'll get more details for your friend and I'm sure we all need more. Just hang loose for awhile. Let me do some more checking, then I'll forward all the juicy details. I would invite anyone you TRUST. In fact I think it's safer than relying on strangers that [the "travel service"] may team up with us. I'll also see if we can't just rent the entire boat. Seems reasonable but we would also need to rent the extra rooms at the B&B. That's why I'd prefer to have more friends with us. Who can we invite and trust from the conference? And who won't go back to Peter? David and Todd, whose email addresses and phone numbers do you have? I have secretary Sam plus davidrbusby and muscleman. Anyone else? And do we want to invite them? What do you think about Sam? I like him but can we trust him? Let's think about it and be smart. I know we can put this together if that's what we all want, and it seems like we do!!

Be safe. Luv ya!!

DADDY

David responded in less than an hour to my e-mail.

Daddy Dearest,

You know that as long as you have $$$$, I could never be mad at you! I assumed that there was a reason for you not returning the call, & you already explained what was going on @ Kink's, er Kinko's. Not to worry.

My concern about Sam is that he is a red flag flying in the wind with his background. In addition, I am not sure he is allowed to leave the country. Todd and I both feel that David Busby (spelling?) probably cannot afford the trip. What about James I-Have-Not-Changed-My-Clothes-in-Three-Days & Future First Lady? I have no contact information for him. Do you think that Sam could get it for you? I do not trust Peter after that phone call. What about the special ed teacher from Pittsburgh? I do not remember his name & have no contact info. The others @ the conference were either too weird even for me, or worse . . . SMELLED.

I am so excited! First week in Feb. works for me. I have to be in D.C. the last day of Feb. thru the first week of March.

Even if it is just the four of us, it would be so much fun. Can't wait!

David

The plan was set in motion, and we were making our preparations. Todd preferred the weekend of February 12 rather than the first weekend, because he had his two children that first weekend. He thought, however, that his ex-wife might switch weekends, if necessary. Todd was willing to modify his plans, knowing that accommodating six people's schedules might be burdensome. "When you're talking about as many as six people's schedules," he said, "my 'ideal' might quite understandably be unachievable, and that's still very cool — especially cool when I contemplate the awesome prospects!!"

David worked hard to find fellow travelers and e-mailed Todd and me on December 6, saying he spoke with a "friend" who was "very interested." Later in the week, he suggested a three-way conference call to work out the details of the trip — dates, leaving from Los Angeles or San Diego, and whether we wanted the four- or seven-day excursion. David wanted to firm up the details so that he could "give some solid info to my two other possible travelers."

Meanwhile, Sam Lindblad and I continued to trade e-mails and arrived at a date for my trip to Albuquerque. I was doing a little "grooming" of my own.

On December 6, I wrote in part to Sam,

Thanks so much for replying to my email. I keep in contact with David from Chicago and Todd, but no one else seems to respond. It hurts because I was really hoping to develop a deeper relationship with those at the conference than just a once-a-year thing.

Sam's December 7 e-mail reply gave me a ringside seat on his life.

Hello Robert,

It is amazing how busy we can get, just trying to pay bills by working, etc. Most guys don't find time to do much developing friendships. The exception to that has been the New Mexico Gay Men's Chorus I sing in. Twenty very sensitive guys. And all extremely intelligent. I feel like the bottom of the barrel when it comes to talent. And none of them have expressed that they are BL's, but still good men. . . .

Prison was very difficult for my whole family. My ex-in-laws severed all ties, but my side has remained supportive. It was hard on my Dad. My 24-year-old son is also still quite angry about it all. He was 15 when I fell, so he had to complete high school with all the stigma attached. Dad's been able to ask me some questions about it all, but mostly now it's "let bygones be bygones."

One cousin is quite concerned about having me in the same room as her 8- and 10-year-old sons. I will do some reassuring in my Christmas letter. My mom died in 1971 at the age of 53. Maybe her body knew she couldn't handle the pain of Sam's imprisonment. She was quite concerned about, "What will the neighbors think?"

Well, it's time for me to get on some holiday cards, and then practice some music. So . . .

Shalom. Sam

33

GETTING THE GOODS

Not all undercover cases cover years of time and involve lengthy preparations, but one thing they definitely have in common is the agent's need to be in the right place at the right time to acquire from the target the key admission or action that will seal his or her legal fate. Sometimes, getting the goods on the bad guys takes a long, long time, and sometimes it happens quickly and can even be fun.

I've already described my little one-act play with Anthony, the New Jersey mobster who was going to break the legs of the producer. Another quick score I was able to help with involved a cameo appearance as a prospective home buyer. Our target was a supposedly bankrupt defendant in a white-collar crime case. The agent who arrested him was relatively new to the Bureau, but she had already acquired a reputation as a tenacious investigator. Her target was convicted, despite his high-priced defense team, but he still had a couple of tricks up his sleeve.

At sentencing the con man argued he had no assets, so any fine would be beyond his ability to pay. In addition, he announced he planned to appeal his conviction and because he was now destitute he was requesting that free appellate counsel be assigned. Neither the case agent nor the prosecutor, Mark Aveis, bought his claims or the financial forms he filed with the court under penalty of perjury.

The case agent learned that the defendant was planning to sell the million-dollar house he claimed he didn't own. She asked me if I would pose as a buyer to see if the Realtor might make some admissions as to the true owner of the house. Since the investigator was known to the con man, having sat in the courtroom throughout the prosecution, she couldn't do the covert investigation.

I decided I needed a girlfriend, just to add some fun to the gig, and asked a cute agent on our squad who had just gotten engaged. She managed to swallow her pride and agreed to pose as my betrothed. Once again, I was way out of my league, but she was a good sport. Also, even on an assignment like this, there was a certain adrenaline rush;

I think she was looking forward to the experience.

We checked out a seized Mercedes from the undercover fleet and headed to Encino, an upscale community in Los Angeles's San Fernando Valley. I made arrangements to meet the Realtor, who had no idea we were agents. My wife and I have sold homes a few times and I know that typically, with a scheduled showing, the family is asked to leave so the potential buyers can roam and speak freely. We assumed we could engage the Realtor in conversation and possibly gain admissions or leads about the con man's true assets.

When we pulled up to the estate, just a few blocks off Ventura Boulevard, I was surprised at the size of the property. It was a beautiful older home on a spacious lot near shopping, with quick freeway access — location, location, location. The home was previously owned by a Hollywood cowboy star, and I only wish I had been able to afford it in real life.

My undercover fiancée and I met the real estate agent out front and spoke briefly before entering the house. I told her I was a screenwriter and was due at a rewrite conference in Studio City later in the afternoon; we wanted a quick tour of the residence and hoped the Realtor wouldn't mind if we fired questions at her about the property. She was only too accommodating to our schedule and our needs.

Using my cane, I hobbled toward the front door and was shocked when who should open the door but the defendant himself. He greeted us and invited us inside. Like every con man I ever met, he loved to talk, and I peppered him with questions about the home and its history. He readily admitted he was the sole owner and claimed he and his wife were planning to remain in the area. He said they were using their sizeable equity in this property to buy a larger home. His admissions, all caught on tape, were perfect. With our objective completed, it was time to have a little fun.

He and the Realtor gave us a tour of the residence, answering questions as we asked. When my "fiancée" inquired about a gardener, I pretended to become incensed. We had already told the defendant that one of the bedrooms would be for her mother, who would be moving from Europe to live with us after the wedding. I said there would be no need for a gardener. My fiancée acted confused. Then I said in the rudest voice I could manage, "She's not living here for free. She can cut the grass!"

My undercover fiancée played the scene beautifully and offered up a quick, though weak, defense for my "future mother-in-law." Later in the conversation, the Realtor asked about children. I immediately responded, "Children will not be a problem." My fiancée said in a quiet, cowed voice, "We have to talk about a family." I responded again in an arrogant, loud voice, "Children will *not* be a problem!" The Realtor, embarrassed for my fiancée and, I suppose, her client, said, "Maybe you two should talk about this some other time." Maybe you had to be there, but it was a classic scene. We quickly excused ourselves to get to my "rewrite conference."

After we left the residence and turned off the tape, we had a great laugh over our successful assignment. And the biggest joke of all was that our "destitute" defendant was now facing a federal perjury rap.

Similarly, my NAMBLA act, though it was going on several years by the time of the Miami conference, was starting to pay off in potentially prosecutable admissions and actions by certain members.

After I returned from Miami, I sent Jeff Devore, the Orange County minister and chiropractor, the following e-mail on November 16:

How about [getting together] the week after Thanksgiving? I'd love to meet with you and meet another BL. I can come to OC or Long Beach. Can't wait to tell you about the conference. It was great. Met some new people who like to travel. Found a very safe haven, that's cheap and close. Maybe you and your friend would be up for a trip. I know it will be FABULOUS!!!!

Jeff never responded, which worried me. There is always a danger in pursuing any subject too aggressively. The line between criminality and entrapment is subjective with each judge. I took one more chance. On December 15 I sent the following:

Haven't heard from you in a long while. Hope all is well. Is this your Friday to be in Beverly Hills? I'll be up there this weekend and thought maybe you and your other friend could hook up. I know it's kinda late notice but let me know. If not, maybe after the first of the year. Want to share with you what happened at the conference and I have some news that may interest you.

If we can't make it this week, have a Merry Christmas. Be safe.

I was surprised when he called the next night, one of the few phone calls we ever had. We agreed to meet. What followed was evidentiary pay dirt. Referencing a conversation we had in February, almost nine months earlier, when Jeff and I last met, Jeff said, "You said you lost your whole collection when your computer crashed. I made a CD with some pictures you might enjoy, if you're interested." My response was an enthusiastic "Yes." I wasn't sure what he had in store for me, but I was looking forward to the little gift he wanted to present.

On December 17 we met at a deli on Sunset Boulevard in West Hollywood. He came alone. His Long Beach BL friend wasn't able to meet with us, but Jeff assured me we would meet soon. Jeff quickly handed me his special present: a CD labeled "Youth 4Bob." A special present indeed: if it contained prosecutable images, he had just violated federal law. I tucked it away. We ordered and Jeff talked about his journey or, I should say, his regression.

He told of meeting an eleven-year-old from the United Kingdom on the Internet and that they "chatted" last night. But they did more than chat. Both had Web cams. Jeff and his eleven-year-old friend "real-timed" masturbation. Jeff, the ordained minister and father of three, said, "We sat there jerking off together." He now described himself as a boy lover who preferred ten- or eleven-year-olds. He was securely back in the BL fold and didn't deny it. He was also escalating by trying something new to satisfy his desires.

He spoke of his work at the church with the youth, teaching a program called "Our Whole Lives," a joint project with the Unitarian Church and the United Church of Christ, a "lifespan sexuality education curriculum." I needed to be sure the boys he was teaching were safe. I inquired and he denied engaging in sexual activity with any of the youth at the church.

When the discussion returned to his online chats, he said, "One of my fantasies has been to be with someone like [his eleven-year-old cybersex partner], and I figure that's as close as I can get. . . . I would never do that . . . get with an eleven-year-old." Then he added, "After I did that, I was so glad that I had; that is something I wanted for a very long time."

Jeff didn't take the bait when I pitched

him on our trip to Ensenada. He said he would think about the invitation and described it as a potentially "life-changing experience." I assured him it most definitely would be. He said he would contact his Long Beach BL friend and see if he was interested. We parted that afternoon, planning to meet again.

We never did. Neither Jeff nor his friend joined us on the "trip" to Mexico. But "Youth 4Bob" contained all we needed for a federal prosecution. The CD contained one hundred graphic sexual images and eight movies of boys in sexually explicit acts, all violations of federal law, the distribution of which carries a minimum mandatory prison sentence of five years. The disc also had twenty-five images of "erotica," images that presented disturbing, full-frontal nudity of boys, though not rising to the level of "pornography" for federal prosecution purposes. Within a few months, if things went well, Jeff might learn that whether or not he joined us on the February trip, his actions on December 17 would have been a life-changing experience.

David, Todd, and I set up the first of several conference calls for December 12. The call was better than anything the FBI could have expected; it lasted almost forty-five minutes, with both Todd and David making valuable admissions. Todd set up the three-way from his office.

David's humor was evident from the beginning of the call as he complained that my "mother," who I said was living with me, was going to inherit the estate upon my untimely demise. When I joked that my real reason for going to Mexico was to find an eleven-year-old to whack my mom, Todd chimed in, "So we're going to be co-conspirators in two different crimes. One we've already discussed and one is murder. This is going to be messy." The divorced dentist from Dallas had just admitted he knew that the purpose of our planned trip was illegal.

David said in an earlier e-mail that he had to go to Washington for a consulting job. I suggested that David worked for the CIA, which became a running joke. At one point, David and I even discussed the type of recording equipment we used to monitor conversations. When David said he used the sixty-minute tapes to record our calls because he didn't "want to bother with changing tapes," Todd laughed, saying we would have to "bs for another fifty-four minutes before we get serious." Little did they know

433

or suspect that all of our calls were being recorded.

Todd talked about his phone call from Peter Herman warning against traveling. According to Todd, Peter said, "Todd, you're a fine, upstanding man, and I just don't want you to do it." This, too, I knew, would defeat defense arguments of entrapment.

Todd and David attempted to contact Paul Zipszer, but were never able to get past his mother, whom David described as "trailer trash." Todd said her voice made her sound as if she had been "smoking since age negative eight." They claimed the third-degree she subjected them to caught both of them off guard. Whatever their complaints, Paul's mother exhibited a mother's protective instinct; she tried to keep her thirty-nine-year-old son out of trouble.

I lied when I told them I had recently read an article in the *Los Angeles Times* stating that criminal matters were a low priority with the FBI because they were concentrating all of their resources on terrorism. David responded, "Thank you, 9/11."

Although I thought through my basic plan for the travel package, I was flying by the seat of my pants during the call. I said I contacted the travel agency and they forwarded me an application requiring a $200 deposit. The total cost of the trip was $620. I told them my imaginary friend described the facility as similar to the bed and breakfast in Miami. Todd asked questions about the size of the boat and the length of the trip. I again punted and said I would check with my friend for all the "juicy details." When David asked what happened to the boat after we landed, I said it remained, so we had access to it throughout our stay. We could use it for whale watching or fishing.

Todd asked if the boys would be joining us on the boat trip from the States to Mexico. I explained that the boys were locals and would meet us at the resort. In fact, we were to specify the age range so we would be matched up with boys within the preferred range who would perform the desired sexual acts. Both Todd and David laughed at this; such "shopping" was different than anything they'd ever done.

David explained about his Acapulco experiences. He had a friend who owned a house near the beach. Either his friend would obtain the boys for David or David would stroll the gay beach and pick up a willing juvenile. David described his success as "hit or miss," depending upon whether the local police had recently done a sweep, limiting the number of boys working the sands. David said when police dragnets didn't interfere, the selection was large.

Todd's desired age range was twelve to fourteen, he said, and David wanted "prepubescent" boys.

David contacted a Bob in Los Angeles. David described him as a BL whom he had never met in person, but David knew through friends that Bob traveled to Thailand. David's second friend was Morgan. He wanted to go but was interested in meeting boys *and* girls. I said I would check and assumed someone had a sister, so that should not be a problem. Why not jail another pedophile, even if he wasn't 100 percent BL?

When the issue of costs came up, I scrambled for the piece of paper on which I had roughed out the figures. I told Todd that when I spoke with the travel agency, I didn't record the call, as David would have, so I had to find my notes. David requested that I just forward my notes after having them notarized and include my fingerprint and DNA analysis. We continued to joke about collecting evidence of our conspiratorial wrongdoing.

It was really my decision to determine how much to charge for the trip. I needed to make it realistic, yet I didn't want to price anyone out if he was truly committed to traveling in violation of the law. Knowing the judicial system, I also knew I needed to make it expensive enough that the travelers couldn't argue in court they merely wanted a cheap respite from Chicago winters. Even though accepting a free trip would still be in violation of the law, forwarding a down payment or partial payment was almost irrefutable evidence of intent. I checked online to determine resort prices in the Ensenada region and determined that $70 per night for lodging seemed appropriate. Since this was a bed and breakfast, I settled on $25 per day for meals, bringing the cost per day to $95. For no particular reason, I assessed each traveler a $240 charge for the boat — hey, it was my trip, right? I also noted that my "friend" suggested that additional entertainment and gratuities would roughly work out to about $50 per day, but would vary with each traveler, depending upon what activities they chose to do with the assigned boy. Those added details provided a sense of authenticity.

Todd wanted to take the four-day trip the first time, with the longer stay on a second junket. I suppose he wanted to make sure he was getting value for his money before committing to the lengthier package.

The issue arose as to whether we could get six travelers and whether we wanted to buy out the boat with just the four of us: David, Todd, my imaginary friend, and me. David described this as a worst-case scenario, still hoping we could find six. Trying to add realism, I expressed concern that I didn't want to be on the boat with people we didn't know or trust. Todd and David agreed.

Todd kept pressing for more details my "friend" relayed. I essentially made up info off the cuff. I said he had traveled twice, and both experiences were similar. The resort furnished the boys who spend the night with the travelers in their respective rooms. You can spend time alone with the boy or team up for group activities, I told them. You could pal around on the beach, lounge in the room, or go into town. The police look the other way as long as there is no abuse. David endorsed my friend's assessment; he described sex tourism as the "biggest moneymaker these boys have" and said the police recognized this, allowing it to happen. I told them my friend said he kept the same boy throughout the trip, but one traveler turned his boy back in and received another. I said the boys allowed themselves to be videotaped, but David cautioned against it — you can't be too careful, after all.

I told Todd and David my friend even said you could get multiple boys if that was your desire. David confirmed that one time he had "three boys in Thailand."

I said the trip sounded "perfect" and Todd agreed: "It sounds great to me."

So far, so good.

34
How Much
Is Too Much?

Both Todd and David were concerned about customs and whether to take passports. They were satisfied with my explanation: since we were not going into Mexico through a port of entry, we would be avoiding customs. We would be slipping in and out of the country undetected, and even if boarded by customs on the high seas, there would be no contraband onboard.

I suggested that when writing a check or money order for the deposit, they should include "Johnny Rockets" in the memo section so we would all be identified with the same travel group. The implication that this "huge travel agency" couldn't keep a few names straight played into the belief that this was a massive organization dedicated to feeding the sexual fantasies of American pedophiles.

Todd complained that his e-mail to the travel agency had not been answered but thought that might have been because he had not mentioned Johnny Rockets. I didn't correct his impression.

Todd and David wanted to invite Steve Irvin, the schoolteacher from Pittsburgh, but neither had a contact number. Todd felt safe inviting Steve after meeting him in Miami.

We agreed to another conference call the next week, playing on my supposed paranoid belief that phone calls were safer than e-mails. They weren't, really, when they were being recorded verbatim, but my phone buddies didn't need to know that.

I wound up the conversation, excited by what I had just recorded. But . . . had the criminal admissions come too easily? The excitement and willingness of both David and Todd was far beyond what I expected from cautious members of a suspect organization. I wondered if this wasn't what we called a "blue on blue" situation — one undercover cop unknowingly pitted against another. David initiated the criminal conspiracy with his travel talk within only a few minutes of arriving at the Miami conference. Although I didn't suspect either of being an actual law enforcement official, I suspected that one, especially David, could be an informant. Miami was the first conference he ever attended, and his actions were far different than the way I behaved in New York the year before, as a first-time attendee. Was he "working off a beef," needing to produce results immediately? I also entertained the idea he was conducting some type of educational study of boy lovers and we were all part of his research. These thoughts would linger in the back of my mind as the investigation proceeded.

In an attempt to placate my concerns, my San Diego case agent researched our files and contacted the Chicago and Dallas offices. Neither David nor Todd was a known informant for the FBI; our counterparts in those offices were unaware of any operation at any level of law enforcement targeting NAMBLA members or "travelers."

The e-mails continued. David contacted his friends Bob and Morgan and was still awaiting a response, he told me. Todd had nothing on Steve Irvin. When Todd tried to e-mail Paul, it was returned as undeliverable, the same response I received. Between a bad address and Paul's mother's vigilance on the phone, I was starting to eliminate Paul Zipszer and his muscular physique from my most-likely-to-be-arrested list.

Todd and I spoke again by phone on December 14. The evidence mounted as the recorder ran. He was preparing to make reservations for his return flight to Dallas following our four-day excursion, and asked me what time the boat would be returning from Ensenada on the Wednesday morning following our sex tour. I wanted to tell him that booking a return flight was the least of his worries, but I resisted the urge.

Todd told me his expectations for the trip included spending time with a "special little friend or a couple." Todd wasn't interested in "multiple friends at the same time" but did "want more than one" while he was there, unless he decided his first kid was "the most incredible thing around."

In most undercover assignments, playing the role of a criminal requires certain legally imposed restrictions as well as practical, self-imposed restraints. Entrapment is always an issue with any undercover operation. For example, is the person predisposed to commit the crime? Did the government merely create the opportunity to violate the law, a violation the individual would have committed if given the opportunity by someone in the criminal element, or did the government somehow induce the violation from someone who was otherwise disinclined?

Self-imposed restrictions are a bit different. A judge or juror might ask, Is the undercover agent more despicable than the criminal? Agents are judged by their language, demeanor, and dress. Whenever possible, I try to imagine my grandmother sitting on the jury. Would she be offended? Would she judge me to be as criminally culpable as the defendant? Typically, I try to let the target drop the f-bombs — although, as I've already said, when you're working the streets and need to blend in, you can't always talk like a choirboy. Still, there's a difference, in my view, between protective camouflage and being gratuitously or habitually foulmouthed. Let the bad guy make the suggestive comments and racial slurs, whenever possible.

The NAMBLA case was especially challenging in this regard. Jurors who have any familiarity with TV may forgive a rough-talking undercover agent and may even expect it. Chances are the juror might also resort to foul language in certain circumstances. But throughout this role, I was burdened with passing as a BL, yet not personally detailing sexually explicit acts that would sicken or disgust the jury. This was especially difficult because we needed the targets to discuss the specific sexual acts they desired to perform. We needed details, not generalities. How could I elicit those specifics from their lips without shocking the jury with my own language? It was a constant dilemma.

I preferred the targets to speak in graphic street terms, but I needed to remain almost clinical. I hoped to get each target to detail his desires in the coarsest language, especially concerning his sexual history with underage boys. Yet, at the same time, I knew that if I explored that topic with a suspect, I might be expected to discuss my sexual history as well. On the one hand, I knew that if I portrayed myself as a virgin, my credibility would be destroyed; yet, if I provided lurid details of alleged previous sexual encounters, a jury might view me as disgusting and just as bad as the defendants I was trying to implicate. It was a most difficult line to maneuver.

Based upon my correspondence with incarcerated members who participated in the pen-pal program, I was convinced that if I graphically discussed my history, our targets would respond in kind. I decided, however, to take the high road and tried to skate around the questions as they arose.

Todd, for example, wanted to know my expectations for the trip. My response was cautious. "I hope that I can find someone that wants to love me and let me love them. . . . It's been a long time since I've really been able to spend quality time alone with someone."

Todd told me he had "never spent quality time. . . . It's been experiences I can count on a few fingers, and then it's been rushed or an environment where it was scary because you were afraid you were gonna get caught. . . . So, never have I spent what I would describe as quality time with the age group that I desire. I'm very excited."

The youngest boy Todd had been with was thirteen, he told me, "ten days away from his fourteenth birthday." Todd met him at a health club when Todd was attending dental school. Todd was working out and noticed the boy inside the club. When the boy left the club, he "motioned with his head to come outside, and, boy, did I drop everything." Todd followed the youngster into the grocery store and stood by the magazine rack, so as not to miss him if he left the store. The boy picked up a magazine and Todd followed him into a closed restaurant deli area of the store. They talked for about two minutes, then went to Todd's car, he said. They drove to a quiet neighborhood where they engaged in mutual oral sex. "It was awesome," Todd said. Todd met him again when the boy was fifteen.

When I broached the subject of anal sex, Todd said, "I'm very into that kind of stuff, absolutely. I can't imagine a typical ten- to twelve-year-old having the ability to accommodate in that way." But he was looking forward to anal sex. I countered, saying that I "just like to be held and caressed. . . . I want to be able to experience everything that I want to experience." I was trying to keep the conversation general yet still encouraging to Todd, in case he wanted to make more admissions.

Todd had known for a long time that he was a BL, but was also attracted to women earlier in life. He grew less attracted to women over the years, however. When younger, he was desirous of having children and thought that he could make marriage work. He loved his wife and described their sex life as "good." But, as the marriage progressed, his wife "gained weight and grew less attractive" to him. This was one of several problems that led to the divorce.

Todd said that while he was working as a nurse's aide there were opportunities to touch the penis "for like a half second" while bathing a kid, and that "was exciting!"

When I said this travel opportunity was going to be exciting and could be a regular event like the one depicted in the movie *Same Time Next Year,* Todd responded with a laugh. "Same time next month. . . . How about May? How about September?"

To maintain my cover story and in order to discourage any homosexual advances, I told Todd, "Body hair just turns me off." Todd said he didn't like body hair anywhere, except "pubic is fine, little bit of underarm is fine and that's all I want. . . . So, really, I guess I ought to request twelve- and thirteen-year-olds and take it that by the time they're fourteen, there could be a greater likelihood of hair."

Todd continued to press me for details of my "friend's" trip. Again, I made up the details as we spoke, glad that I would have the opportunity to review the conversation in order to keep my facts straight for subsequent calls. My friend went with a group, I told him, but knew no one prior to the trip. I described individual rooms featuring king-size beds in a large, well-appointed hacienda atmosphere. When I said he traveled as recently as October, Todd was relieved to learn there was no police action resulting from the excursion.

The one aspect of my work that has always

troubled me is that almost all my efforts result in destruction rather than growth. I'm not an architect who can point to an edifice I designed; I'm not a writer who can pull my book from the shelf and display it to friends — well, until now, that is. The point is, my work, my arrests, often lead to destroyed families and shattered lives — oftentimes innocent lives.

At some point in this investigation, the day would come when at least two children, an ex-wife, parents, and loved ones were going to see on the evening news or read in their morning paper that their dad, their friend, their son, their ex-spouse had been arrested for planning to have sex with boys. It would be devastating to have to face the neighbors, the children at school, the friends at church or at the market. Yet, time and time again, men and women are willing to subject their loved ones to such humiliation because their desires to commit crimes outweigh their love of decency.

Make no mistake: I know my work may make the streets safer. I was honored to carry a badge and aid the incarceration of those who seek to destroy the fabric of society . . . but I still have feelings for the innocent casualties of my work — especially the families of those who choose to step outside the boundaries the law imposes on society.

Our next "three-way" was on December 19. David enjoyed making a sexual reference to our group calls, and I enjoyed the overwhelming evidence I collected with each conversation. Todd's office phone had the capability to make the conference call, so he always made the connection. There was some delay in getting us all connected on this particular evening and I joked it gave David enough time to turn on his recorder. Mine was already running.

David complained about the six-degree-below-zero temperature he was experiencing in Chicago, and I was reminded that I needed to move the trip along for fear he might take advantage of one of his free flights and visit me in warm Southern California. I was not prepared to entertain a pedophile for much more than the time it would take to arrest him, so I hoped to redirect the conversation away from his complaints about his local weather.

Early in the call, David dropped an unexpected bombshell. The FBI was still attempting to fully identify those we were targeting and based upon all David said, we assumed he was an international flight attendant. However, David revealed he only flew part-time, enough to maintain his flying privileges with American Airlines, and that his full-time occupation was as a psychologist. He mentioned having a degree in psychology at the Miami conference but never said anything about practicing. As it turned out, though, in addition to working at several Chicago-area hospitals, he did consulting work for the Department of Health and Human Resources in Washington, D.C. In a way, David was a Fed.

We were still trying to attract more passengers for our Mexican excursion. David said neither of the two friends he invited to join us on the trip would be coming. I expressed my concern — genuine — that the friends might object to the actual purpose of our trip and contact law enforcement. David assured us they were not concerned with the activity itself, just the timing. They would be available for a future trip. Todd was pleased when I said I contacted Jeff Devore and he was interested. Todd said he "hung around him quite a bit in New York" and hoped Jeff would join us. David had not yet contacted Paul, but said he would. When I suggested Bob, the attorney from Atlanta, both Todd and David opposed contacting him but never clearly explained why.

Their opposition raised another problem with the investigation. Obviously, the FBI wanted to snare as many as would commit to the scenario, since it was our position that all members of NAMBLA, especially those who attended the conference, were predisposed to have sex with minors. But, as the undercover agent, I could not overtly go against the wishes of Todd and David without possibly alienating them from participation. I also needed to be careful that my greed would not result in someone sensing the sting, then alerting all the others and blowing the investigation.

Both Todd and David were having problems connecting with the undercover travel agency and had not yet sent their deposits. I offered to assist in contacting the agency. In an effort to get David to commit to the type of sex acts he wanted on the trip, I asked him what he was expecting. With a hearty laugh, he said, "Warm weather." I offered that Todd wanted anal intercourse, and David responded, "That would be nice, but not necessary . . . icing on the cake, but I'm not holding my breath." Todd interrupted to say that he didn't believe a typical ten- to twelve-year-old could "accommodate that." David, however, didn't see that as a problem.

The Los Angeles and San Diego offices of the Bureau were still determining how to handle the prosecution of the case. My San Diego case agent and I met with Assistant United States Attorney Anne Perry, and we were awaiting a decision by her office as to whether they would prosecute. The San Diego U.S. Attorney's office had only done a limited number of travel cases, and even though Anne was extremely eager to prosecute, her bosses expressed some reluctance in assuming the prosecutorial lead. Los Angeles, on the other hand, regularly prosecuted travel cases and was fully supportive of our efforts. It was another administrative issue I was hoping to avoid. I was the undercover agent in three separate operations — one with national security implications — and had little time or patience for bureaucratic haggling. In fact, by now you may have figured out that even if I had only one case I was working on alternate weekends, administrative procedures would not be high on my priority list.

As I was awaiting a prosecutorial decision, I was trying to coordinate Todd and David's commitment to fly into either Los Angeles or San Diego. Todd had already made reservations to fly into L.A. The boat would supposedly leave Los Angeles for a four-hour journey, making a stop in San Diego, prior to heading for the ultimate destination at Ensenada, three hours south of San Diego. I convinced him the shortened travel time on the boat made San Diego the preferred launching spot, and Todd agreed to change his reservation to San Diego. David said he could use his connections to get us reservations at a Hilton Hotel the night before the scheduled departure.

Everything was falling into place. The trip had developed into a team effort, with each of us accepting certain responsibilities. A conspiracy completely orchestrated by the undercover agent may result in a legal collar, but it always gives rise to defense arguments that the client was entrapped, coerced, or an unwilling participant in a government sting operation that smacked of "gross governmental misconduct." So far, Todd and David were willing and equal partners in our travel-for-sex conspiracy, and that was just the way I wanted it.

35
SWARMING TO
THE BAIT

NAMBLA prided itself on maintaining the privacy of its membership list. Even the letter praising my "courageous step" for joining the organization stated, "Be assured that our records are confidential and will not be released to anyone." Neither David nor Todd had Steve Irvin's contact information. Steve and I had not exchanged e-mail addresses or phone numbers while in Miami. On December 20, I took a long shot at trying to obtain the information from Peter Herman. Although, I had not sent Christmas cards nor had Steve Irvin agreed to help on the privacy pamphlet project, I e-mailed Peter the following:

Peter,
Hope your holidays are going well. I sent my cards out and hope they are received in the spirit they were sent. It always saddens me to know that so many

of our brothers are there because of archaic beliefs. Someday society will be enlightened.

At the conference, Steve from Pittsburgh offered to help me with the privacy pamphlet and I lost his email address. I know you don't like to give those out but could you either give me his address or give him mine. I'd really like to connect with him so we could finish up this project.

Peter took the bait and two days later responded with Steve's e-mail address, a major coup.

David reported on his promise to attempt to call Paul with a December 20 e-mail. It was really pretty humorous.

Howdy from the Frozen Tundra of the Upper Midwest!

Not sure if I should laugh or cry over my attempt to speak to Paul. Hope this translates onto paper. I called shortly after 6:00 pm EST & got his father (he identified himself as his father — this is an important point). I of course asked for Paul & was told he was not home but to call back later that "afternoon." I pointed out that it was already after 6:00

pm & could he be more specific when to reach Paul. He finally stated that I should call back in 90 minutes. He then asked me who I was & I identified myself as Dr. Mayer. "Father" then asked what kind of doctor I was, stating that Paul was not under a doctor's care. I stated it was confidential & would not discuss the matter. We went through that scenario two times. Not pretty. I was able to intimidate him & he took my # stating he would have Paul call me as soon as he got home. End of Part One. Part Two:

In less than ten minutes my cell phone rang with caller ID showing the number in Florida. "Yeah!" I thought to myself . . . wrong! MUMSIE calling. This nasty woman starts screaming at me that "my husband Paul has been dead for two years" & why am I calling! I must admit that she threw me for a second, however I made a rapid recovery . . . in between her screaming at me I asked why "Father" stated he (Paul) would be home in 90 minutes, etc. That shut her up for three seconds . . . then she started asking what kind of doctor I am, etc. I again stated that it was confidential; she then screamed at me that her husband is dead & don't ever call again. CLICK.

End of Part Two.

Either of you care to place a bet if Paul got the message? I am fearful that Mums is making his life miserable over the calls. However, there must be some way to rescue this guy. Daddy — how about the same technique for Paul as for Pittsburgh? Can you ask Sam for help? By the way, you can tell Sam that Peter's email address is on the web site. I think Paul should go live with Daddy on his estate; I am sure you must have a spare bungalow on the property. Maybe he can be the pool boy?

Not a problem for me to mail you a check. Just let me know the amount. I will also need full name, address, etc. (aren't we just getting intimate!). By the way, as of today's mail I still have not heard a word from [the undercover travel agency].

Daddy — another project for you. Could you go to the Hilton Hotel web site (which will also include all other property such as DoubleTree, Hampton Inns, etc) & let me know which hotel we want for the one night — I do not know SD @ all. Did not know if we wanted to stay @ airport, in the city, by the water, etc. Select the hotel & I will make the arrangements.

Nothing else to report @ this time. If by some miracle Paul calls I will call both of you. Don't hold your breath! Also, if Paul does call, do you want me to give him both of your #'s or just have me be the contact?

Speak to you both next Monday evening if not sooner. Merry Christmas.

On December 27 David e-mailed to say he had still not heard from the undercover travel agency. He also asked, "Daddy, any word from any of the others: The First Lady? Kathy Bates' son, Paul? David of Miami (could you send me his e-mail? I will also try to convince him to join us). How is the hotel search going?"

When I checked my undercover post office box later in the day, I was pleased to find a letter from David containing one more nail for his coffin: a personal check in the amount of $620.

Todd set up another three-way conversation that evening, a call that would continue to bury David and Todd in the criminal conspiracy. Todd spoke of his desire to bring the "boys" back with him. David finally received the application from the undercover travel agency and would forward the completed application to me. He also would make reservations for us to stay at the San Diego Airport Hilton on February 11, the night before our maiden voyage.

As we discussed other potential travelers, David referred to David R. Busby as a "slut," but that apparently didn't preclude him from being invited. David said he would contact Steve Irvin. And as if Mexico were not enough, Todd and David initiated plans for a Costa Rica trip after Ensenada. They also wanted me to ask "Sean," the name I made up for my imaginary friend, what gifts and trinkets they should bring the boys to insure appropriate sexual favors.

Todd and I spoke briefly on December 28. Most noteworthy was the fact he said Steve Irvin approached them at Miami about going on a trip. I was unaware of that fact and was glad Steve followed up on my suggestion during our brief encounter at the conference. When I asked Todd if he knew of men other than those who were in Miami that might interested, he reiterated the mantra of NAMBLA: "I don't know anybody of like mind but know that there are plenty of us out there. . . . It's not like you can put a sign on the front yard: 'Hey, all BLs, call me up. Let's go on a trip.' "

On December 30, David e-mailed me to

say he was leaving that evening for Frankfurt, Germany, and had e-mailed David R. Busby and Steve Irvin. His December 27 e-mail to Steve was brief and somewhat circumspect.

Just a quick reminder that we met in Miami a couple of months ago @ a conference. You asked me to let you know if I was planning on any holidays. Three of us from the conference are planning a trip to Mexico in February. You are more than welcome to join us — it will be for four days. If you are interested, let me know; I can give you more details. Cost is around $620.00 including lodging and meals.

Steve responded to David's e-mail a few days later.

Sure I remember you. Yes, I would definitely be interested. Thanks for asking. I really didn't get a chance to visit a lot when we were at the conference. I guess I should have just taken a day off work, and not rushed my trip. . . . I start my sabbatical from work in February. . . . Anyhow, thanks again, David, for asking. Since I didn't really talk a lot to anyone I thought maybe you wouldn't write. I'm just overall pretty quiet. Smiled when I got the email!

David forwarded me Steve's response, and we began preparation for another traveler. Steve's primary concern was the cost of airfare. Since we had set up the boat trip to begin in L.A. with a stopover in San Diego, it provided a perfect alternative. It allowed the travelers to choose their departing locale. Since flights into LAX were generally less expensive than those into San Diego, each could travel to either city. By providing a choice, it may have also minimized any suspicions that this was a sting. From an evidentiary standpoint, it also added a free-will element to the decision each traveler made.

The same day I received David's e-mail with Steve's forward attached, I e-mailed Steve, setting out the details of the trip and providing my undercover cell phone number, suggesting we speak over the phone rather than trade e-mails. Steve responded with his cell number and a home number, setting in motion our next traveler: the special education teacher from Pittsburgh.

Steve's e-mail provided valuable evidence for predisposition. The e-mail confirmed

what he told me at the conference and what
the FBI suspected was happening at these
gatherings: Steve had traveled previously
and arranged that travel through a contact
at the NAMBLA conference.

I'll call you later today. I just keep
smiling! Really looking forward to the
trip. Went to Santo Domingo several
years ago with someone from the conference and had a great time. One of the
best times of my life. I looked on the
computer under cheaptickets and found
flights to San Diego for $250. Smile!
When I talk to you, we can discuss sending the $620. I am so happy I was
invited along. I was quiet at the conference and then the way I planned the trip
it was pretty fast. Didn't really get to
know anyone very well, but thank you!

In the morning, on New Year's Eve, Steve
called me and left a voice mail message.
That afternoon, I returned the call. My
contact with Steve at the conference had
been minimal. I remembered him as tall,
thin, quiet, and in his mid-forties. On the
phone, he displayed a gentle nature I'm sure
made him well suited to teach special
education. He reminded me of Sam Lind-

blad, who also taught special education prior to his conviction. Did both these men have a genuine love for mentally, physically, and emotionally handicapped children, or were these youngsters just easier to manipulate and victimize?

Steve last attended a NAMBLA conference in 1988, where he met Bob Rhodes. Rhodes's name was known to me, having been featured in the movie *Chicken Hawk* and on several Web sites discussing NAMBLA. He was also named in the Jeffrey Curley wrongful death civil lawsuit. A rotund individual, I thought of Rhodes as a "central casting" pedophile; he looked like someone you'd want to keep an eye on, should he show up at a park or playground. I didn't remember Steve in that way. Steve said he and Rhodes went to Santo Domingo and had a "great time . . . at a bed and breakfast . . . and got boys there." Steve's experiences sounded similar to those shared by David. Steve had already checked into airline prices and was "definitely interested" in traveling with "like-minded people." Again, in the almost providential way this case was coming together, Steve was to begin a one-year sabbatical from his teaching responsibilities in February. Had Todd, David, and I chosen a January weekend,

Steve would have been unable to join us.

Steve had been a member of NAMBLA for many years but had not been active recently. He marched at Stonewall and attended conferences in the mid-eighties. He also spoke of his hatred for George W. Bush and "Ashcroft cronies." I didn't ask, but I assume he did not think highly of the FBI, either. Steve said he had been inactive in NAMBLA and had only recently communicated again with Peter Herman, who encouraged him to "not live your life in fear." Thanks to Peter's encouragement and invitation, Steve decided to attend the Miami conference.

Although his age of preference was "around fourteen," he described himself as "very versatile" and that he did "different things with different people . . . very easily pleased. . . . Of course, I love good sex, but I'm not very demanding."

Steve admitted to coming to the Miami conference with the idea of finding someone with whom to travel and told me he approached David when he learned David might be putting something together. Another tally mark in the "NAMBLA networking" column.

He was open on the phone, but I was reluctant to push too hard. He said teaching provided the benefits of being near boys and that many boys came on to him. He denied having any "special friend" at the time we were talking. When I provided him with the Web site information about the travel agency, he promised to send his deposit to reserve a spot. "I am really looking forward to the trip and have a smile on my face."

For the next week or two, Steve and I exchanged e-mails and engaged in several telephone conversations. After some initial problems with the travel agency, he was able to connect, work out the details, and set up his flight into Los Angeles. I suggested Steve invite Bob Rhodes, but he had lost contact. Even when he asked Peter where Rhodes was, Peter claimed not to know.

The new year meant continued investigative and undercover responsibilities in all three of my then-current undercover operations. It did not take long for the Ensenada conspiracy to grow. On January 2, I was able to contact Paul Zipszer, something the others had been unsuccessful in doing. Paul and I briefly exchanged pleasantries before I sprang the invitation. He hesitated, but only momentarily. Again, his concern was finances, not criminal culpability. I laid out the details of the trip and relayed David

Mayer's offer to help with airfare to California. Paul took David's number and promised to call him to discuss the details.

In just a few days, our party of traveling pedophiles had grown from three — David Mayer from Chicago, Todd the "divorced dentist from Dallas," and me — to five, if both Steve Irwin and Paul Zipzser followed through on their professed interest. And, I would soon learn, there were more fish eyeing the hook.

36
GREG NUSCA, AKA
DAVID R. BUSBY

David Mayer was overseas, but I called Todd that evening with the news I contacted Paul. I was fighting a cold, and when Todd noted that I sounded different on the phone, I said I was using my "heterosexual voice." Todd laughed at this, then told me he was pleased one of us was able to connect with Paul. I attributed my success to the cold and the fact that I claimed to be a friend from the gym seeking a personal trainer.

Although David R. Busby had been ignoring my communications, he did respond to David Mayer's e-mail, and David forwarded it to me.

> Great to hear from you!! Mexico sounds great, I'd love to go. I'm not sure I can come up with that kind of money, although getting off work will not be a problem. Let me hash it over, and I'll

get back to you ASAP.

By the way, you told me that you knew of a good website featuring boy feet. Would you e-mail me back a link?

I'll email you soon. A very Happy New Year to you!!

A new target emerged, and I needed to prepare.

On January 4, I sent David R. Busby the following:

So excited that you may be able to join us for the trip. I really hope finances won't get in the way. We may be able to help. As we get more travelers, the price goes down. One thing: it's probably cheaper to fly into LAX than San Diego. Several of us will be getting on the boat there, rather than in SD. Don't be shy, let me know. Love to help you join us.

I said the magic words: "we may be able to help." After practically ignoring me for almost two months, David R. Busby responded in fewer than eight hours.

Can you give me a call? I want to talk about a few details of the trip. For example, I didn't know that we were talking about a cruise until you mentioned it in this email. . . . I'm excited about the prospect of going if I am able, I just want to ask a few questions. Thanks!

The next day, on January 5, I called the number David gave me, and when the voice mail picked up, it identified the person as "Greg Nusca," or at least I thought that was what it said. I could not quite make out the name on the voice mail greeting. I checked the number he provided and redialed. Again: "Greg Nusca." I did not recognize the voice and decided it was best not to leave a message. Instead, I immediately e-mailed "David R. Busby" and told him of the voice mail encounter. Within minutes, my cell phone rang, it was "David R. Busby" — or, as I would subsequently learn, Greg Nusca.

No one was forced to fully identify himself at the NAMBLA conferences, and as I learned there, Tim from Michigan was not necessarily "Tim," "Peter Herman" was actually Peter Melzer, and "Rock Thatcher" was an alias. I never suspected David R. Busby was not my target's real name until encountering the voice mail message on his phone. He carried himself and his lie with thorough deceit. I guess I should have recognized the work of another professional, but I didn't.

Greg explained the ruse but refused to give me his true name. It was only later we fully identified him. To the real world, he is known as Greg Nusca. In BL circles, he uses the name David R. Busby, an alias consisting of a "conglomerate of four boys that I've been with that I thought were tens" — a sort of memento of his conquests, I guess.

Even though he would not provide his true name, he had little problem incriminating himself in our phone conversation. A production manager at a Miami-area print shop, he hoped to go to massage school and become a physical trainer working with boys' athletic teams. He told me he found "Mexican and Brazilian boys very arousing," and after I explained the details of the trip, he said that he would sell his mother to go. Before that sale was completed, however, he needed me to spot him the money until his tax refund check arrived. He agreed to pay the two-hundred-dollar deposit, and I fronted the rest.

Greg's age of preference was nine or ten, and he wanted the "whole enchilada" — he was looking for anal sex.

I provided him the Web site and e-mail

address of the travel agency and asked him to invite Sam from Miami. Greg Nusca, aka David R. Busby, one of the newest members of the NAMBLA steering committee, was excited about the upcoming trip and a more-than-willing participant. I was confident we had snagged another sexual predator on our "Mexican sex cruise."

On January 6, Greg left a lengthy voice mail message while I was in the air, flying to meet Sam Lindblad in Albuquerque. With time to ponder his decision to join us, he thought of several questions. Greg detailed his concerns in the voice mail: He had still not heard from the travel agency and wondered how I heard of it. Although he trusted me, he was preparing to make nonrefundable airline reservations and wanted to make sure the trip would, in fact, happen. Sam from Miami would not be able to join us and Greg assured me he promised not to tell Peter Herman. Greg added that even if Peter told him not to go, he would still join us.

I was a little worried on the flight in, since I was traveling with my San Diego case agent. I didn't know how big the Albuquerque airport was, and didn't want to risk running into Sam Lindblad while in the company of another FBI agent, in case Sam got overeager and decided to surprise me by picking me up at the airport. He stuck to our plan, however, and I was able to score a Mustang for my rental car — a decided improvement over the "soccer mom" ride I'd had at the Miami NAMBLA conference.

Our Albuquerque contact briefed my case agent and me on the scope of the Lindblad investigation, which he had been pursuing diligently, despite certain administrative hurdles presented by the Bureau. He was eager to assist us in any way and agreed to cover me in my meeting with Lindblad that evening, along with my San Diego case agent.

Once I settled into my Albuquerque hotel room, I called Greg. He said Sam from Miami wouldn't be able to join us because it was too difficult for him to travel. He noted that Sam's advanced age prevented him from engaging in much sexual activity, but Greg told Sam he would allow him to watch Greg have sex with a boy if Sam desired. What a pal! I put Greg at ease, answering his questions and reinforcing the validity of the trip.

New questions arose the next day, however, after Greg received an e-mail from the travel agency, asking for a mailing address so they could send him the brochure and application. Greg did not want to identify himself to the travel agency or provide an address. He even had reservations about the manner in which to provide the two-hundred-dollar deposit — cash, check, or money order? My frustration growing with each contact and with his endless questions, I almost wanted to say, "Don't worry about it, you're going to jail under any name you use." I maintained my composure, and after what seemed like a lengthy discussion, I convinced him that I would mail him my extra copy of the brochure to any name and address that he provided. His solution was an intelligence-gathering coup: he provided the name and address of Sam from Miami — another NAMBLA member identified. Greg repeated that his age of preference was "nine to ten" and bragged that he once had an eight-year-old "go down" on him.

I got off the phone, his boast still ringing in my ears: eight years old. As I wrestled with my anger over the thought of Greg Nusca debauching a boy so young, I remembered another eight-year-old whose innocence was erased — but for a very different reason.

It happened while I was working gangs in L.A. We had just conducted one of our all-too-frequent searches, hoping to locate a gang member wanted for murder. We hit the house with a court-authorized arrest warrant in hand. We successfully found our teenage murderer asleep in his bed, and as two police officers took him away, several members of our task force spoke to the grandmother with whom he was living. I walked back out to the car and found the gang member's eight-year-old brother sitting on the curb, crying. I sat down next to him without saying a word.

After a while, he dried his tears and asked, "Did my brother kill someone?"

I sort of dodged giving him a direct answer. "We just need to talk with your brother," I told him. "We have to ask him a few questions and need to clear up some things."

"My dad killed my mom," he said. "That's why I'm living with my grandmother." He paused and added, "I hope my brother didn't kill anybody." He then began talking about guns and how plentiful they were in his neighborhood. "I hear gunshots all the time."

What he said didn't surprise me. In the early sixties, Los Angeles averaged about six gang-related homicides a year. By the time I got involved in gang investigations in the late eighties, local law enforcement tallied gang-related homicides at well over five hundred per year. By any standard of measurement, this little boy was living in a war zone.

I followed up one of his comments by asking him how many people he had seen killed. He looked down at his open hand and began counting his fingers. He looked up and asked, "You mean shot, or killed?"

A lump began to form in my throat as I thought about my own son, who was also eight at the time, and the boys I coached on our youth league baseball team. This little guy should have been playing ball, watching cartoons, and dreaming about his future. Instead, he was dodging bullets, just hoping to survive long enough to be nine. After a few more calculations, he said, "I've seen eight people killed."

His innocence was stolen, just as BLs stole the innocence of the boys they seduced.

In the world of the BL, a question frequently asked early in any encounter is, "What's your age of preference?" In the outside world it might be like asking a teacher which grade she preferred to teach or asking me which age group I preferred to coach. But for the BL it has very explicit sexual implications. Although some men I met or corresponded with were satisfied with any underage boy, most had very specific desires. In one conversation a BL said, "Eight to ten, nothing older, nothing younger."

I was thinking about all this as I prepared for my interview with Sam Lindblad in Albuquerque.

Sam was right on time, a good sign. We made our way through the lobby of the hotel to the Rancher's Club, where I had made reservations. I said I wanted a quiet corner to conduct business, and the hostess was most accommodating. The rustic setting provided a perfect atmosphere for a business dinner: saddles, Western artifacts, and artwork adorned the walls. I was not disappointed by the meal, either. The Rancher's Club had received numerous well-deserved awards for fine dining, and it definitely received my personal Undercover Agent's Gold Star Seal of Approval. The meal was expensive, but price is no object when you have an undercover credit card.

Sam ordered the New York sirloin and red beets. As a twenty-six-year veteran of the FBI, having spent many of those years in various undercover roles, I can categorically say I have never dined with a target who ordered red beets. I'm not sure I've ever been to a restaurant that offered red beets. My choice was a bit more exotic, taking advantage of the unique menu. Selecting from the mixed grill, I chose the double-bone antelope chop, grilled wild boar sausage, and venison tenderloin, with baked sweet potato and sautéed mushrooms — a five-star meal to go with the five-star admissions I would gain that evening.

The joint project for the *Bulletin* provided the perfect vehicle for allowing Sam to openly discuss his past. Keeping with my handicap cover, I asked Sam if it would be okay to record our conversation, since writing was sometimes difficult because of my "condition." He readily agreed to my request, never inquiring into the exact nature of my medical problems.

I placed a small recorder on the table and began asking some prepared questions. At appropriate times, I turned off the recorder to inquire about more intimate details. What Sam didn't know was that I was wearing a separate recording device, and when the table-top recorder was off, my body wire was still running. That evening I obtained a wealth of information — most of it rather disturbing.

37
Diary of a
Sexual Predator

Out of prison less than fourteen months, Sam Lindblad made criminal admissions throughout the evening, including a statement that he molested over twenty boys. As a twenty-year-old camp counselor, he let a boy sleep in his sleeping bag. While on a cruise with his wife, "a ten-year-old caught my eye and before I knew it I was sleeping with him on the deck." Even after being released from prison, he attended a church where he "hung around the older brother [an eighteen-year-old] 'cause I liked the younger brother [a thirteen-year-old]." Once, while at their home during the mother's working hours, Sam was in the kitchen helping the thirteen-year-old and his sister with the dishes. The mother called and Sam instructed them "not to tell their mother" that he was there. I'm sure if the mother had realized her children were at home alone with a recently released sex offender, she would have found someone to cover her shift.

Sam had a master's degree in special education and worked with the developmentally disabled. Obviously, such employment provided him with a target-rich environment and he took advantage of his position. He denied engaging in oral or anal sex but said he enjoyed "fondling." His age of preference, "nine- to fourteen-year-olds," was a pretty broad range compared to most of the men I encountered. Since many boys begin puberty before fourteen, few men I met targeted both pre- and postpubescent boys.

Our discussion of the prison rehabilitation program brought into question the value of any organized effort at rehabilitation, at least as far as it applied to boy lovers. Sam said something that never occurred to me.

The mandated prison counseling program he attended consisted of approximately fifty inmates, all sex offenders. By Sam's estimates, 10 to 20 percent were boy lovers. Here, for the first time in his life, thanks to the required prison counseling, he met other BLs. "I made some good friends in the program," he told me. Even more enlightening was the fact that despite the counseling and therapy, he still considered

480

himself a BL. "I don't know anybody that's gone through the therapy [who changed sexually as a result]. . . . You don't get cured and they know that. . . . You play the game. . . . It's not what's between your legs; it's what's in your brain."

Sam's frank admissions reflected the views expressed on the NAMBLA Web site regarding their "Prison Program."

Some states conduct "therapy" programs for inmates, and for parolees once they are released. The therapy ranges from drug therapy and aversion therapy to group counseling. For parole or early release, an inmate's "cooperation" with the prison therapists conducting these programs is required. Prisoners are required to enroll for a "cure," to participate, and to seem to be rehabilitated. . . . These programs have *never* [emphasis added] been shown to have any lasting value for the prisoner or for society.

I once heard Vin Scully, the voice of the Los Angeles Dodgers, say that statistics are like a lamppost to a drunk: they are used more for support than illumination. Sam's "therapy" program and his admissions of offending multiple times since his release reminded me of a study I read in preparing for this investigation. The Sex Offender Treatment Program established by the Federal Bureau of Prisons at the Federal Correctional Institution in Butner, North Carolina, studied ninety inmates who volunteered for the treatment program. During their presentence interviews, these ninety prisoners, who were admitted or convicted child sexual offenders, admitted to 106 sexual contact crimes. After completion of the federal treatment program, these same ninety inmates admitted to 1,728 previously undocumented sexual contacts. Each offender admitted to an average of 19.2 additional and previously undocumented sexual contacts. How many of the men we were targeting were truthful in admitting, either to me or their counselors while in therapy, to the number of sexual contacts they had with minors?

For Sam, the therapy sessions provided him with insights into his own psychological malaise, but he remained a sex offender — albeit a sex offender with a better understanding of why he offended.

Sam's admissions reinforced what I discovered throughout this investigation. The sexual offenders with whom I was dealing were not those who, under cover of darkness, slipped past sleeping parents into the bedroom of an unsuspecting child. These offenders began their quest in full view of an unsuspecting public. They were our sons' teachers, doctors, therapists, neighbors, friends, and relatives. Their responsible behavior in public causes us to drop our guard. We somehow believe we are smart enough to recognize the pervert lurking in the shadows and, as a result of that confidence, fail to see the predator in our midst.

Since relocating to Albuquerque, Sam joined a gay men's chorus. Recently, the group performed at a Unitarian Church. A seventh grader, the son of the man from the church who organized the performance, sat in the front row. At a postconcert reception, Sam served the boy punch, and they began a discussion. "He was so pleased to have somebody respond to him and share opinions," said Sam. Sam wrote a thank-you note to the father and included a note to the son. Sam's own words best describe his motivation: "I haven't heard back, but I was grooming."

Some sex offenders with whom I communicated enjoyed the planning stages of the seduction almost as much as the actual sexual experience. Sam's attempt at grooming seemed textbook. He sought the child's friendship, as well as the friendship of the parents. The grooming process began with a "look" at the concert, it continued when Sam provided the boy with refreshments following the performance, and it certainly continued with the conversation, in which Sam lavished praise on the boy for his insights and maturity. Sam was attempting to build trust. Maybe his only mistake was in choosing a boy whose father was in a position to see through Sam's attempts. As I learned so often in my correspondence, the most easily conquered target is one without a strong, loving, caring father figure.

I take a deep, personal satisfaction at succeeding in my undercover role. During the evening's conversation, two comments brought an inner joy reflecting that success. First, as Sam was complaining about law enforcement's interest in him following his release from prison, he noted he often believed he was being watched. When I asked if he thought he was being watched while we ate, he didn't respond until I added that I chose the pricey restaurant because I knew "no cop could afford to eat here." He laughed and readily concurred. Meanwhile, my surveillance agents were two tables away.

But the second line I will always remember

came when I asked what piece of advice he wanted to impart to the membership through our article. His answer was an undercover classic. He made a fist for emphasis, looked me in the eye, and pleaded, "Be aware that there are many, many sting operations going on. I was not aware of that ten years ago." He still wasn't!

As the evening was drawing to a close, I sensed the time was right to give Sam Lindblad a sniff of the bait.

Me: I'm a little reluctant to ask you this.

Sam: I don't have to answer.

Me: Would you be interested in going on a vacation? We have a place in Mexico that is a bed and breakfast and a friend of mine has been twice, as recently as October. He's going with us. It's a BL's delight. I don't want you to get in trouble. . . . But I want to throw out the invitation to you.

Sam: I've heard about such things. . . . It sounds like something I can't say no to. . . . I'm very glad you did ask me, even though you were reticent about asking, if for no other reason than just to know that such things exist, not only in Thailand.

Sam asked if he could invite Dick Stutsman because he was "lonely too." How could I refuse? Sam said he would call Stutsman the next day and let me know the answer. He also promised not to tell Peter.

I left the Rancher's Club that evening a very satisfied agent: I enjoyed a truly memorable meal, I afforded my two backup agents the same opportunity, I acquired incriminating admissions from a convicted sex offender, and I potentially gained two more members for the Ensenada BL tour. Altogether, a rather fruitful day's work.

Meanwhile, I was trying to navigate around a few shoals and other obstacles in the path of the investigation — some being placed by the Bureau. A few days earlier, some administrative issues arose that forced me to place my UC activities on hold until the regulatory difficulties could be resolved; form over substance as far as I could tell. I quickly concocted a cover story that I was taking a trip to Australia on some business for one of my family's "foundations," and would be out of contact with Todd, David Mayer, and the others until I returned. When my San Diego supervisor concluded with me that HQ was wrong about their self-imposed issues, we resumed the operation — without Headquarters' concurrence — and I "cancelled" my Australia trip.

I communicated this to Todd and David Mayer, and recapped for them my recent successes in getting past Paul Zipszer's fiercely protective mother and potentially recruiting David R. Busby for the trip. I mentioned to them that in both cases financial assistance would likely be required.

In a return e-mail, Todd casually mentioned that he had been informed that his deposit and trip application had gone to the wrong PO box. He immediately called and e-mailed the undercover travel agent to determine if his materials were ever received.

This was worrisome: The travel brochures apparently had a wrong address printed on them, and one of my suspects' all-important indications of intent had gone astray. But my cover story needed protection as well, since I repeatedly told my targets I was in mail contact with the travel agency. I quickly concocted a cover for my cover: the travel agency had printed "new" brochures with a wrong address. I had been using an "old" brochure with the correct address. I told Todd I called "my friend Sean" about the problem and received assurances the travel agency knew about the mistake and was taking steps to resolve it with no inconvenience to its customers. In other words, Todd didn't need to stop payment on the check he used to purchase his money order.

Our group was growing. Just before I left for Albuquerque, I was awakened by an early-morning phone call. I groped for my phone, groggy since I had been up past three am on a phone call related to the national security case I was also working on at the time. I had been speaking to a foreign general, negotiating a multimillion-dollar "weapons deal." I could barely focus on the caller ID as I tossed a tape into my recording device.

The caller wasn't the general, it was Paul Zipszer, who apparently didn't quite grasp the concept of time differences between Florida and California, but the early-morning wake-up call was worth the disturbance. Paul wanted to join the cruise. Although finances were a problem, he would forward me the two-hundred-dollar deposit and asked me to front him the rest. I gladly accommodated that request. He provided me with his address and said that twelve to thirteen was his age of preference. He also stated that he liked "anal sex but not with a boy this young."

Likewise, it didn't take long for Sam Lindblad to respond to my invitation to join us in Mexico. The day after our meeting at the restaurant, Sam telephoned me and left a voice mail message. He had called Dick Stutsman and both would be going on the trip.

In my return call to Sam, his excitement was evident and apparently contagious. He told me he called Dick earlier in the day and convinced him to join us on the trip. Their plans included Dick driving from South Carolina to Albuquerque, picking up Sam, and driving together to Los Angeles. The interstate travel element of the offense would be easy to prove. Dick was willing to drive over three thousand miles across country, pick up a co-conspirator, and then take an eight-hour boat trip to have sex with underage boys.

Sam did say he would need my financial assistance to make the trip. Dick was going to make Sam's two-hundred-dollar down payment, and Sam asked that I finance the rest. Sam agreed to repay me at fifty dollars a month, even offering to sign a promissory note. I gladly accommodated his request.

38
MY LIFE AS A
GHOSTWRITER

In keeping with my stated purpose for the
trip to Albuquerque, I actually wrote an
article for the *Bulletin* I never expected to
publish — until now. In a perverse way, I
was sort of proud of it, since it provided a
"BL-approved" example of the topsy-turvy
ethics and logic of boy lovers. Since everything in the *Bulletin* is published under some
sort of incomplete or assumed name to
protect everyone's identities, I guess you
could say I did it as a ghostwriter. Here is
an abridged version, appearing for the first
time on the printed page, with Sam Lindblad's name changed to Daniel — to protect
the guilty.

The judge's gavel crashed onto the
mahogany bench and Daniel's heart
sank. The sentence had been imposed. . . . Less than six months ago,
what began as an act of kindness ended

in a prison sentence. At 48, a man who had devoted his life to helping boys was going to spend the next 7 years separated from the objects of his vocation and avocation.

Even at an early age, he found himself attracted to young boys. As a 15-year-old member of 4-H he loved the opportunity to work with the 9- and 10-year-olds. As a 20-year-old, he used his knowledge and skills to mentor boys. Although he married in his early 20s and fathered a son, his attention was always drawn to boys. . . .

Daniel knew he was different from the others. He knew that he loved boys in a way that society failed to understand. He knew that he had to constantly fight to satisfy the natural desires that he had for boys. Maybe someday an enlightened society would understand . . .

[H]e began a teaching career. Catering to the special needs of mentally handicapped boys, he could not only manifest his love in a format acceptable to society, he was able to spend every day with the boys he loved. Over the course of the next decade he was able to develop loving relationships with many boys, relationships that meant as much to him as they did to the boys. Only once was a complaint lodged because of his desires to be near a boy . . .

One day, a mother in need came into [his] business with her son. Daniel was able to help the mother. He also developed a friendship with her son, a friendship that began with the innocent sharing of letters. The youngster lived over 80 miles from Daniel and a regular correspondence resulted. Daniel noticed that the fatherless boy sought his advice on a variety of topics and Daniel was only too eager to help. One day however he noticed that the boy's latest note came from a post office box. The boy said that he opened the box to prevent his mother from reading his mail. . . . Daniel should have listened to that inner nagging voice, especially as the letters became more sexual in nature. . . . As the relationship blossomed, the boy's requests and demands seemed too sophisticated. . . . When Daniel agreed to meet the boy, Daniel was met by the police and arrested on child enticement charges. Daniel had been snared in a trap sprung by a mother who read her son's letters and misinterpreted Daniel's genuine and sincere advice . . .

That night he learned that the mother had contacted the police who opened the post office box and took up the correspondence that the boy had started . . .

What had he done! The news of his arrest spread throughout the county. The reaction of family and friends fell into three categories: abandonment, disbelief, or support. . . . Daniel's acts of kindness have cost him his job, his pension, his livelihood, and his freedom.

He thought of fighting the charges. . . . He could explain each and every sentence he wrote. But taking the stand meant disclosing the prior arrest. . . . A court-appointed attorney encouraged him to take a plea. . . . He reluctantly took the deal offered by the District Attorney.

He began his prison sentence in Colorado but his incarceration resulted in imprisonment in five different institutions over the course of seven plus years . . .

As a sex offender, he was singled out by the prison system. Although he was the target of an attack by a fellow inmate, he managed to survive. Fortunately he was able to participate in a sex treatment program of approximately 50 sex offenders, ten of whom were BLs. The program was most simplistic in its approach, with a Nancy Reagan–type mantra of "just say no." The program demanded that BLs "swear" off boys and tell everyone with whom they come in contact that they are sex offenders. . . . The genius who drafted such an approach had obviously never been the victim of hatred, prejudice, or abuse.

Rather than obtaining an early release, Daniel served the entire sentence. . . . Daniel was, however, a registered sex offender. When he finally settled after his release, he was forced to register with the local police. That registration placed him on the radar screen of the law enforcement authorities. . . . Despite their efforts he was able to meet boys and he even began corresponding until the day they searched his residence. . . . Now he continues to live under the threat that he might be targeted by the local police. He . . . longs for the day that an enlightened society will see the many benefits the BL community brings.

David Mayer and I spoke again on January 7. We shared a laugh when I gloated over the fact that I was able to connect with Paul when he, "my CIA operator," couldn't get through. He told me that his next attempt at reaching Paul had also been thwarted by Paul's mother, whom David called "Kathy Bates," referring to her Academy Award–winning role in the Stephen King thriller *Misery*. "Stupid, she's not," he said. "She may be a drunk. She's probably out of a trailer park somewhere. But, dumb this woman is not."

David began issuing orders I gladly accepted, since they demonstrated his leadership role in the conspiracy. He told me to call Paul again. David needed to set up a time when Paul could call him so the two of them could make arrangements for Paul's American Airlines family pass flight to San Diego. David asked me to make the arrangements because "Kathy Bates ain't gonna let these phone calls go through." David was also concerned that Paul didn't have the application for the trip that needed to be submitted in a timely fashion. I told David I mailed Paul an extra brochure and application. David suggested I fill out the form and forge Paul's signature by signing it with my "opposite hand." David's final question concerned a return flight from San Diego to Dallas, Chicago, and Florida. This question had arisen before. I hoped a return

495

flight would not be an issue because my plan called for all three of them to be in custody not long after getting off the plane in California. However, I responded by detailing our return trip from Mexico with potential arrival times in San Diego, suggesting we might even want to go to Los Angeles after the Mexican trip, extending our vacation time together.

Paul and I spoke on January 8. He was looking forward to joining us for the trip and was going to repair his mother's roof to get the necessary funding for the trip. On January 10, I received his deposit check for two hundred dollars, made out to my undercover name. I had an undercover bank account in a Los Angeles bank. The only San Diego branch for that bank was in Carlsbad, thirty miles away. I needed to cash the check and enter the money into evidence, so I placed those tasks on my to-do list.

We all continued to trade e-mails and voice mails, keeping each other updated on the progress of the trip. David, who was willing to obtain a family pass or use his frequent flier miles for Paul, the bodybuilder, had no desire to assist Steve Irvin or David R. Busby. The reason appeared obvious: David Mayer had a schoolboy crush on Paul and may have been hopeful of taking his romantic adventures beyond the youngsters awaiting him in Mexico. From an investigative standpoint, everything was falling into place.

On January 15 I received Paul's application and a letter.

Hi Robert!

I have filled out the reservation request as you needed. I will be starting my mother's roof repairs this weekend at which time she will pay me and I will forward you the remaining $420. . . . I look forward to seeing you in LA. Thanks again.

Paul

The irony was apparent: His mother, who had so diligently protected him from David and Todd's attempts to invite him into the criminal conspiracy, was now unknowingly providing the funding for him to join us.

Meanwhile, I was still deeply involved in a Los Angeles undercover investigation targeting international weapons dealers and narcotics traffickers and was now trying to minimize my NAMBLA contacts. On January 17, I had a meeting with one of those involved in the weapons deal and was en route to a second meeting with a faction of an Asian organized crime syndicate when my cell phone rang. It was Greg Nusca, aka David R. Busby.

I took the call, quickly switching from my macho, weapons-dealing persona to "Robert," the lover of prepubescent boys. Greg proudly told me he had taken a second job to pay for the Mexican trip, an indication of how important it was to him. I almost laughed out loud as Greg explained that he completed the travel agency application using his alias, David R. Busby, combined with Miami Sam's address — then used his true-name credit card to pay for the trip! Even though we already had him identified, his attempts at secrecy and concealment vanished with that move. I've always joked that I want my target's IQ to be a few points lower than mine. It still makes the project challenging but also gives me a leg up on success. I've never claimed to be the sharpest knife in the drawer, but even I see the futility of trying to conceal my identity when I provide a credit card with my real name on it.

As a way of covertly discussing our planned excursion into Mexico, Sam Lindblad and I began referring to our upcoming "fishing trip." On January 19, Sam responded to the *Bulletin* article I rough-drafted.

Hello, fishing buddy,
   I thought you did an outstanding job of putting our interview into well-chosen words. . . .
   I did receive a brochure from Tim as per our fishing trip on the Iguana. I did pen out a promissory note spelling out my payback to you. I am going to stick it in the mail to you so you have a signed hard copy, but . . . I find I don't have your snail-mail address. Please email that to me. I am excited also. I must admit that I have wondered if there could be any kind of STING here??? It's called paranoia.
   Start cutting bait.

                                  Samuel

In an attempt to ease his fears, I responded, "I'm excited that so many like-minded 'anglers' will soon be together for an unforgettable fishing trip! The only STINGS we'll encounter will be compliments of the jellyfish off the Mexican coast."
   True to his word, on January 25, I received a letter, a check for $50, and a promissory note that read,

To: Robert Wallace
From: Samuel Lindblad

I agree to repay Robert Wallace for the loan of $420.00 or $320.00 (cross out invalid amount) at $50.00 per month till paid in full. Interest rate _____.

Signed: Samuel Lindblad
Date: January 18, 2005

The evidence against Sam, a three-time convicted sex offender, was mounting.

39
LOSING IT?

As the undercover investigations progressed, my health was failing. I was having trouble kicking a cold, but of greater concern was the large amount of blood I was passing in my urine. I made an appointment with a urologist, who performed a cystoscopy. I was still holding Paul's deposit check for two hundred dollars and needed to go to the bank branch where I had an undercover account. I was putting off the trip because it was thirty miles out of the way and more pressing matters were at hand. After one of my doctor's appointments and another unpleasant procedure, I headed to the bank. I was still experiencing a great deal of discomfort and decided to reward myself with a stop at a bookstore that was having a sale. I returned to the car and continued to the bank.

When I arrived at the bank I realized I did not have the check. I searched the car as thoroughly as I would have gone over a drug dealer's vehicle, but to no avail. The check was gone. I had lost evidence, something I had never done before in my career.

Juggling three undercover cases was no excuse. Such mistakes are what defense lawyers use to blister you on the stand, and even though the check was only one small piece of the puzzle and actually insignificant in the overall investigation, it was sloppy work.

Now I had to decide how to handle the revelation to Paul. Obviously, his check would not clear, so he would know something was wrong. Would this arouse his suspicion?

I told my case agent of my mistake, but we didn't have to wait long for resolution. On January 17, Paul left a voice mail telling me that someone had mailed him the check from a bookstore where it had been found.

I called Paul back that evening. Apparently, the check dropped out of my car when I stopped at the bookstore. An employee found it and had the courtesy of returning the uncashed check to Paul, whose address was on the document. My mistake actually became another asset to the investigation: Paul had a second chance to back out but didn't, making clear his intent to go on the trip. During our conversation, Paul said that rather than sending the two-hundred-dollar deposit he would send the entire amount. We discussed the trip in detail. Paul, a four-year member of NAMBLA, said his age of preference was eleven to thirteen and he "just came out of the closet as a BL" a few years ago.

On January 21, his check in the amount of $620 arrived. I called to let him know I received it. We spoke of sexual preferences, but he was reticent in discussing it over the phone; he was the only traveler who expressed any reservations about the topic. I wanted to solidify the evidence but didn't want to push him away. He continued to inquire about how safe the trip was. Rather than deal directly with the travel agency, he wanted me to act as his intermediary. Because my exposure to Paul in Miami was minimal, I could understand his reluctance to deal even with me. But as the conversation continued, he relaxed somewhat. He expressed concern that the FBI could be monitoring the calls and that they had infiltrated the organization. His instincts were correct, but would he follow them? As happened so often in my investigations, the target's personal greed — in this case, the desire to have sex with boys — overcame his natural caution. His comfort level grew as the conversation continued. By the end of the call, he admitted to wanting to fondle and have oral sex with the boys. Paul Zipszer was safely back in the fold.

I was relieved my screwup apparently wasn't going to jeopardize this investigation, but I couldn't relax until it was all over. I invested several years of my life and untold hours of thought in this case, and it was coming down to the wire. I couldn't afford any lapses in judgment.

In fact, one of the reasons the NAMBLA case meant so much to me personally was that I spent so many years gathering the evidence and carefully accumulating actionable admissions from members. Possibly, the mounting pressure was contributing to some of my health symptoms. At times like these, I had to remind myself of my conviction that the beginnings of my FBI career had as much to do with divine guidance as any career plan I'd conceived for myself.

By the time my Marine Corps commitment was over in August, 1979, I knew a courtroom career wasn't for me. I applied to the FBI and did well on the written and oral examinations. I was disappointed soon thereafter, though, when the applicant coordinator told me the Bureau had just announced a one-year hiring freeze. I did ask that he keep my application on file and hoped for a phone call the next year.

I was a little surprised one morning when I saw an ad in the sports section of the *Los Angeles Times* seeking CIA case officers. I thought maybe it was a joke; wouldn't the CIA recruit covertly? Still, I answered the ad, and soon began a months-long, multi-tiered recruitment process. All the correspondence I received was on plain bond paper and my first interview was with a man who had a scar stretching across the front of his neck from ear to ear — impressive. I imagined he had been garroted in the back alley of some third world country. Probably, though, in his youth he ran into a clothesline playing touch football in the backyard. Whatever the reason, he had my attention. This seemed to be the excitement I was seeking and I enthusiastically pursued the Agency.

The recruitment process included multiple flights from L.A. to Washington, D.C., traveling under an assumed name, meeting in safe houses, and taking a battery of tests. I kept being called back, moving through the application process. I thought a job offer would be forthcoming and was looking forward to my training at the Farm.

Imagine my disappointment, then, when I was notified the CIA declined my application. I contacted an official with the Agency who told me that being a lawyer, having never lived overseas, and scoring a zero on their personality test entered into the decision-making process.

I was crushed but can laugh about it now. I mean, a zero on a personality test? The test was graded on a scale of zero to ten. The way they explained it to me, a "zero" could live on a deserted island for months on end and a "ten" needed to be in the constant presence of people. I admit, I skewed my answers, thinking they were looking for paid assassins who could parachute behind enemy lines and remain secreted for weeks. Wrong! The psychologist who scored the test told me he had never seen a zero and the Agency was looking for threes and fours. Go figure. My wife occasionally reminds me I have been rated as a zero personality by the federal government.

With the CIA passing and the FBI in a hiring freeze, I knew I needed to find a job. I would be out of the Marine Corps on August 15 and the summer was quickly coming to an end. I finally accepted a position in Los Angeles with a small broadcasting company. The exact job description was never completely spelled out, but my enthusiasm for the position was still less than what the employer deserved.

My parents came out to California the second week of August for vacation and stayed in our tiny three-bedroom home. During the job search, I was frustrated with my wife. I really didn't want to take the L.A. job and wanted her to understand. She enjoyed being the wife of a Marine and secretly wanted me to stay in. She was frustrated with me because after six years of marriage — two while I was in law school and four while I was an attorney in the Corps — I was now making an about-face on the job front. Although I wouldn't characterize our talk that evening as an argument, it is fair to say we each expressed our frustrations with the other.

We were letting my parents stay in our bedroom. My wife slept with our one-year-old daughter in the spare bedroom and I slept on the couch. That night, before going to bed, I gave it all up to God: "Okay, God, I really don't want to take this job in L.A. The pay's good, so your 10 percent will be more than if I got the CIA job or the Bureau hired me, but I really don't want to do this.

I'll leave it in your hands, but I sure wish the FBI or the Agency would call."

The next morning, I was — how can I put it? — seated in the place where I do most of my best reading, when the phone rang. My wife answered, then hollered into the bathroom that it was for me. We were selling our VW van to another Marine at the time, and I assumed that was what the call was about. I yelled, "It's Larry; tell him it's five thousand dollars." She then cracked open the door and said, "It's the FBI."

As quickly as possible I ran to the phone. I was told a spot had just opened in the September academy class and was asked if I could report by September 17. There was no hesitation in my response.

God truly answered my prayer with that phone call. I reflected often on that evening in those frustrating days when the legal and administrative hurdles seemed overwhelming. I am convinced God had a purpose in putting me in the FBI. Maybe it was to expose the boy lover agenda — or just to get a few bad guys off the street.

When I next spoke with David Mayer, I had to raise an issue that concerned me. Going into the conversation, I felt as if I were walking on eggshells. Sam Lindblad committed to the trip, and he was one of several persons David did not want me to invite, fearing Sam's three-time-loser status and recent release from prison might put him and everyone with him on the law enforcement radar screen. Knowing what I knew about his activities since his release, I wanted Sam arrested. I was concerned, however, that David or Todd would learn from one of the others Sam was coming and react badly, jeopardizing the cohesiveness of my group of targets. It made more sense for them to hear it from me rather than through the back door, which would likely arouse even more suspicion.

I presented it to David Mayer and the others as "good news, bad news." The good news was we had ten travelers; the bad news was I invited Sam and he accepted. David was not thrilled with the news, even if it meant our group was at ten and it included Dick Stutsman. David said, "My heart bleeds for him. . . . There, but for the grace of God, goes each of us." Nevertheless, David's knowledge of the law and experience counseling registered sex offenders made him very uncomfortable with Sam accompanying us. Had I gone too far? Would David back out and take Todd with him? Would my greed destroy the investigation? I quickly went into my reassuring sales pitch, and even though the topic would reemerge, David seemed to be somewhat at ease by the end of our conversation.

Despite his misgivings about Sam, David was pleased so many would be joining us, referring to the trip as a mini-convention, minus "Peter, Tim, and the insane." David even questioned whether he was still in NAMBLA. He had not heard from Peter or the organization, nor had he received a *Bulletin* since the conference. He thought Peter might have kicked him out.

We spoke more about his sexual travel adventures. In the Thailand "boy bars" he saw a five-year-old working, and in Mexico, he told me, he did not tip for specific sexual favors. Instead, he would pay for meals in exchange for sex and tip fifty to seventy-five dollars for several days and nights of non-stop company. He described some of his adventures as "one-night stands" and others as "one-hour stands."

As was typical of all our conversations, the criminal admissions rolled off his tongue. It just seemed too easy. Was I the subject of some study by the Department of Health and Human Resources or maybe David's doctoral dissertation?

I was still struggling with health issues

including a nagging cough, sore throat, and insomnia. At this point, even two or three hours of uninterrupted sleep was a lot. I would wake thinking of the dozens of individuals we were targeting and the particular issues surrounding each of the three undercover investigations. Keeping it "real" in my undercover role, I mentioned the sore throat to Todd and David in an e-mail, using it as an excuse to beg off scheduled three-way phone calls. This provided a convenient dodge, because at this point in the investigation, each contact meant one more opportunity to lose the case rather than win it. The evidence was there; the only nail left for the coffin was the pedophiles' arrival on the West Coast, confirming their intent. A slip in a phone conversation or e-mail could mean our whole house of cards tumbled. I wanted to avoid that if possible — especially given my deteriorating health.

Just to keep the channels of communication alive and not arouse suspicion, on February 1, I sent an e-mail to Todd and David detailing a dream that never occurred.

I have to tell you about a funny dream I had last night. I dreamed we bought the B and B in Mexico. David was working the front counter and Todd was practicing dentistry in one of the rooms. I said to Todd, "You don't have a license," and he said he was licensed in Texas. I said, "This is Mexico." Todd said that Texas used to be part of Mexico so he could still practice. We decided to have our fall conference at the B and B but didn't invite Peter. Then I woke up. By the way, I got my voice back. Sorry, guys, but it looks like I'm gonna live . . . Daddy

Later that day, David responded.

Daddy Dearest,
   I would have written sooner, however, I was so distraught at the thought of your terminal, er, sore throat, that I went out and started buying lots of black ensembles — in cashmere, along with a few trinkets from Tiffany's. Just in case I needed to wear something to a memorial service, & for the probate reading (you do have the correct spelling of my last name? Do you need a Social Security #?) . . . however, with your full recovery . . . which of course, I cannot begin to tell you how thrilled I am about that . . . I will have to return all my

items . . . including the new BMW. . . .

I will try and call Paul tonight and see how he is doing. Remember, all of this is very overwhelming for him . . . this is someone who has never been on an airplane! Anything new with "David" . . . has he heard from the future first lady?

Got to run — talk to you this week.

David

Todd also replied.

I would love to own a B and B. I'll leave my dental equipment behind in Dallas this trip, but next time I could bring my stuff and you guys could be my assistants. This could augment the modest income the boys would bring in. . . . I could sing on the side and . . .

I spoke briefly to Greg Nusca, aka David R. Busby, one more time before the February 12 trip. On January 30, he called to say the travel agency received the application. He again expressed his excitement and appreciation for being invited.

The chickens were all coming to roost. Now, if I could just keep it together long enough to close the door to the chicken coop. . . .

40
KEEP THOSE
PLATES SPINNING

On February 1, I experienced one of those moments that can happen to an undercover agent while participating in multiple operations. In addition to posing as a NAMBLA member and an international arms merchant targeting Chinese, Russian, and Iraqi organized crime figures, I was the undercover agent in a San Diego investigation of Vietnamese drug traffickers. That afternoon, I was negotiating a crystal methamphetamine transaction with the Vietnamese. I was between meetings, sitting in a parking lot with my San Diego case agents, when the phone rang. I assumed it was my Vietnamese target and prepared to record the call.

To my surprise, it was Dick Stutsman from South Carolina. The call was pure dynamite, erasing any defense he might even hope to mount during a trial.

Dick was a talker and I let him talk.

Maybe my ego should have been bruised, but he didn't remember me from the Miami conference. With only seventeen members present and me having actually talked with him on several occasions, you would have thought I would have made an impression. Apparently not.

Dick was going on the "fishing trip," he said, but he was scared. "I can't resist temptation, but I've been doing a lot of thinking. Back in the mid-eighties, I was the target of a sting operation. So I'm a little bit hypersensitive to the possibility that this is a sting operation. . . . Even if there is a one chance in a thousand that it is, it really wouldn't be worth the risk."

When I responded by telling him I wasn't sure I would back out knowing the odds were that much in my favor, Dick said, "If you do something this risky a thousand times in your life, you're gonna get caught. . . . I don't want to lose my freedom. . . . I'm almost sixty and something like this could just ruin the whole rest of my life."

I expressed my appreciation for his caution and said that if I did not completely trust my friend, "Sean," I would not be going on the trip either.

Dick continued to express his concern. As

part of the NAMBLA pen-pal and holiday card program, he corresponded with twenty prisoners, many of whom were incarcerated through various sting operations. In a conversation that was almost unbelievable, Dick said,

You know that Bush passed a law that modified and made stronger the law that Clinton passed in '94. Bush signed a law in 2003 that further criminalizes people going overseas to do stuff illegal that might even be legal there. . . . Apparently, though, the way sting operations work, you don't actually have to commit the crime. You only have to have exhibited intent. So now, here's a scenario. Somebody is going to offer a . . . let's say a sex tour. And you send them a deposit check with your signature on it. And they get on the phone with you, and they ask what kind of person would you like to have sex with? You specify, "Well I'd like . . . a fourteen-year-old kid, maybe." Now, you've expressed intent to commit a crime. I think that might be all that's necessary in a sting operation. So then, we all gather at, say, some meeting place, where other people have [sic] similarly have been invited and have the same kind of thing, and we all write checks for the rest of the amount. And while we're all there, a paddy wagon drives up, and we all get on it. We're all under arrest. I can see that . . . that's why I'm scared. . . . If I were a member of the Justice Department who wanted to catch people like this, this is how I would do it . . . ten people at a time. That's still gonna make the news, and it's gonna get votes for the administration.

Dick Stutsman had just written our operation order! Amazing! He laid out the entire undercover proposal. Would he still succumb to temptation?

I needed to get going, because I had to return to my Vietnamese drug dealers. I told Dick I was in the middle of a real estate transaction and had to go to the bank to sign escrow papers, but I promised to call him back that evening.

He said he had one more horror story he would tell me when we spoke later in the evening, but before he hung up he wanted to read me an article he found on the Internet while researching this subject. The article was entitled "U.S. Law Enforcement Targets Child Sex Tourism."

Dick began,

On April 30, 2003, President Bush signed into law the Protect Act aimed at strengthening U.S. law enforcement's ability to prevent, investigate, prosecute, and punish violent crimes committed against children. Many of the provisions of the Protect Act focus on protecting children within the United States, but the new law also reaches well beyond U.S. borders to protect young people and combat child sex tourism. Since the law was enacted, eight U.S. residents have been placed in federal custody on charges of child sex tourism. U.S. Immigration and Customs Enforcement (ICE), the largest investigative arm of the Department of Homeland Security, conducted the investigations leading to these arrests. In addition to the indictments brought under the new provisions there are many more investigations in the works, ICE spokesman Dean Boyd told the blah, blah, blah . . .

Dick didn't finish reading the article to me, but he made his point. We said our good-byes with a promise to speak later in the evening.

Undercover agents love the thrill, the chase, and the confrontation. Dick's call made the endgame of this investigation even more exciting. Entrapment wasn't an issue, but successfully convincing him to join me on the "fishing expedition" was a challenge — and I love a challenge.

I rushed to my meeting with the Vietnamese, refocusing and putting on my drug dealer game face. My target spoke in detail about his involvement in a previous drug deal I did with one of his associates. From surveillance, we knew of his participation, but his admissions on tape insured his indictment when the investigation was complete.

Returning to the office, I completed my paperwork on the drug negotiation and prepared for my second call with Dick. I retreated to a large conference room in the San Diego office and closed the doors. Most of the agents had gone home for the evening, but I shut off the overhead paging system and made the call. Once again, the call produced more than any prosecutor could hope for. For an hour and ten minutes, Dick continued to paint himself into the corner, just as he had begun in the earlier call.

Criminal intent and entrapment issues

were completely eliminated by his admissions. For a cautious man concerned about a potential sting operation, Dick's open conversation was remarkable, to say the least.

He thought I was perfectly safe in going on the trip. Although he "did not want to offend" me, his reasoning went, "I don't know if you and Sam are part of the deal. . . . You know people who have done this before and nothing has happened. And if that's really true, then you have nothing to worry about. It's just: do I believe you? I don't know and I want you to convince me, because I really want this, you know? I want to do it. I just want to be safe."

I said, "No, I appreciate your honesty. I really don't know what to tell you. Because even after we go on it and have a great time and we call you back, you still may think, oh, they got arrested, and now they must be working with the cops."

Dick then told me about his brother, a social worker for the city of Charlottesville, Virginia, in whom he confided. His brother warned him not to go on the trip and recited stories of other sting operations.

Remarkably, Dick remained undeterred by his brother's warning, insisting he still wanted to go. He then began to instruct me on the legal system.

Now, I've always had this fantasy that if I were charged with some kind of crime of which I wasn't really guilty or even if I was technically guilty of intent of something, if I hadn't done anything wrong, I think I could get the jury to exonerate me. But that means you have to have a trial by jury. Now, the court system hates jury trials.

If arrested, Dick planned to represent himself in court. He continued to detail his strategy.

I'm a very strong believer in the fully informed jury, and the judge will usually instruct the jury that they have to base their judgment as to whether you're guilty solely on the evidence of whether you've committed that crime. But, in fact, juries have the power to nullify the law if they think the law itself or the sentencing that's based on the law is unjust. So even if there's undoubtable [sic] evidence . . . if they don't think that the crime [is really a crime], that there should be a law [against the crime] in the first place, or [don't believe] that there should be a strict penalty, had you violated [that particular law], all you have to do is convince one jurist to not find you guilty. That's all . . . but a lawyer won't do that. You know why? Because he is defying the judge. He is telling the jury they can ignore the judge's instructions with impunity, which they can and they don't know that. I can tell them.

After educating me on his potential legal strategy, Dick continued to express his desire to be convinced that the trip was safe.

Me: I don't know what to say to you.

Dick: I know, there's hardly anything you can.

Me: I don't want to talk you into it if you don't want to do it. . . . Here's a couple of things that I've said to some other people. And you can take it for what it's worth. . . . There was an article in the *L.A. Times* within the last couple months about how even the FBI and all of their resources are being devoted to terrorism and there was even a complaint, an anonymous FBI person, who said that they couldn't even do criminal wiretaps because all their resources are being diverted to terrorism. They didn't have enough money and personnel.

I previously laid out the fictitious *L.A. Times* story to Todd and David Mayer, but would Dick buy it? The answer was quick in coming.

> *Dick:* And I believe that. . . . What you just said makes me feel much less fearful. In fact, I've never heard of a case of wiretapping being used to convict a child molester. . . . That's why I speak freely when I'm on the phone.

Dick went on to criticize the U.S. government, Presidents Bush and Clinton, the handling of the Branch Davidian affair at Waco, and the war on Iraq. I finally managed to turn the conversation back to the trip by saying, "I will miss you very much on the trip."

Dick quickly responded, "Oh, I'm not saying I'm not coming. I may come. I haven't cancelled it at all. I'm really wanting to be put at ease."

I told Dick "they have had other trips since Sean's October excursion." Dick liked that answer. "And if this is really true," he said, "then I have nothing to worry about."

Me: My biggest concern isn't that this is a sting operation. My biggest concern is that somebody down in Mexico is going to do something stupid and that's why to me it was important that we had people that we knew.

Dick: What's different about this trip is . . . a lot of important people that work for NAMBLA or are with NAMBLA [are going]. The government hates NAMBLA. You know that they would love to get rid of us.

As we continued our conversation, I complained about how the organization was being run and said I considered not even renewing my membership. "My only reason for continuing my membership, quite frankly, is the annual conference, where I can network with other people, because I don't get that opportunity often."

Dick then asked, "Can I ask you how many conferences you've been to and how long ago you went to your first one?"

I made a potentially costly mistake with my answer, but my instincts said I needed to close this deal with a strong record of membership. Although I had only attended the New York and Miami conferences, I lied by saying, "I've been to about five, you know — six or seven years." I reasoned that if confronted later with the lie, I could say I misunderstood the question, and that I had been a member about five years but had not attended conferences in each of those years.

Dick: Okay, if that's true, and I'm sure I can confirm that with somebody —
Me: Yeah.
Dick: Then that puts me at ease, right there. Because that means you're not an unknown. Because, you see, when Sam mentioned you, he said, "Well, he was kind of quiet and he didn't really say much at the meeting." And I thought that was suspicious, but I didn't know if that was your first meeting.
Me: No, no, no.
Dick: For all I knew, it was, and you could have been the government plant.
Me: No.
Dick: But if it's true that you've been to five and really nothing has happened . . . then I think maybe that's a good thing and I feel much better. I really want to go.

Dick even went so far in the planning stages of his trip as to arrange for someone to care for his cats while he joined us in Mexico. It became clear to me that despite his professed and exceedingly well-informed caution, Dick Stutsman really wanted to be convinced it was safe to go with us to Mexico to have sex with underage boys. That's how strong the pull of his obsession was.

Paul Zipszer's mother tried to protect him. Dick Stutsman's social worker brother offered good advice as well. But neither Paul nor Dick heeded the well-intentioned efforts of family members.

Dick cited another problem that arose with the undercover travel agency: "I thought it was suspicious that [the undercover travel agent] said, when I wanted to use a credit card, that he didn't think his machine worked. . . . See all these things, if you're paranoid enough?"

And yet, despite his paranoia, he continued to express a desire to join us on the trip. I complimented him on how much he opened my eyes during these two conversations and told him I would like to set aside an hour for him to present his ideas in a formal setting at the next conference, which I was hosting. "The membership needs more of this."

When I told him the boat was picking up

passengers in Los Angeles and San Diego, he joyfully responded.

Oh, I didn't know that. . . . That's more good news. In other words, I'm really beginning to feel okay about this now, because, first of all, you're a member in good standing, you're with Peter, you're involved in this western conference next year. . . . In my mind, if you're trustworthy, then I know that this is not a sting operation. . . . I don't think the feds would have invested five years of somebody's time to get inside of our organization.

When he said these words, I know a smile came over my face as I sat in the dimly lit conference room. I had him hooked and now only needed to reel him in. I responded, "You know what? . . . I would sure hope not. If we had 9/11 . . . I mean, if they've got some crippled white guy out there that wants to be an undercover cop, I wish they would have put him in some Arab terrorist organization, rather than NAMBLA."

As we began to wind down the conversation, Dick had three questions he wanted me to research. "I want to make sure that these valets are not under duress, that they are free agents, however old they are, that they're not doing this 'cause they're working for some scummy pimp. . . . I don't want to be part of this problem where a large number of children in the world are in fact very abused." He also wanted to know what an appropriate gratuity might be, and whether we would be able to express affection in public. I promised him I would find the answers.

He then discussed his relationship in college, when, as an eighteen-year-old, he had his first sexual encounter with a thirteen-year-old paperboy. He was expelled from New Mexico State University when the affair was discovered.

He wrapped up the conversation with "I want this trip. I want it!"

I hung up with a great sense of satisfaction. Dick Stutsman was in and he was bringing Sam Lindblad with him.

41
Intensive Care

The next day, I headed up to Los Angeles for a series of meetings with the subjects of our Chinese organized crime investigation. With the help of my East Coast counterpart, this undercover operation netted eighty-seven indictments later in the summer. For the moment, I was no longer the lover of prepubescent boys, but a tough international arms dealer and narcotics trafficker — a role, frankly, I was more comfortable portraying. On February 2, I met with two of the subjects in the Ritz-Carlton Hotel in Pasadena. We enjoyed a fine dinner in my hotel room and exceptional criminal conversation. Both subjects made valuable admissions to be used in their indictment and subsequent conviction.

After spending the night at the Ritz, I met with a third subject and again discussed an international weapons transaction. Following that meeting, I returned home. My brother was visiting from back east, and my wife and I wanted to take him to dinner. Before leaving the house, I gave Dick Stutsman a call, answering his questions from our phone call two nights earlier.

I shocked Dick when I opened the conversation with the fact I was mad at him. I said I had trouble sleeping after our conversation because I now was questioning whether or not this could be a sting operation. I told him, however, I spoke with "Sean" and was much more comfortable after that conversation. I answered Dick's questions, and he, too, seemed satisfied. He mentioned he was debating taking pictures while there but was fearful; he "didn't want to leave any evidence." He was also concerned about taking a valuable camera or computer on the trip, fearing that if it were stolen he wouldn't be able to report it to the authorities, since our presence at the bed and breakfast would be for illegal purposes. As the conversation was waning, I was pleased when he said, "I'm starting to get a little better picture of this and I'm starting to feel comfortable with this."

As we finished up the call, Dick said he was looking forward to "re-meeting" me, since he could not recall my presence at the Miami conference. Since he left himself wide open, I took a not-so-subtle shot: "Well, maybe I'll do something so you'll remember me." His response was classic: "I'm sure I'll remember you this time." Do tell.

Steve Irvin and I went several weeks without any contact. I was busy balancing the other undercover cases and concentrating most of my NAMBLA work on the San Diego travelers, David Mayer, Todd from Dallas, and Paul Zipszer.

On February 3, Steve e-mailed me.

Hi Robert
How are things in California? Cold in Pittsburgh.

I haven't heard anything from anyone for a while, since I talked to [the undercover travel agent] a few weeks ago. Is everything ok? Just wasn't sure if there was a problem. I did tell him I was a little concerned about law enforcement. I just don't trust our current administration and their right-wing moralists. At any rate, I hope I didn't offend him, and am looking forward to the trip. . . .

I just started my sabbatical yesterday! I'm ready for the break. . . .

I have to take two computer classes starting the 17th, the day I get back in

Pittsburgh. Both on web page development.

Well, Robert, better go for now. Please
let me know if there is a problem. . . .
I'll see you on the 12th. Smile.

Have a good week.

Steve

I finished the call to Dick and read the
e-mail from Steve. I then joined my wife
and brother for dinner. Less than three
hours later, I was lying in an emergency
room.

For some unknown reason, I passed out
and woke seconds later, bathed in sweat.
I had severe cramping, diarrhea, and internal bleeding. The hospital stay lasted four
days, two of which were spent in intensive
care. All kinds of scenarios ran through my
head. Had I been poisoned by the Chinese?
It made no sense. Besides, I ordered the
food and they had nothing to gain by my
death. If they suspected me of being an
undercover agent, the prudent move would
be to return to China; killing undercover
agents in hotel rooms usually leaves a trail
of evidence. A series of medical tests and
procedures suggested a few possible problems, but the condition was never defini-
tively diagnosed.

I remember one humorous incident during my hospital visit — at least it's humorous now. I was lying in bed when I heard alarms going off and people rushing down the hallway. I thought, "Boy, some poor guy is in trouble." About then, medical personnel came charging into my room, pushing a crash cart.

My pulse was at twenty-six and my blood pressure had fallen to dangerously low levels, and as they worked on me, I prayed, "God, if it's my time to go, fine. But you're really going to mess up three pretty good investigations if you take me now." I guess the Lord either listened to me or has a sense of humor, because the staff was able to stabilize me.

My biggest fear was getting out of the hospital in time to meet the travelers on Friday, February 11. Without me being at the airport, I'm not sure we would have a case. I couldn't wait for more procedures or tests. Fortunately, I didn't have to wait long. I was released from the hospital early Sunday evening. I missed the Super Bowl, but it could've been worse.

On February 7, I sent the following e-mail to Sam Lindblad, "David R. Busby," and Steve:

Hi,

Had a scare this past week and don't know if you have been trying to contact me. I went to dinner with friends on Thursday night and as I was driving home had a severe stomach cramp and passed out. I didn't wreck the car but they rushed me to the hospital where I spent two days in the ICU. No contact with anyone but doctors. I'm home now and the doctor said if I rest for a few days I should make my cruise. My voice mail was full so I don't know if you tried to contact me. Short of death, I WON'T MISS OUR TRIP!!! See you Saturday. I'm really looking forward to this. I hope you have a better week than I did. Take care and be safe.

Robert

Steve responded that evening.

Robert,

Good to hear from you. Did wonder where you were. Glad to hear you're doing okay and can make the cruise. I talked with [the undercover travel agent] and have arrangements to meet on Friday.

If I don't talk to you before, I'll see

you on Saturday. Smile!

Steve

It was the last I heard from him.

"Chief," or "Schmohawk," as David Mayer dubbed John the "gaytheist," presented an interesting, if frustrating, issue. John was a two-time convicted sex offender and NAMBLA member. At the Miami conference, he even admitted to me he molested a third boy who did not cooperate with the police when questioned.

Shortly after returning from Miami, I sent a card to John, hoping to keep the lines of communication open, thinking I might be able to travel to San Francisco and determine whether he was currently involved in criminal activity. In the card I wrote,

John, It was so great meeting you this past week at the conference. Hope you had a good trip home. . . .

Maybe sometime if you ever get this way or I get up there we can get together and I'll buy dinner. I'd love to just talk and share. Ever thought of traveling to some safe haven? We're trying to put something together down south. A friend has been there and says it's fabulous.

Well, be safe. Happy Turkey Day . . .
Robert

He did not respond to the note, and, as with those to whom I'd sent unanswered e-mails, I wasn't even sure he provided me a correct address at the conference. John went on the back burner as the investigation heated up with David, Todd, and the others.

John's Mohawk haircut and lack of personal hygiene habits kept him off the A-list as Todd and David Mayer discussed possible invitees. My mission, however, was not to please my two traveling companions but to target anyone willing to violate federal law. Given his record and admissions at the conference, we had plenty of predication to ask John. The issue was how to invite him without the others learning of the invitation. At Miami, he appeared more of a loner than the rest, and I doubted he was in communication with any of those who agreed to travel. I decided to take a chance and invite him, believing we could hide the invitation from the others.

In Miami, John provided a mailing address but no phone number or e-mail address. I reviewed the tapes from the conference and retrieved the name of the San Francisco residential hotel where he was staying. Directory assistance had no listing for John, but did have a number for the hotel. My first attempt to contact him via phone was unsuccessful. Although someone answered the phone by identifying the hotel, that person said there were no telephones in the rooms and I could not leave a message. It obviously wasn't the Ritz.

My next effort was more successful. On January 20, I sent him a second card that mentioned the trip and included my glowing hopes for it. I included my cell phone number and awaited a call that never came. On January 27, though, I did receive a letter from John that seemed promising.

Hello Robert,

Since returning home here I have been very busy. I am very much involved in the Gay and Atheist life styles here in SF. . . .

You stated in your card you are trying to put something together "down South" and it's "fabulous"? Whatever could that be?

Getting together with you sometime sounds just great. I want to talk and SHARE. I think we all need that release.

I just went down for my mail and

found another card from you and as I read it and incorporate my answer to it I am watching the beautiful Steven [sic] King production of "IT" with all of those beautiful BOYS featured.

I love the idea of a "special vacation" for Feb 11 to 14. I am up for it. This letter will reach you prior to 1-31-5. Call me any night at midnight you will always reach me at that time. I do want to join you. That particular weekend is perfect.

All love,
John

It looked like we gained another traveler, but John's letter failed to provide a phone number. Although there were no deadlines for the trip other than the actual day planned for the arrest, time was running out. Since it had taken him so long to respond to my letters, I wasn't sure we could make the appropriate arrangements and get the necessary criminal admissions in place if we used snail mail. That day I sent a Federal Express letter to him.

John,
Got your letter but you never sent me a phone number. I need to talk to you about the "vacation." I'll certainly in-

clude you but I want to make sure you're okay with all the details. This will be HEAVENLY DIVINE!!

Call me at [my phone number] or send me your number ASAP!!!!

Robert

Because John prided himself on his atheism, I included the "HEAVENLY DIVINE" bit as a subtle jab. By February 1, I still had not heard from him. I made two more attempts to contact the residential hotel and leave messages, saying it was important that I contact him. Whether he received the messages or not, I don't know.

On February 7, he called and left a number on my voice mail. That evening, I returned the call, assuming we were about to add another defendant to our growing list of NAMBLA members. But it was not meant to be; he either sensed a sting or genuinely did not want to participate. When I provided the details of the trip and the fact that boys would be furnished for sexual favors, he declined. He cited his two prior convictions and reminded me that if caught he would spend the rest of his life in jail. I certainly could not argue with his reasoning and was careful to avoid entrapping him.

We provided the opportunity and he

passed; it was as simple as that. Possibly, John's prior convictions and the fear of going to prison again served as the deterrent it was meant to be. His reaction was certainly different than Dick Stutsman's.

After I completed the call, I immediately phoned my San Diego case agent with the news. Although we thought we had another traveler, we did not. The effort was worthwhile, if for no other reason than to show a jury, should it become an issue, that some who were invited chose not to attend. In other words, those who came did so voluntarily and in full knowledge they were breaking the law.

42
FINAL PREPARATIONS

After my medical Waterloo on February 3, I sent e-mails to David Mayer and Todd, informing them of why I hadn't been in contact for a few days. I assured them, though, that wild horses couldn't drag me away from the pier where we would board the boat to "paradise." I did want to provide a reasonable excuse for not joining a pre-trip conference call, as requested by David. After all, I was exhausted from all the testing and medical procedures. I needed a few days' rest in order to be ready for Friday, when Todd, David, and Paul arrived in San Diego. The Los Angeles office would be handling the L.A. travelers, which suited me fine; in my weakened state, I was glad we had not set it up so that I would have to be in L.A., as well.

January was a rainy month. February began dry, but soon the rains came. Several days before the scheduled departure of the travelers, a winter storm hit Southern California. The San Diego case agents asked me to attend the briefing on Thursday at the dock where the arrests were scheduled to take place on Saturday. I reluctantly went, though I was still recovering from whatever had just put me in intensive care for two days. We held the briefing outside, and it rained the entire time. Adding pneumonia to my other problems didn't seem at all unlikely.

We arranged through hotel security for my room at the Hilton to be on a separate floor from the others. The room adjoining mine was also ours. Technical equipment was being installed as we briefed on the dock. Cameras and sound equipment would record my meetings the next day with David, Todd, and Paul. A surveillance team would monitor the meetings and provide security, if needed, but that was doubtful. Everything but the weather seemed to be falling into place.

I returned home after the briefing, hoping to get a good night's sleep in preparation for the next day, but doubting sleep would ever come.

This case took several years of my life, and was exhausting physically, emotionally, and mentally. It challenged all my resources of self-control and forced me to think about things personally disgusting in the extreme. I sat with pedophiles, smiling and encouraging them as they talked about their desires and wishes.

The NAMBLA case was especially difficult for me because there was no one — and I truly mean no one — I could sit down with and talk about the case in order to decompress; no one with whom I could share my frustrations, fears, and moral outrage. With my Bureau colleagues, I had to remain professional, focused, and factual, or risk being evaluated as some sort of liability to the investigation. And my wife let me know in no uncertain terms she was not emotionally prepared to chat with me about my adventures in the BL world. Not that I can blame her. I could talk with my son, but he was on the East Coast and face-to-face sit downs were impossible. But the point is, this case wore me out in a way I never thought could happen.

And now, within the next forty-eight hours, the final act would be played. By the end of the day on Saturday, we would either have a number of sexual predators in custody, or we would face the sickening realization that the last several years were for nothing. I was personally confident in our preparation, our procedures, and our eventual outcome. But I knew too well that once the case got into the courts — if it got that far — unexpected things could happen. I had only to remember the rude awakening we got in the case of Darrel, the Canadian heroin trafficker, to realize that many aspects of the case's eventual outcome were beyond my control. That was the thing that kept me awake on Thursday night and into the wee hours of Friday morning as I awaited the moment when I would meet Todd, David, and Paul after their flights to San Diego.

By 5:30 am, I gave up trying to sleep, so I showered and prepared for the most important day of this investigation. The rains increased, making road conditions hazardous and raising my fear the travelers would back out before the conspiracy was complete. After all, would even a boy lover, desperate for unrestrained sexual adventures south of the border, actually get on a boat during a driving rainstorm?

A legal issue was raised highlighting a conflict between the Los Angeles and San Diego Bureau offices. Los Angeles said the travelers had to board the boat; the San Diego U.S. Attorney's office did not require it. The mere travel to and arrival in San

Diego was all that was required for the San Diego office to demonstrate intent. It was understood that boarding the boat provided an extra piece of evidence, but that also meant each traveler had one more evening to ponder his fate and withdraw.

The law seemed clear to me. United States Code Title 18 Section 2423 (b) states, "Travel with intent to engage in illicit sexual conduct — A person who travels in interstate commerce . . . for the purpose of engaging in any illicit sexual conduct with another person [under the age of 18] shall be . . . imprisoned for not more than 30 years."

So, to me, actually boarding the boat did not seem a necessary element of the statute. In a conspiracy, the subject can withdraw at any time prior to completion of the act. The policy of the U.S. Attorney's office would probably prevent prosecution should any of the travelers decide to return home prior to boarding, especially if they expressed remorse. But what if the bad weather made them pull out, fearing for their safety on the boat? What if they thought they might get seasick and decided to postpone getting on the boat until the next excursion? My other concern was the fact the FBI brought to Southern California sexual predators and was allowing them to spend the night, when, in the legal opinion of some government attorneys, the crime had been completed. What if one of our travelers decided to seek sexual satisfaction with a juvenile the night before the arrest? None of these questions was answered to my satisfaction, but I was in no mood to argue. I resigned myself to the fact that on Friday, when my travelers arrived at the airport, the day was only beginning, and I had to insure their "safe-keeping" for almost twenty-four hours.

I developed phlebitis at two of the injection sites for the IVs I received at the hospital. The veins had become inflamed, hardened, and quite painful. The doctor recommended wet-heat packs for half-hour periods every two hours. Clearly, I was not 100 percent. I certainly did not have to worry about acting or looking sick; I had lost about ten pounds while in the hospital and was gingerly eating soft foods. I looked weak because I was. However, as I drove to the Hilton San Diego Airport/Harbor Island hotel, I realized the heat packs could be used to my advantage.

I checked into the hotel in my undercover name and made my way to the room on the sixth floor. The surveillance agents were already in the adjacent room, and we examined the technical equipment. The room's compactness insured I could concentrate all three subjects well within view of the hidden cameras. We rearranged the furniture, setting it up so I would stay out of the way as the camera focused on David, Todd, and Paul. It helped that an outlet was on the wall close to where my chair would be positioned, making it reasonable that I should always be seated in the same place so that I could plug in the heating pad for my moist-heat compresses.

We made our last-minute preparations. The surveillance teams were in place, the technical equipment was in working order, and I was ready to go. I strapped on the recording equipment and headed to the airport, less than half a mile from the hotel.

The American Airlines flight out of Dallas–Fort Worth was scheduled to arrive at 11:10 am. When I pulled in front of the airport, my three friends from NAMBLA were eagerly awaiting. We greeted each other with hugs and drove back to the hotel.

It was clear I was not well, and all three examined my phlebitis-stricken arm. My hotel room provided the perfect venue for a relaxing afternoon. They were a somewhat captive audience; I needed to keep the compresses on my arm, their rooms weren't "ready," and the torrential rains persisted.

Once we settled in my room, a unique discussion took place, offering insights into not only the boy lover mentality but the child sex trade. Three relaxed sex offenders, believing they were safe from the inquiring minds of law enforcement, commenced a textbook look into the world of the sexual predator.

Since Paul had not been with us at Johnny Rockets restaurant in Coconut Grove, I was able to use that as my reason for having Todd and David repeat their travel experiences. There was no hesitation on the part of either man.

Todd was the first to share. Several years ago, he arranged a couple's retreat for himself and his office staff in Jamaica. By the time the trip came around, he was going through his divorce, but chose to make the trip anyway. He flew alone in his airplane and met his staff and their spouses in Montego Bay.

One evening, Todd was at a local bar on the beach, having a beer and listening to music, when he saw "some people over on the beach, selling stuff." He decided to investigate. He approached "this one old, black guy, who was probably in his sixties . . . [who] said, 'What can I getcha — a man, a woman, a boy, a girl?' "

Paul, as shocked as I was, interjected, "He said that?"

"Actually, you know what? He didn't. He said, 'What do you want? Man? Woman?' And I'm like, 'Well, no, actually . . . that's not what I want.' I kind of beat around the bush. I was real uncomfortable, because I'd never done that before. And I finally said, 'You know what, I want a boy.' "

The old man, whom Todd referred to as "the pimp," said he could help and instructed Todd to follow him. It was late, "nine thirty, maybe ten o'clock," and they took a cab to another bar. At this second bar, Todd gave the pimp seventy dollars and was told to wait. Todd did as instructed but questioned whether he would ever see the pimp or the money again. A short time later, to Todd's surprise, the pimp did return, asking for more money. Todd reluctantly complied. The pimp escorted Todd to another cab, and in the backseat sat Charlie, an eleven-year-old boy. Todd told us he "wanted somebody like fifteen or sixteen, but this eleven-year-old looked pretty good." Todd, Charlie, and the pimp then drove for a long time to what Todd described as a "really poor part of Jamaica."

Paul interrupted again. "Aren't you worried this guy is gonna rob you or something?"

Todd admitted he was afraid. He had about three hundred dollars in his wallet and knew that was a lot of money in Jamaica. They eventually arrived at "just a dump of a shack" and the pimp asked for more money. Todd had already paid $195 and refused to pay any more. They argued briefly and the pimp stormed off, leaving Todd and Charlie alone. At this point in the story, Todd mentioned that Charlie had a large open sore on the left side of his head, the result of a beating by the pimp. Todd, though a medical professional, didn't offer to treat the wound or take the child for medical care. Instead, he offered this assessment: "Charlie's a good-looking kid, except for this open place."

Charlie took Todd into the house and suggested they could spend the night together in his bedroom. Todd said, "I walk in this room, and the bed, if you want to call it that, is just covered with stuff. . . . And it just looks really filthy, and just really scary. . . . There's no way I'm gonna spend the night here."

Charlie added to the suspense by informing Todd that the pimp killed people. Charlie even wanted to show Todd a skull that was buried in the back, just to reinforce how dangerous the pimp was. As this discussion took place, a car returned with, according to Charlie, the pimp's girlfriend, who Todd believed was looking for him, perhaps to collect more money on orders from the pimp. Todd was terrified, fearful both he and Charlie might be killed. Todd began to panic and looked for a place to hide. When the opportunity arose, he and Charlie ran toward the highway. They found a cab and headed back toward the resort.

As Todd described it, "It just kept going downhill from there." Todd and Charlie returned to the hotel where the couple's retreat was being hosted, but the retreat's policy barred children, and the security guard denied them entrance to the complex.

Despite all Todd had been through that evening, he renegotiated with Charlie. "So I've negotiated with this kid, I'll pay him sixty-five dollars if we can make one last ditch effort to hook up somewhere, somehow. So, basically, long story short, over here in front of some bushes on the highway I talked him into letting me touch him through his shorts for like three seconds, once . . . and that's the end of it. I didn't die."

Paul seemed shocked by Todd's admissions. I believed Paul when he said, "The youngest [I ever had sex with] is seventeen. . . . I've never done anything really young like this." Paul turned to David. "How about you? Tell some stories."

Before David could begin, Todd added, "I have [had sex], one other time, very, very briefly with a thirteen-year-old. And then again when he was fifteen, but extremely rushed . . . no long-duration stuff like this trip. I'm fantasizing about this coming four days."

Next up for true confessions was David.

43
PREDATORS TELL ALL

David Mayer proceeded to educate all of us on his sexual travels, burying himself with his words. "Been to Thailand four times, and Mexico numerous times, more than I can count. . . . Acapulco was hit and miss . . . until I hooked up with Frank [the cook at the bed and breakfast], then it became much more consistent in 'Rockapulco.' There's a gay beach that's infamous for having boys. [Unless the local police department has just conducted a sweep] the boys will be there. And even if they have done a sweep, then the boys will be back, but you just never know in what period of time that they'll come back."

Todd, our ingénue, was confused by David's continual referral to Acapulco as "Rockapulco": "I'm curious, why do you keep calling it 'Rockapulco'?"

David looked at him in disbelief. "*The Flintstones.* They went down to Rockapulco." Todd had never watched *The Flint-stones* but admitted to being a big fan of SpongeBob.

When Todd asked me about my experiences, I said I had never traveled outside the United States but had experiences with four boys, eleven being the youngest — but only fondling. David said, "So, you never consummated the marriage?" I hesitated, and David smiled, saying, "Oh, a little blush there . . . a little color in the cheeks." What he interpreted as a maidenly blush on my part was actually the rise in my blood pressure as I suppressed the urge to end the investigation right there by throwing him out the window. *Another twenty-four hours,* I kept telling myself. *Just keep it together another twenty-four hours.*

Todd wouldn't let it go, though; he kept inquiring about my relationships. I said that all were developed over a period of time through long-term friendships with the boys. I figured sticking to the time-honored NAMBLA mantra of "building loving relationships" would be safe.

David took just the opposite tack, and seemed proud of it. His relationships, he said, were purely sexual: "Mine were always sexual . . . a very transient relationship . . . it's purely sex."

David did cite one boy whom he saw on multiple occasions over several years. Frank, the cook at the B and B, also had sex with the boy, so as a favor to both Frank and the boy, David once brought a PlayStation, "because Frank liked him and I liked him, so we kind of both were tag-teaming."

Then David talked more about his trips to Thailand: "The bars that I was in, where the boys were, there was literally, like, a show. They just kind of paraded by. . . . The youngest I saw was five. The average was, probably, ten . . . to thirteen."

David described most of the customers in the boy bars as Germans and Americans. He denied having sex with the five-year-old because the child "didn't do anything for me, but I can't be . . . a hypocrite and say, you know, 'Don't do that.' But as I told Todd, the five-year-old, literally you needed a stick. . . . I mean, there were, like, twenty people trying to get to him, but [the boy] didn't do anything for me."

David said, "There were rooms, either upstairs or somewhere relatively close, and a hell of a lot safer than Jamaica, mon. . . . I never felt threatened in Thailand."

Not to be left out of the discussion, Paul also wanted to share. He joined Big Brothers and was matched up with a twelve-year-old boy. The boy's mother was divorced but dating. She viewed Paul as a convenient babysitter and Paul certainly didn't mind. Paul had a variety of toys that interested the boy, including his four-wheel-drive truck and a five-foot-long remote-control boat. Paul said he and the boy "went . . . all over the place. . . . The mother never suspected anything."

He and the boy went camping together and would sleep in the same bed. He denied ever doing anything illegal with the boy but admitted to holding and hugging him. Paul admitted it could have led somewhere had the relationship continued. He said it was "moving in that direction little by little."

That situation came tumbling down when Paul's roommate reported him. The roommate was going to accompany Paul and the boy to Daytona Beach for Bike Week. When the boy came over to the apartment, Paul allowed the boy to sit on his lap while the roommate was getting ready. When the roommate came out of the bedroom and saw what was happening, he became suspicious of the relationship and later called the Department of Children and Families. The sheriff's department conducted an investigation.

During the inquiry, the boy told officials

that Paul had spoken to him "about masturbation." Big Brothers terminated Paul after
only three months in the program, but according to Paul, there was no evidence of
criminal conduct. Sometime later, while
Paul was jogging in the park, he saw the
boy again. He was with his mother. When
the boy spotted Paul, he came running. The
mother became concerned, pulled the boy
away, and left the park. Paul interpreted the
boy's actions at the park as meaning he
wanted to continue the relationship. "The
kid's not upset with me and I wasn't doing
anything wrong with him. He actually
was . . . well, I would say he was eating it
up."

David was getting hungry but I didn't
want to terminate the video-recorded conversation. David checked on the rooms and
they still weren't ready. Surprisingly, no one
questioned why my room had been ready
and theirs were not. David suggested we
eat, but he refused to eat in the hotel. My
suggestion of Seaport Village, an outdoor
shopping area in downtown San Diego near
the water, received a unanimous yes vote.

Before we broke for lunch, Paul had
another story he wanted to share. As we
learned in Miami, Paul drove a Corvette.
He told us he would drive to the park, then

jog. One day, when he returned from his run, Paul met a twelve-year-old boy who had taken an interest in the car. They began talking. According to Paul, at one point in the conversation, the twelve-year-old invited Paul to join him in "monkey-bar fighting."

When David asked Paul to explain monkey-bar fighting, Paul described it: "You grab the monkey bars and you wrap your legs around each other. . . . You fight, wrap your legs around each other . . ."

Todd smiled, saying he thought that wrapping your legs around a child sounded like fun.

David asked, "Do you keep your clothes on?" Paul, who never seemed to catch on to David's humor, stared back incredulously. "Yeah . . . it's at the park."

David liked the idea of monkey-bar fighting and asked, "Does the B and B have monkey bars? Even if they don't, we'll make our own."

Paul went on with his story. The boy lived several blocks from the park and would show up every day on his bike. As Paul jogged around the park, the boy would follow.

David interrupted again, commenting that Paul was being "stalked by a twelve-year-old."

Paul agreed. He and the boy spent a great deal of time together in Paul's car, listening to music and talking. Paul learned that the boy's father was an alcoholic who was "always drunk" and abusive. One evening Paul joined the family for dinner. "His mother is cooking food. She was a little leery, I could tell. The father didn't give a damn."

Paul continued to meet with the boy almost every day at the park. He denied doing anything sexual with the boy, but said, "[The boy] knew what was going on. I mean, he knew . . . where things seemed to be leading."

Paul seemed surprised that his activities and constant presence at the park sparked law enforcement interest. Paul said, "Believe it or not, the police got called out there twice on me. They said, 'We have complaints that you keep seeing this kid.' Because I have this highly recognizable car. There's neighbors all around, seeing this car every-day, me with this kid, [we're] sitting in this car every day at this park. . . . They call the Sheriff's office. . . . The deputy goes, 'Well . . . Mr. Zipszer, I just have to investi-gate, we've got a complaint. . . . You're seen talking with him and some other kids.' Because other kids kept coming up to me, young boys."

Thank God for alert neighbors, I thought.

David interrupted, smiling. "Young boys?"

Paul said, "Yeah. . . . They were just flocking to me, for some reason. I don't know, it must've been the car. I don't know what it was. They like Corvettes or something."

To Paul's credit, when Todd asked, "Did you have a hard time not acting upon all that wonderful stuff?" Paul responded, "I'm kind of weird this way, because I was just enjoying the company of him. . . . I didn't want to progress it too quickly."

I never quite understood Paul. He denied ever having a sexual relationship with a boy as young as the boys he was describing, but his "grooming" technique and his words appeared to be describing a slow, methodical seduction through trust. Whether he knew it or not, he was following the same strategy espoused by many pedophiles — the grooming method employed by Sam Lindblad and others.

Paul said, "But [the boy] knew what this was kind of all about. . . . I don't know if he was certain in his own mind that I was gay, because I haven't really approached him that way. But he knew there was something going on. So I don't know if he was afraid to try to bring things up like that. And it ended before it got to that point. It was like a period of six weeks."

David brought the conversation back to the imminent trip with a question about the boys. "Who selects who, for whom?" When I said I thought the boys had already been matched, based upon the age of preference each had stated, it allowed me to review that element of the offense. I could make it clear for the evidentiary cameras that each of my traveling companions knew this was an opportunity to have sex with juveniles.

David joked that his age preference was "twenty-seven." I looked at Todd and he said, "Ten to twelve." I then looked at David and said, "Ten to twelve?" David agreed: "Right." And, as they both had previously requested, I added, "And anal sex, if they'll do it." Both Todd and David concurred and were pleased the boys were willing to provide anal sex.

David was surprised when Todd requested boys that young. Todd explained, "I started out twelve to fourteen, then it was eleven to thirteen."

Paul answered the question: "Eleven to thirteen — eleven, twelve, thirteen."

When pressed as to what the others desired, I said "Sean" wanted twelve to fourteen, but that I was uncertain about the others' tastes.

We joked about David R. Busby, and I explained to Paul the entire story behind Greg Nusca's alias, repeating our encounter at Johnny Rockets in Coconut Grove. We also used this opportunity to review for Paul how David had arrived at his monikers for the various members who attended the Miami conference. David mentioned how Steve Irvin, the special education teacher from Pittsburgh, who would arrive later that evening in Los Angeles, was "sooo funny, he just literally — we were out having breakfast. . . . Truly like the CIA, he slips me a note [about wanting to go on a trip]. . . . He's cute."

I told Paul how we had trouble with his mother screening his calls, preventing Todd and David from getting through. David pointed out that I was the only one who was able to get past her. David told Paul if I had not gotten through, Paul "wouldn't be sitting here." In words I hoped he would soon have cause to regret, Paul said, "Yeah, I'm glad you guys are persistent. . . . I wonder how she knows, how she can have a sixth sense of that stuff?"

David said, "Well, I probably should not have asked her if you were out on a date with a six-year-old boy. . . . You know, 'Is he in that park with that six-year-old again? Exposing himself. When he's done, can you have him call me?' I have no idea if that upset her or not."

The subject turned to Sam Lindblad, and I became wary. I was in no condition to joust with Todd or David and knew that it was still possible for them to withdraw from the conspiracy. I needed to reassure everyone that Sam's attendance on the boat would not be a problem. I told them he was not on probation or parole, nor was he under state-imposed monitoring of any kind. I also said that under New Mexico law, he was not required to report that he was leaving the state, especially for such a short period of time.

Although David assured me he liked Sam, he repeated why he and James, "the future first lady," voted against him as a steering committee member: "The future first lady and I were the only two that didn't want him elevated, because we didn't want the notoriety. We were both concerned that as a sex offender . . . that this was just not gonna look real good for us."

A true sense of satisfaction ran through me and I had to conceal a smile when David said, "You know, obviously, I mean on a serious note, there should be some sort of . . . background check on us . . . make sure that we're not, you know, the FBI or police or something."

Growling stomachs prevailed over more discussion of NAMBLA politics, interfering law enforcement, or trysts with underage boys. David led the parade to the door as I unplugged the heating pad that so conveniently kept them on camera. Their luggage remained in my room and we headed to lunch.

The rain subsided long enough for us to get to my car, but "America's Finest City" was experiencing one of its wettest winters in history, and I feared that each raindrop was hollering to my travelers, "Cancel the boat trip." I knew the forecast called for continued showers well into the week but maintained an optimistic façade, claiming the weathermen had difficulty predicting the weather more than a day in advance because of ever-changing offshore conditions.

I excused myself when we reached our table in the restaurant, and when I returned from the restroom, Todd and David told me the three of them decided to exchange boys each night and asked if I wanted to participate. They reasoned that it would enhance the experience if, over the four-night stay, they had four different boys, offering a variety not available from spending the entire trip with the assigned boy. I agreed to participate in the exchange and complimented them on their ingenuity. One more nail for the coffin.

During lunch, Paul excused himself several times to go to the restroom and complained of not feeling well. He blamed the long trip and the nutritional supplements he had taken without sufficient food in his stomach. At the time, we thought little of his complaints, and David suggested it was probably an accumulation of stress and excitement over the upcoming experience.

We finished lunch and I suggested a short trip by car through the downtown area prior to returning to the hotel so I could resume my warm compress treatment on my arm. The damage from the IV was real; the massive bruising on my arm and nearly rock-solid veins at the injection sites had an authenticity that could not have been recreated by a Hollywood makeup artist. My need for resuming the compresses was authentic, but convenient as well.

We drove past the convention center and Petco Park, the home of the San Diego Padres. As we drove through the historic Gas Lamp District, Paul interrupted our conversation, saying he had to go to the restroom immediately. I pulled in front of the Marriott, and he raced in. The three of us remained in the car. Todd and David commiserated over Paul's health. In my mind, I was questioning the legal consequences should he be too sick to board the boat in the morning.

Paul eventually returned to the car, and we headed back to the hotel, where he could rest and I could resume my compresses. As the rain continued to fall, I wondered if all of my traveling companions might not back out of the trip. Would a combination of inclement weather and upset bowels undermine the case I had so carefully built over the last several years?

44
SPRINGING THE TRAP

At last, Paul's and Todd's rooms were ready. Paul rushed to his with a look that said he would be hugging the porcelain throne for most of the afternoon. David and Todd joined me in my room as our videotaped conversation continued.

David returned to his discussion about his travels to Thailand. He went into more detail about the boy bars, where, he said, the boys "were just strolling . . . like a runway type of thing. 'I'll take one of those, I'll have one of those. . . .' "

In response to a question from Todd, David said, "Variety is the spice of life," and indicated that he had had more than one boy simultaneously "a couple of times."

In an exchange that sickened me, David complained of the ever-present cigarette smoke he encountered overseas. David said, "I really despise cigarettes. I hate the smell of them. . . . Even the kids were smoking at ten or eleven. . . . Well, it was a turnoff and . . . I'm sitting there . . . lecturing him about smoking at ten or eleven, but I'm [having sex with] him also."

When I said, "Well, but smoking will kill you," Todd replied, "The other one just gives you hemorrhoids."

"A little surgery, you'll be fine," David responded.

Todd said, "Just rectal incontinent later on, but —"

"Don't worry about it," David interrupted, "you're young."

Todd: "You'll shit in your pants when you're twenty-two, but that's all right."

David: "We've got diapers. There's people we put into adult diapers. . . . We'll ship some over from the States. Yeah, it's really not that big a deal."

It was a conversation that would almost guarantee conviction, if played before a jury.

The rest of the afternoon's topics ranged from deep to light. At one point, I tried to lead the discussion toward whether boy lovers could be cured. David never responded directly, but did say, "Life certainly would be a lot easier if I was heterosexual. . . . Life would be a piece of cake . . . but that's not the case."

Todd asked about favorite TV stars, asserting that David's was Haley Joel Osment. I went with my standby — "Ricky Schroder, *Silver Spoons*" — and Todd responded with a breathy, "Oh, yeah. Mm-mm!" Then Todd talked about a commercial he saw on TV before his flight left: "This morning, I saw a Sylvan Learning Center commercial while I was eating breakfast, and I just about fell out of my chair. This boy on, I guess a national commercial — you have to see it! I replayed the thing, slowed it down, and froze it."

In one final admission of guilt, Todd responded to my comment that I didn't think what we were about to do in Mexico should even be considered criminal. Todd said, "Well, by society's standards, about as criminal as it gets. But, we still feel good about it. Sadly enough, if you go to prison for doing what we're about to do, you're viewed as being just about as despicable as it can get. You know, in prison, [among] the prison population, you're lucky to come out alive."

The rain continued, making even a drive to a restaurant for dinner a fool's mission. We decided to dine downstairs and remain close in case Paul needed us. We had a leisurely dinner with little, if any, criminal conversation and headed back to our respective rooms preparing for tomorrow's "life-changing experience."

That evening I contacted my Los Angeles case agent and learned that Sam Lindblad, Dick Stutsman, Steve Irvin, and Greg Nusca, aka David R. Busby, had arrived in L.A. and had met with other undercover agents posing as fellow travelers and travel agency personnel. In fewer than twelve hours, we would learn the success of the undercover operation.

It was another restless night. I never got more than one or two hours of sleep at a stretch. I kept replaying the investigation over and over in my mind — how it all began, where it led, and what insights I gained. I also rehearsed what would happen in the morning. The Los Angeles arrests were scheduled for 6:00 am, when the travelers there boarded the boat. I had to wait until 10:00 am, the four-hour difference supposedly being the time it would take the boat to travel from L.A. to San Diego. I was worried that those four hours just allowed that much longer for David, Todd, or Paul to withdraw from the conspiracy.

It rained throughout the night, at times pounding on the sliding glass door that connected my room to the balcony. No person in his right mind would board a boat for a casual cruise to Ensenada in this weather! There was nothing I could do but perhaps have a suitable alternative available, should they balk at taking the boat.

I decided to make a preemptive strike and offer to drive everyone across the border in a rental car. My reasoning would be that it would be more difficult for the authorities to trace us in a rental car, and as long as we remained calm while being questioned — if in fact we were questioned — we would merely be tourists. It seemed like a plausible solution and possibly the only one I had. I also believed it would still circumstantially demonstrate the firm desire these men had to travel to Mexico in order to engage in sex with minors. Of course, getting on a boat in inclement weather might also make the same point to a jury.

I spoke with my Los Angeles case agent early Saturday morning and learned that all four L.A. travelers had been taken into custody without incident as they were about to board the boat. Jeff Devore would be arrested later in the day, on the charge of distributing child pornography.

Before parting ways with Todd and David Mayer the night before, the three of us set a time to meet for breakfast. As I made my way into the dining room, which also held numerous FBI surveillance agents, I was pleased to see David, Todd, and Paul, who was back among the living and ready to join us on the journey. I was wearing a bright, multicolored shirt given to me by a friend from Africa. It seemed festive and made me easily identifiable should the arrest scene turn into chaos. David, however, had out-done me in the selection of his ensemble for the day: his pink short-sleeve shirt and lime green pants were over the top. To-gether, we made quite the fashion state-ment.

We engaged in light conversation through-out breakfast, joking about being part of next year's NAMBLA Christmas card project and naming our favorite prison songs. Todd was absolutely giddy, like a schoolgirl preparing for her first prom. I told the group that I had spoken to Sean, and he was on the boat heading south for San Diego with the other travelers; in other words, all was right with the world, even as the rains continued. When I offered to drive the group across the border, everyone balked, suggesting it was too dangerous. They were clearly ready to board the boat, regardless of the weather.

We agreed to meet in the lobby, check out, and head over to the boat ramp for the 10:00 am pick up. As we were waiting for everyone to complete the checkout process, I took a prearranged call from my "friend," a final piece of stage business. I relayed his "message" to the others: the boat was nearing the dock. David remarked that it was right on time, and I headed to my car.

The plan called for me to drive the travelers just a short distance, from the hotel to the boarding-area parking lot, where I had allegedly arranged to leave my car during our trip. I pulled my undercover Lexus in front of the hotel to pick up the group and assisted them as we loaded luggage in the trunk. Jokingly, David, feigning concern for my health, said to Todd and me, "Now, if the two of you want to stay here at the hotel and get through the recovery, Paul and I will get through this by ourselves." With a straight face, I replied, "But wouldn't that take us out of the conspiracy?" David responded, "No, don't worry about that, it's too late!"

He was right — it was.

My passengers were unaware that in the background, on my car stereo, Linda Eder was singing "The Children of Eve," a song she helped write "to comment on children caught in the crossfire of physical abuse, starvation, and war." It seemed more appropriate than "Jailhouse Rock."

It took less than three minutes to drive to the boarding ramp. Paul was unusually quiet; Todd and David seemed oblivious.

FBI agents don't believe in fair fights; we want to overwhelmingly out-man and out-gun the opposition. I knew that more than a dozen agents had concealed themselves, waiting to spring a trap set in motion years earlier.

We exited the car and retrieved our bags from the trunk. As we headed through the rain toward the boat dock, the arrest plan was executed to perfection. Agents jumped out from behind trees, bushes, and buildings. All four of us were taken into custody. If it were Hollywood, I would report that all three subjects ran, a foot pursuit erupted, and shots were fired, but like most arrests, this was uneventful — the best kind.

Two SWAT agents, friends from my squad, arrested me. I dropped my crutch, feigned collapse, and was caught before I hit the wet pavement. In what I can only describe — with utmost modesty — as an Oscar-worthy performance, I sobbed fake tears as the two agents cuffed me and dragged me to their car. My SWAT team buddies fought back laughter, unprepared for my antics. I was so caught up in my theatrics that I didn't learn until later that the other three were arrested "without incident."

I honestly worried that at the arrest I really would get emotional. I had poured myself into this investigation, fighting near-constant urges to inflict my own brand of justice on the men we targeted, while simultaneously balancing two other undercover operations fraught with their own administrative headaches — finally incurring physical illness requiring hospitalization.

But a sense of relief was the main thing I felt, as well as a profound sense of satisfaction. Of the twenty-plus undercover operations in which I participated as the undercover agent, this was the most rewarding. Even though there were no real boys involved in this particular sting, I truly believe we saved lives. We saved boys I may never know or ever see from going through the hell of abuse and exploitation. It was well worth the effort.

Next, though, we had to successfully negotiate the case through the courts.

45
AFTER THE ARRESTS

Once the targets were in custody, my first worry was about David Mayer and the ease with which he had implicated himself in our conversations. I held my breath while awaiting the results of his interview, dreading he would proclaim his innocence with some proof of a study or dissertation he was conducting. My fears were unfounded; he "lawyered up."

Unlike on TV, we don't "close by arrest" and move on to a new episode next week. Although the undercover operation was successful, the judicial process awaited. My work was not complete.

The investigation netted eight members of NAMBLA:

Sam Lindblad, former schoolteacher and steering committee member
Gregory Nusca, aka David R. Busby, steering committee member

Steven K. Irvin, special education teacher
Richard Stutsman, businessman/substitute schoolteacher/mentor
Jeffrey Devore, ordained minister/chiropractor
David Cory Mayer, psychologist/international flight attendant
Phillip Todd Calvin, dentist
Paul Ernest Zipszer, personal trainer/warehouse worker

We were surprised that following the arrest there was no known immediate communication between the members and NAMBLA leadership, notifying them of the sting operation and arrests. In fact, it was not until the next issue of the *Bulletin,* published five months later, that there was even a public acknowledgement of the arrests.

An article, less than a full page, distanced the organization from the criminal acts. Appearing on page thirteen of the nineteen-page publication and lacking even a headline or byline, the article seemed more of an afterthought. It stated that during the Miami conference, "a police operative (perhaps an FBI agent) initiated contact with some of the attendees during the 'off hours.' " The "police operative later inveigled the men" to join him on a trip to Mexico. Describing the members arrested as "extremely naïve," the article called the undercover operation a "classic entrapment" for which the men would "bear a heavy burden." The unnamed writer cautioned members of potential sting operations and explained the federal law. Minimizing the offenders' criminal actions and intent, the article warned that "no victims are needed to prove the case, only a demonstration that one intended to travel overseas and thought about doing something naughty while there." As with Peter Melzer's characterization of murderer Charles Jaynes — who suffocated Jeffrey Curley, sexually assaulted the body, and threw the deceased child off a bridge — as a "real decent guy," anal and oral sex with prepubescent boys apparently falls into NAMBLA's category of "naughty."

The seven-paragraph article, "A Report & Proposal from the Steering Committee," appeared within a section of the *Bulletin* titled "Spotlight." Of significance was a three-paragraph notation carrying the subhead "Conferences & Membership." According to the report, the general membership conferences were "labor intensive" and afforded "the seasoned leadership . . . little opportunity to address a wider public." The steering committee was "considering having fewer General Membership Conferences, and then only when there is a compelling reason to meet." The article went on to say, "We have always been a convenient target for right-wing ideologues and fanatics. The virulence of the opposition is evidence of the power of our message. We trust their venom will have the contrary effect of empowering, inspiring and strengthening the force of our movement. We are confident our members and supporters will rise to the task."

It sounded to me as if Peter Melzer and his cronies were making a virtue of necessity. But whatever their motivation, in this case I was proud to identify myself with the "right-wing ideologues and fanatics."

I hoped all the defendants would plead guilty. The evidence against each of them seemed overwhelming, and I thought it doubtful any would choose to air in front of a jury the recorded conversations in which they discussed their prior sexual history and their sexual desires for the boys they believed to be awaiting them in Ensenada.

Guilty pleas came rather quickly from Greg Nusca, Steve Irvin, Jeff Devore, and, to my surprise, Dick Stutsman. If anyone chose to fight, I assumed it would be Stutsman, who had laid out his defense plans to me in our February 1 phone call.

My initial assessment of Nusca at Johnny Rockets during the Miami conference was correct. He had previously offended. He had a prior conviction and was sentenced to fourteen years. Devore received the minimum mandatory sentence for distributing child pornography, five years. Irvin had no criminal record and was sentenced to thirty-seven months.

The San Diego defendants circled the wagons and rode the coat-tails of David Mayer's retained attorney, who, along with Todd's lawyer, filed several motions challenging my initial infiltration of the organization. They claimed that the government — specifically, Bob Hamer — had violated the defendants' First Amendment right of freedom of association and their Fifth Amendment right to avoid self-incrimination by engaging in "gross governmental misconduct." In one motion, David's attorney admitted "Mr. Mayer and his co-defendants belong to an organization that is hated for espousing beliefs that are distasteful to virtually all in American society. Yet, despite the repugnance of their beliefs, they are entitled to the same First

580

Amendment and other constitutional protections as anyone else."

In characterizing my behavior as "gross governmental misconduct," the attorney wrote, "It is shocking that the undercover agent, realizing that Mr. Mayer would not take part in illegal conduct with underage boys in this country, would go to such lengths to instigate the criminal activity by suggesting conduct that would be tolerated by local police in a foreign land."

My personal favorite line in the motions filed by the defense was the allegation that I "inappropriately played on Mr. Mayer's psychological condition." The attorney never quite defined his client's "psychological condition," but the client to whom he referred was in fact a Ph.D. and a practicing psychologist. I never even took psychology in college. I admit to having a bit more than my share of self-confidence, but I must be better than even I thought.

Just prior to the evidentiary hearing on the motion, both Todd and Paul entered into a plea agreement and changed their pleas to guilty. Each was sentenced to twenty-four months. David Mayer remained the sole San Diego defendant at the table. Anne Perry presented the case for the government and we were most fortunate to have drawn Federal District Court Judge Jeffrey T. Miller. He saw through the smoke and mirrors of the defense motions and ruled against them. After that, David Mayer had very few weapons remaining in his legal arsenal, and was subsequently sentenced to thirty-seven months.

Los Angeles defendant Sam Lindblad, a three-time convicted sex offender, also chose to fight the charges. Even a guilty plea meant a possible lifetime period of incarceration, so he had little to lose by going to trial.

It is difficult to put into words the roller coaster ride I was on throughout the week of December 12. Although I have had longer trials, spent more time on the stand, and was subjected to more rigorous cross-examination, I fought to keep my emotions in check.

Within three weeks I would be retired from a twenty-six-year career with the FBI. I would no longer carry the badge and gun that had become like parts of me. Although I joked about it with family and friends, every time the phone rang throughout my career I thought it could be that one great undercover assignment that would make Mel Gibson or Bruce Willis jealous — full of danger, excitement, and intrigue.

Now I knew that call would never come. I also knew the upcoming trial was one of the most important of my career. Sam Lindblad was a predator who needed to spend the rest of his life in jail. I had a major role in seeing to it he never saw the daylight of freedom again, and I wanted more than anything to go out with this win under my belt.

On Sunday I drove up to Los Angeles from my San Diego home and spent the evening in a hotel, listening again to my recording of the January 6 dinner conversation with Lindblad in Albuquerque. The next day I was to meet with the prosecutors to prepare for the trial. Even though I had dealt with hundreds of federal prosecutors during my career, I had never met the two Assistant United States Attorneys handling the Lindblad matter. I would soon learn that their excellent reputations were well earned.

On Monday, I met with Tom O'Brien and Jennifer Corbett. Tom was the chief of the Criminal Division and had the final say on all prosecutions coming out of the Central District of California. Never had the "chief" ever gone to trial in any of my cases, and I had been involved in some major investigations.

My confidence level rose immensely as soon as I met Tom. A Naval Academy graduate and former naval flight officer — Tom had been a backseater in an F-14 — he left the Navy, became a prosecutor in the Los Angeles District Attorney's office, and prosecuted hundreds of gang-related cases before jumping to the federal system. My first question to him when we met was why. Why was he assisting in this case? His answer was brief and said it all: he had a son.

I spent the morning explaining my role in the investigation and giving him my insights into NAMBLA. We were joined in the afternoon by Jennifer Corbett. She had an outstanding grasp of the investigation. A Yale Law School graduate from New York, she spent most of her time in the U.S. Attorney's office prosecuting federal sex offense cases. Her self-confidence was evident and refreshing. She, too, was more than ready for this trial. The burden was now on me to prepare myself for tomorrow's testimony.

Prior to leaving for the day, I accompanied Jennifer to the courtroom of Federal District Court Judge Nora N. Manella. Judge Manella, a former United States Attorney before being appointed by President Clinton to the federal bench, would be presiding over the Lindblad trial starting the next day. This afternoon, however, she was sentencing Richard Stutsman, who had pleaded guilty several months earlier. Because of federal sentencing guidelines, the sentence was no surprise. Stutsman, who had no prior convictions, was sentenced to thirty-seven months in prison, a $7,500 fine, and to seven years' federal probation upon completion of the prison term. The sentence was far less than I thought he deserved, but I was even more disappointed when the judge seemed to characterize the contemplated sex acts as consensual and the price of the trip as minimal, almost enticing, almost a "sex light" type of crime. The implication was that tomorrow's trial might not be as easy as we would hope.

After a quick dinner in Los Angeles' Little Tokyo, I returned to the hotel room and pored over my reports, attempting to refresh my memory on all that had taken place with Sam Lindblad. I was up late into the night, prepping for the next day, trying to anticipate possible cross-examination. Based upon discussions with defense counsel, Tom and Jennifer knew Lindblad's defense was going to be that he merely went on the trip in order to "walk on the beach with a boy," read him stories, and touch him. Sam was going to claim he had no desire to engage in any sex act with a child.

As you know by now, my undercover career took me into some pretty dangerous situations. And after all that, I still say I would rather wear a wire into a meeting of armed murderers than testify in court.

I hate being on the stand, hate being subjected to the scrutiny of every word uttered, hate the attempts by the defense to twist every statement, and hate the frequent disregard for the truth in pursuit of a legal victory. I have never lied under oath, yet, based upon the decisions of some judges and jurors, there have been times when I was perceived as not telling the truth. I learned from those times that testimony by any witness has nothing to do with the truth: it has everything to do with whether you are believed to be telling the truth. In fact, the trial is not about the truth; a trial is about each side attempting to place into evidence that which helps its theory of the case and preventing the other side from presenting those facts most favorable to their cause. I am always afraid my nervousness on the stand will be perceived as lying, and I am constantly seeking peace as I testify.

Judge Manella's courtroom 11 was in the old courthouse at 312 North Spring Street. Built in the 1930s, the courtroom was large and ornate; its vintage furnishings and beautiful wood paneling would provide the perfect setting for a Humphrey Bogart period piece. But when court began at 8:30 on Tuesday morning, it was no movie. Lindblad, who had been in custody since the February 12 arrest, was ushered into the court by two federal marshals. He was charged in two counts of a three-count indictment with violation of 18 USC 2423(b), travel for the purpose of engaging in illicit sexual acts with a minor, and 18 USC 2423(e), conspiracy to do the same.

I took a deep breath and said the latest of the large number of silent prayers I'd uttered over the last few days.

46
THE TRIAL OF
SAM LINDBLAD

In the morning session, Lindblad was wearing a multicolored sweater and looked somewhat like a like a thin, balding college professor. By the late morning session, he was wearing a shirt and tie and blue sport coat. To me, he now looked more like a molester. Whoever was responsible for the wardrobe change had my thanks.

What did concern me was Stutsman. Dick made bail several months after his arrest and was still free, pending his reporting to federal prison on January 31. He appeared in court and would be present throughout the three days of trial. One valuable piece of evidence would be the videotape of the February 11 motel room meeting between the Los Angeles undercover agents and the three co-conspirators, Lindblad, Stutsman, and Steve Irvin. If the jury realized that Stutsman, who was on the video, was sitting in the courtroom, they might assume he was acquitted of the charges or that no charges were filed against him. Although the judge would instruct the jury to judge this case only on the evidence presented at trial, there was no telling what factors could enter into a juror's decision-making process. Although I doubted an outright acquittal was possible, it only takes one juror to force a retrial. There was little we could do to keep Stutsman out of the courtroom and could only hope for the best.

Somewhat ironic was the fact that four very attractive women were present in the courtroom throughout the trial. If cast for the movie, Michelle Pfeiffer could play Judge Manella. The prosecutor, Jennifer Corbett, and my two female case agents from the Los Angeles office were three of the most attractive women in federal law enforcement — but maybe my macho, male sexism is surfacing, attempting to overcome the pedophile persona I assumed for several years.

It took the lawyers all morning and part of the afternoon to select a jury, one of the most ethically diverse panels I saw in all my trials — blacks, whites, Hispanics, Asians; male and female; young and old. It was truly a cross section of Los Angeles's multiethnic communities.

Another concern I always have with trials near the holidays is that the Christmas spirit might enter into the verdict, though that can cut both ways: overwhelming evidence might result in quicker guilty verdicts, enabling jurors to get back to Christmas shopping.

Contrary to most TV courtroom scenes, witnesses do not sit in court listening to the evidence being presented, then come from the gallery to testify. Typically, courts "invoke the rule," excluding witnesses from the courtroom until called. I paced the hallway, waiting to be called and rehashing in my mind the testimony I was about to give. I was to be the first witness.

I was sworn in and took the stand as Tom O'Brien began direct examination. Lasting more than an hour and a half, we played portions of the January 6 Albuquerque recording, including Sam's statement that he liked to "fondle." We also introduced two telephone calls Sam and I had the next day, January 7. NAMBLA and "boy love" was a central part of our presentation. I testified to the two conferences I attended and Sam's role at the Miami conference. I was even able to put into evidence the minutes from the Miami NAMBLA conference Lindblad wrote as the "acting secretary." My direct testimony was relatively short compared to the many times I've testified in the past, but I was nervous and was afraid it showed in my voice. I was telling the truth and could only hope the jury believed me.

During a break, I ran into Dick Stutsman in the hallway. He smiled and said, "Now I remember you. I guess the crutch was fake, too." I returned the smile but said nothing.

Following my direct examination, Lindblad's attorney began his cross-examination. His questions were often confusing, sometimes using double and triple negatives. On one occasion, even Judge Manella interrupted, asking the attorney to clarify. As 5:00 approached, the judge called for a recess and stated that we would resume at 8:00 am, the next day.

Tom, Jennifer, and I, along with the case agents, returned to Jennifer's office to discuss the day's events. Although Tom wasn't lavishing praise on my testimony, he said I did fine and that we were where we wanted to be in the presentation of our case.

I returned to my hotel room, grabbed a quick dinner, and went back to the room, once again reviewing the recording of my January 6 dinner with Lindblad.

Judge Manella began court precisely at 8:00 am and I was back on the stand. The cross-examination continued for well over an hour. I held my own, and Tom said my testimony was much stronger than it had been the day before.

The undercover travel agent was the next witness. He introduced the video recording of the February 11 meeting, the night before the arrests, and also introduced a three-way call he had with Lindblad and Stutsman. His cross was minimal.

Another agent, who posed as a traveler and was present for the arrest, also testified. He seized and searched Lindblad's luggage and testified about what Lindblad brought on the trip: two books on boy love, a guide to Spanish, and a box labeled "Olympics." Its contents would not have been menacing had he been an elementary-school teacher, but knowing he was a participant in a sex tour that he thought would involve under-age boys, the contents were disturbing. A small piece of paper listed the "Olympic" games he wanted to play with the boys: "discus throw" with paper plates, "inch worm," "tickle me Elmo" with feathers, "stand on head," "crawl over the broom," "limbo" with a long piece of rope, "front/back rolls," and "javelin throws" with plastic straws. Included in the box were cookies strung with ribbon to be used as gold medals and presented to the winners of each event.

The agents who arrested Lindblad and subsequently interviewed him testified to the confession they elicited. The recorded confession would prove invaluable. Lindblad acknowledged that the "special trip would include some boy love." He defined boy love: "for me, it is cuddling and contact and possibly some fondling, but that is not necessary. No sex . . . doesn't have to include sexual contact." When asked if it might include sex and what that would depend on, Lindblad responded, "The boy involved, partly, and my own feelings and opinions, but I certainly would not have oral sex or fellatio or anal sex or raping the child." Later in the interview, in a follow-up question on the cuddling and fondling comment, Lindblad said, "Cuddling means holding hands, being close, running my fingers through the boy's hair on his head, tickling him, possibly wrestling, not in terms of a hurtful wrestling but just . . . roughhousing, I guess, may be the word. . . . If the boy didn't object or if he allowed or made available to touch his penis, I would. . . . If I tickled his stomach, and he said, 'Tickle me lower,' I would."

Knowing he was being recorded by the

FBI, Lindblad also repeated a theme I heard expressed throughout much of my NAMBLA experience. Lindblad discussed how a relationship with a boy who is being groomed moves beyond friendship to a sexual encounter.

> We are all sexual beings, and [I'm] certainly not barring a ten-, eleven-, twelve-, thirteen-year-old boy from being sexual. . . . It's on their minds a great deal, so they have questions. . . . There's sexuality on the periphery of many things, you know. So when they say something as a compliment to you . . . on the side of that, the edge of that, is a bit of sexuality.

Finally, the police officer from Grand Junction, Colorado, testified to the 1996 conviction. The officer's testimony was compelling and painted a very vivid picture of the type of predator Lindblad was.

The government rested. The case seemed solid. A conviction should have been guaranteed based upon any three factors individually: his statements to me at the Albuquerque dinner, his statements to the undercover travel agency, or his confession.

Everyone, however, was shocked when the

defense presented its only witness: the defendant. Sam Lindblad took the stand and for the rest of the day testified on direct examination by his attorney. The answers were eerie and surreal. Seldom does a three-time convicted sexual predator under oath detail his life and his sexual history. Sam did.

Having spent parts of three and a half years posing as a boy lover, it was difficult for me to be unbiased as I watched Sam on the stand. I could only hope the jury was seeing the same things I saw.

Sam began his testimony by saying, and repeating often throughout his direct and cross examinations, that he had a "deep emotional need to relate to and be with young boys, and it's something I've dealt with all my life." His reason for agreeing to go on the trip to Mexico was "not sexual. It's companionship, sharing, playing, teaching. . . . I wanted to have a good time with a young lad." He planned to "avoid all sexual activity with that boy."

He testified to his meeting with the boy involved in his 1996 Colorado conviction. Sam described the fourteen-year-old boy as "a bit on the naïve side, but also inexperienced and shy." They played footsie under the table at the Burger King where they first met. As with other boys he encountered, Sam contemplated a time when he could put his "hands in their hair, hold hands, rub their shoulders, give them a push . . . on the swing . . . horsey-back ride . . . wrestling."

Sam had difficulty putting into words his own emotional development but described himself as being at the "twelve-year age. . . . I wish there was a good way to explain it. Whether it's called the 'Peter Pan syndrome' or arrested development, or there are some of us adults that never really make it to adulthood, I still feel and respond to many things as a twelve-year-old . . . or an eleven-year-old." Yet this teacher with a master's degree admitted to remaining married for twenty-five years and fathering a child. He also admitted he hoped the relationship he had been developing with the victim in the 1996 conviction would've grown into a sexual relationship.

Sam's defense was somewhat unique, maybe the only one a three-time convicted sex offender could attempt. Essentially, he was saying he had been wrong in the past, had learned his lesson, and would never again engage in a sexual act with a minor because of the harm it would bring to the child. His purpose for going to Mexico was non-sexual contact with a boy, and his definition of "fondling" did not include the touching of the penis.

He admitted to his prior bad acts, but prison changed him: "I spent time in prison. It was not comfortable. It was a great deal of time for self-introspection. There was also therapy, which I can't say changed my emotional need for boys, but it did dampen my sexuality. . . . As a sexual human being, I am a failure. With my wife — we were tremendous platonic friends, but 'platonic' does not meet the criteria for marriage, and it made marriage difficult. Sexuality with adult men . . . I feel like I'm in the wrong place. I do the out-of-body experience, I guess. Not that I've had many, but, you know . . . not pleasant. And with minors or children or young boys, it's nothing but pain for both of us. I see the look of fear on a child's face, and I realize it's the same look I have on my face when I'm in an uncomfortable sexual situation."

Later in his testimony, he described himself as "an emotional-sexual failure" and denied ever having sexual intercourse or engaging in oral sex with a minor.

Sam claimed that while in Miami, he heard "rumbling" about a sex trip. He denied ever being on a "sex trip" but admitted to knowing about them. He also admitted that when I first broached the subject of the trip with him at our January 6 dinner in Albuquerque, he knew the trip was a "sex trip" and illegal, but as he maintained throughout his testimony, he had no desire to engage in any sexual act while in Mexico.

Sam and his attorney concluded the direct testimony that afternoon. Jennifer would have the evening to prepare her cross-examination. We returned to her office to evaluate Sam's appearance on the stand. Although we unanimously concurred that his testimony didn't pass our "smell test," it only took one juror to believe his story enough to raise the specter of reasonable doubt. The reasonable doubt burden sets a very high standard for the prosecution. We needed to meet it on each element of Sam's offense.

47
THE VERDICT

Jennifer enjoyed an excellent reputation with all of us in the L.A. FBI office, but I had never been in court with her. I wasn't sure what to expect. Obviously, direct examination is all about preparing the witness. It takes work, but the script is written. Cross-examination is where the good trial attorneys are separated from the weak. I learned the next day that Jennifer was beyond good; she was great. She eliminated the wiggle room in Sam Lindblad's testimony and laid a solid foundation for the jury to return a guilty verdict, if they were inclined to do so.

Referencing the 1996 Colorado conviction, Sam admitted he met Thomas McQuade, who also went by "about six other names," at a court-ordered sexual offenders' therapy program. When McQuade had to leave the program to begin a prison sentence, "he, in essence, turned the child over to me." You could almost hear a gasp from those in the courtroom when Sam Lindblad nonchalantly said this.

In describing his relationship with the Colorado teenager who had been "turned over" to him, Sam said he wanted a "platonic friendship" in which "any topic could be discussed." Jennifer elicited that the topics included pornography and condoms.

Sam wrote in various letters to the fourteen-year-old things like, "[I would] greatly appreciate it if you would destroy this letter when you are done with it . . . so it doesn't fall into the wrong hands" and "I certainly will do everything in my power to keep you from getting into trouble, if you will do the same for me."

In his letters to the teenager, Sam asked some provocative questions: "Are you comfortable in the shower at P.E. or quite self-conscious?" "Do you enjoy looking around at the other bodies with you?" "Have you ever gotten handsy with another boy or girl?" "Have any boys or girls touched your penis when you were younger?" "What about an older person getting handsy with you?"

Sam admitted he initiated these questions. He also told the boy to lie to his parents about a proposed outing they were going to have, to see a play. He admitted to sending the letters in envelopes with no return address and on one occasion putting the return address of a local church.

Under questioning by Jennifer, Sam admitted he told the boy he masturbated thinking of the fourteen-year-old and also while thinking of another ten-year-old boy.

Sam admitted to writing, "I do want to see you and touch you. That is the handsy part. I just want to put my hands all over you, in your hair, scratch your back, feel your legs, feel your chest, touch your penis when you have [an erection] or even if you don't."

When Jennifer asked if the treatment program he attended with McQuade was his first, Sam replied, "I have had hundreds and hundreds of hours of a variety of counseling and therapy and hypnosis therapy and spent thousands and thousands of dollars. . . . I know that I still have a very strong emotional need for companionship, camaraderie with little boys."

Jennifer followed up: "Were you cured of your sexual desire for them?" Sam said, no and admitted he still had a sexual desire directed toward boys.

Steering committee member Sam Lindblad did not dispute Jennifer's assertion that

NAMBLA was an "organization whose primary function revolves around sexual behavior." He admitted he discussed the NAMBLA organization with members of his sex offender therapy groups even though the therapist saw it as a "negative organization . . . sexually." Even with that warning from the therapist, he admitted to rejoining NAMBLA upon his release from prison.

Jennifer then took him through a series of written promises he made less than three years earlier, following his release from the seven-and-a-half-year prison term in Colorado for the 1996 conviction.

> I will take myself out of positions where I can look at children.
> I will not be around children to wrestle or horseplay with them.
> Wrestling with a child is part of a buildup to a sexual assault.
> I know that inappropriate fantasies are the road to assaultive behavior.
> I will not work with any children.
> I will not use my jobs to access children.
> I will tell adults that I am not trustworthy around children.

Sam admitted to initiating "assaultive touches that were very inappropriate" sixty or seventy times over the course of his adult lifetime, and that he inappropriately touched the same boys more than once. He admitted to inappropriately touching his son "a time or two." He admitted to having been caught by his wife when he intentionally "tweaked" his son while bathing him and that his wife said, "Don't ever let that happen again." He admitted that "repeated sexual contact with young boys" was the reason his marriage ended.

Despite this series of admissions, despite the fact he admitted to placing himself in "high-risk behavior" situations following his release from prison less than three years ago, and despite the fact he admitted to "grooming" boys since his release from prison, he maintained that his intent in going to Mexico was "to have an emotional relationship with a child, but my specific intention was no sexual activity." Even though he participated in a three-way call with Dick Stutsman and the undercover travel agent in which Stutsman detailed the sexual acts he wanted to perform, Sam denied wanting to engage in sexual activity with the ten-, eleven-, or twelve-year-old he expected to meet in Mexico. Sam claimed that, by his definition, "fondling" did not include sexual contact. "I was eliminating sexual contact, sexual activity from our hoped friendship."

Every contact I had with Sam was recorded — my contacts in Miami, my phone calls, and the dinner in Albuquerque. In discovery, the prosecution turned over every recording, every e-mail, and every written report. Sam had a chance to review that evidence, as did his attorney. Although parts of the recording that night in Albuquerque were somewhat inaudible, it was possible to make out almost all of the conversation. Certainly, the general nature of even the inaudible portions was evident. Given all this, what followed next was surprising.

In response to Jennifer's query — "[Isn't it true that] in fact, you never mentioned during the first conversation you had with Robert about the trip that you had any concerns whatsoever about the legality of the trip" — Sam lied. He stated, "I said very specifically, 'I do not.' My words were, 'I very strongly believe in NAMBLA's tenet that states, "We do not advocate any breaking of the law" ' . . . and [the undercover agent] responded, 'Well, you certainly don't have to do anything you're —' wait. 'You don't have to participate in anything that you don't want to. You don't have to participate in any activity that you choose not to.' . . . And I realized then, that means I can choose not to break the law, and I realized, I guess that's the first good advice I've gotten from Robert."

Jennifer followed up that answer with another question: "And was that conversation recorded?" Then she asked, "Have you listened to the recording of that conversation?" Sam said he heard that conversation on the recording, and then he took the lie further by saying he heard himself say on the tape, "I am very concerned about living up to the tenets of NAMBLA of doing . . . of not . . . NAMBLA states, 'We do not advocate breaking any laws' . . . and then I said, 'Robert, I'm not sexual with men, women, or boys,' and he [the undercover agent, me] looked at his watch and hurriedly got up to leave the area."

I thought I was done testifying, but Sam's lies forced me to take the stand one more time to rebut his testimony. The conversation he said took place never happened, except maybe in his wishful thinking. I listened to the tape of the January 6 meeting at least six times and even helped transcribe parts of it. Sam lied. Did the jury believe him? Had he raised a reasonable doubt? Only time would tell — the time it would take for them to deliberate.

Both sides rested their respective cases. It was now time for the closings, the chance for the prosecution and defense to discuss the evidence and explain to the jury what it all meant. Even though the jury is cautioned that the attorneys' comments are not evidence, and that they should decide the case on only the evidence presented, the impact of a closing argument can sway a jury.

Because the prosecution has the burden of proving the case "beyond a reasonable doubt," they get two opportunities to speak to the jury: the opening argument and the closing argument. In between those two presentations, the defense has its opportunity.

Tom O'Brien gave his opening argument, detailing the evidence and describing how each element of both counts as charged in the indictment had been proven beyond a reasonable doubt. His opening was matter-of-fact but made our case.

Sam's attorney presented his closing. There is an old adage taught in law school: when the facts are on your side, pound the facts; when they aren't, pound the table. The attorney pounded the table, loud and long. I wasn't the least bit convinced but was unsure if possibly one or more jurors bought his theory that Sam's only desire was to cuddle on the beach and read stories. I carefully watched each juror. Several often looked away, as if they couldn't take another discussion point from the lawyer. Several looked angry. But "reasonable doubt" meant that one juror, though not completely believing the defendant, might buy enough of his story, enough to be uncertain. I was hoping and praying that wouldn't be the case and that Tom, who had one more chance to speak with the jury, would settle any lingering misgivings about a guilty verdict.

I was not disappointed. Tom gave the finest closing argument I have ever heard. It was almost TV-perfect. Not once did Tom refer to any notes; he spoke from the heart — that of a father who never wanted Sam Lindblad to walk the streets again as a free man. Whether his eloquence was necessary, I'll never know, but Tom resolved any doubts that Lindblad's attorney raised. I was confident that as the jury left the courtroom to deliberate, they would return with the verdict I was seeking.

Judge Manella recessed at noon, allowed the jury to break for lunch, and asked them to return to deliberate. By 2:30 they had a verdict: guilty on both counts.

I fought hard to contain my emotions. Following the announcement of the verdict, the two alternate jurors, who were now sitting in the gallery, came up to me, congratulated me, and thanked me for "going undercover." Never had I received a higher compliment. For almost four years, I poured myself into this investigation. This verdict validated all of that effort.

When Lindblad was later sentenced to thirty years in federal prison, it was the best ending I could possibly imagine for my last undercover.

ABOUT THE AUTHOR

Bob Hamer spent twenty-six years as a "street agent" for the FBI, many of those years in an undercover capacity. In assignments lasting anywhere from a day to more than three years, he has successfully posed as a drug dealer, contract killer, fence, pedophile, degenerate gambler, weapons dealer, and white-collar criminal.

Bob has worked undercover against such diverse groups as La Cosa Nostra, the Sicilian Mafia, Mexican Mafia, Russian Mafia, Asian organized crime groups, and Los Angeles–based street gangs. His successful infiltration of NAMBLA (North American Man/Boy Love Association) resulted in the arrest of what one defendant called eight members of the "inner circle."

He has received numerous awards throughout his career, including the FBI Director's Award for Distinguished Service, four United States Attorney Awards for

Distinguished Service, and numerous letters of commendation including one from then U.S. Attorney Rudy Giuliani.

Now retired, he is a member of the Writers Guild of America and the Writers Guild of Canada and has written for TV. He also worked as the technical advisor for *The Inside* and *Angela's Eyes* and has consulted for *Law & Order: SVU* and *Sleeper Cell.* He appeared as a guest on *The Oprah Winfrey Show* to discuss his role in the NAMBLA investigation.

A Marine Corps veteran and law school graduate, he is married and has two children.

The employees of Thorndike Press hope you have enjoyed this Large Print book. All our Thorndike and Wheeler Large Print titles are designed for easy reading, and all our books are made to last. Other Thorndike Press Large Print books are available at your library, through selected bookstores, or directly from us.

For information about titles, please call:
(800) 223-1244

or visit our Web site at:
http://gale.cengage.com/thorndike

To share your comments, please write:
Publisher
Thorndike Press
295 Kennedy Memorial Drive
Waterville, ME 04901